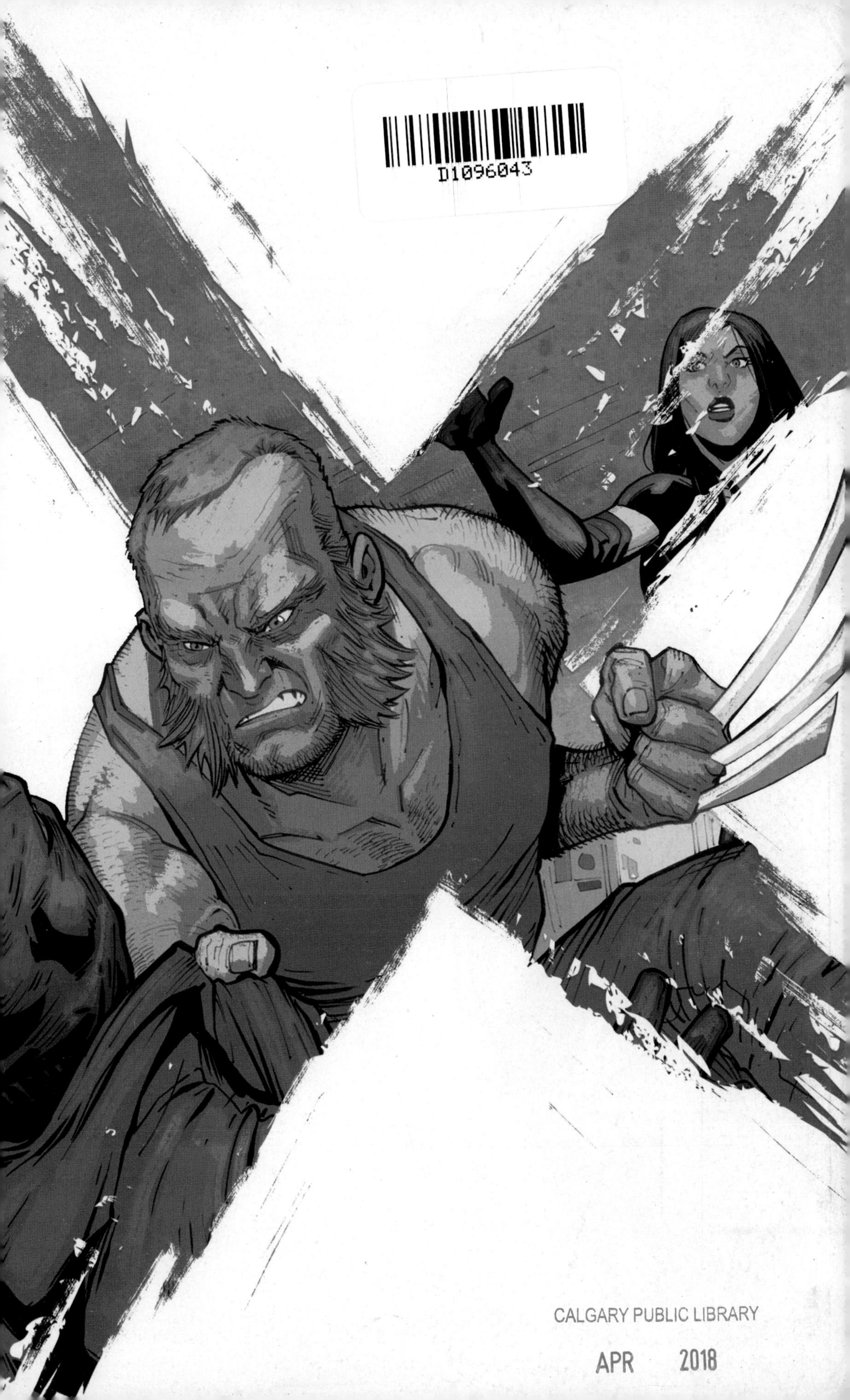

collection editor **JENNIFER GRÜNWALD**
associate managing editor **KATERI WOODY**
associate editor **SARAH BRUNSTAD**
editor, special projects **MARK D. BEAZLEY**
vp production & special projects **JEFF YOUNGQUIST**
svp print, sales & marketing **DAVID GABRIEL**
book designer **ADAM DEL RE**

editor in chief **AXEL ALONSO**
chief creative officer **JOE QUESADA**
publisher **DAN BUCKLEY**
executive producer **ALAN FINE**

ALL-NEW WOLVERINE VOL. 2: CIVIL WAR II. Contains material originally published in magazine form as ALL-NEW WOLVERINE #7-12. First printing 2016. ISBN# 978-0-7851-9653-2. Published by MARVEL WORLDWIDE, INC., a subsidiary of MARVEL ENTERTAINMENT, LLC. OFFICE OF PUBLICATION: 135 West 50th Street, New York, NY 10020. Copyright © 2016 MARVEL No similarity between any of the names, characters, persons, and/or institutions in this magazine with those of any living or dead person or institution is intended, and any such similarity which may exist is purely coincidental. **Printed in the U.S.A.** ALAN FINE, President, Marvel Entertainment; DAN BUCKLEY, President, TV, Publishing & Brand Management; JOE QUESADA, Chief Creative Officer; TOM BREVOORT, SVP of Publishing; DAVID BOGART, SVP of Business Affairs & Operations, Publishing & Partnership; C.B. CEBULSKI, VP of Brand Management & Development, Asia; DAVID GABRIEL, SVP of Sales & Marketing, Publishing; JEFF YOUNGQUIST, VP of Production & Special Projects; DAN CARR, Executive Director of Publishing Technology; ALEX MORALES, Director of Publishing Operations; SUSAN CRESPI, Production Manager; STAN LEE, Chairman Emeritus. For information regarding advertising in Marvel Comics or on Marvel.com, please contact Vit DeBellis, Integrated Sales Manager, at vdebellis@marvel.com. For Marvel subscription inquiries, please call 888-511-5480. **Manufactured between 8/26/2016 and 10/3/2016** by LSC COMMUNICATIONS INC., ROANOKE, VA, USA.

10 9 8 7 6 5 4 3 2 1

X-23 WAS CREATED TO BE A WEAPON.

For a time, that's all she was. But Laura Kinney escaped that life with the help of the man she was cloned from, the man who became her mentor: THE WOLVERINE. Tragically, the original Wolverine has fallen, and the mantle has been left empty.

Laura will live as Logan's legacy, and she will fight for her brighter future.

She will leave behind her old life and make a new one. She is the...

Laura recently discovered that she had been cloned by Alchemax Genetics. The surviving three "sisters" wanted revenge against their torturers, and together Wolverine and the clones took AG down. Two clones were lost in the fight, leaving one, a preteen girl named GABBY, with an uncertain future...

writer
TOM TAYLOR

ISSUES #7-9

artist
MARCIO TAKARA

color artists
JORDAN BOYD (#7-8) & MAT LOPES (#9)

ISSUES #10-12

penciler
IG GUARA

inkers
BOB WIACEK (#10), VICTOR OLAZABA (#10) & WALDEN WONG (#11-12)

color artists
JOHN RAUCH (#10) & MICHAEL GARLAND (#11-12)

letterer
VC's CORY PETIT

cover art
BENGAL

assistant editor
CHRISTINA HARRINGTON

associate editor
DARREN SHAN

editor
MARK PANICCIA

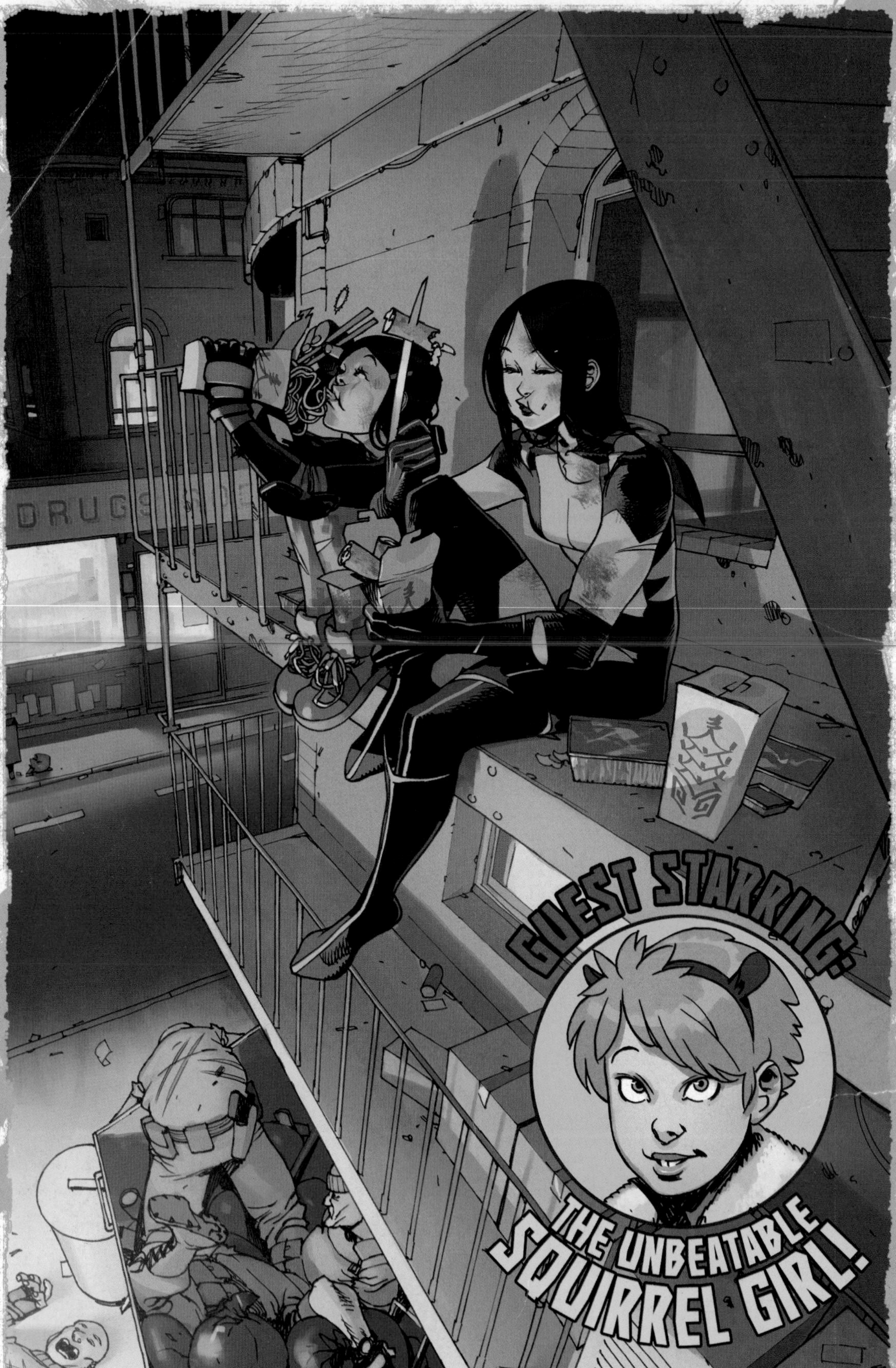
DRUGS
GUEST STARRING:
THE UNBEATABLE SQUIRREL GIRL!

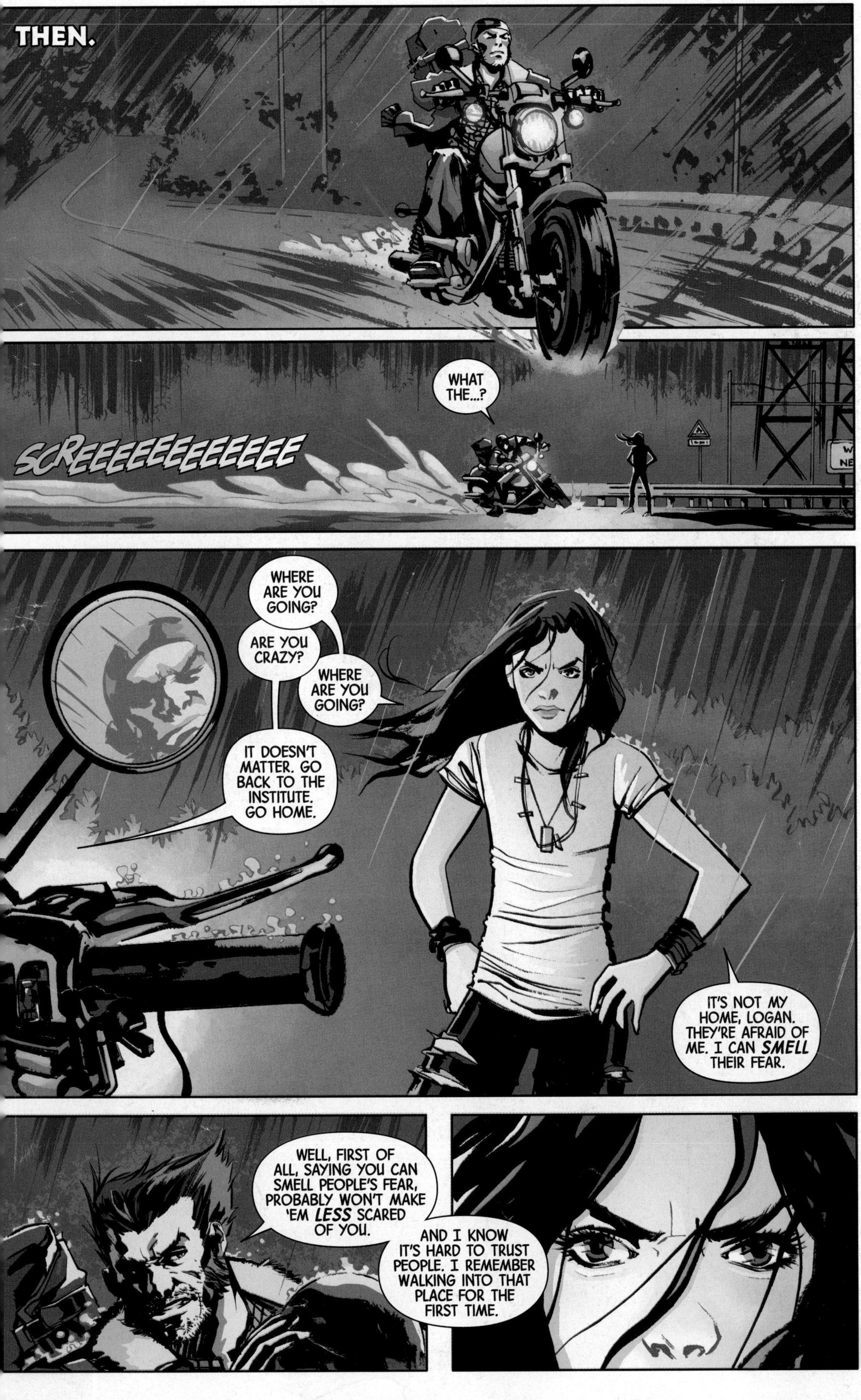
THEN.
SCREEEEEEEEEEEEE
WHAT THE...?
WHERE ARE YOU GOING?
ARE YOU CRAZY?
WHERE ARE YOU GOING?
IT DOESN'T MATTER. GO BACK TO THE INSTITUTE. GO HOME.
IT'S NOT MY HOME, LOGAN. THEY'RE AFRAID OF ME. I CAN SMELL THEIR FEAR.
WELL, FIRST OF ALL, SAYING YOU CAN SMELL PEOPLE'S FEAR, PROBABLY WON'T MAKE 'EM LESS SCARED OF YOU.
AND I KNOW IT'S HARD TO TRUST PEOPLE. I REMEMBER WALKING INTO THAT PLACE FOR THE FIRST TIME.

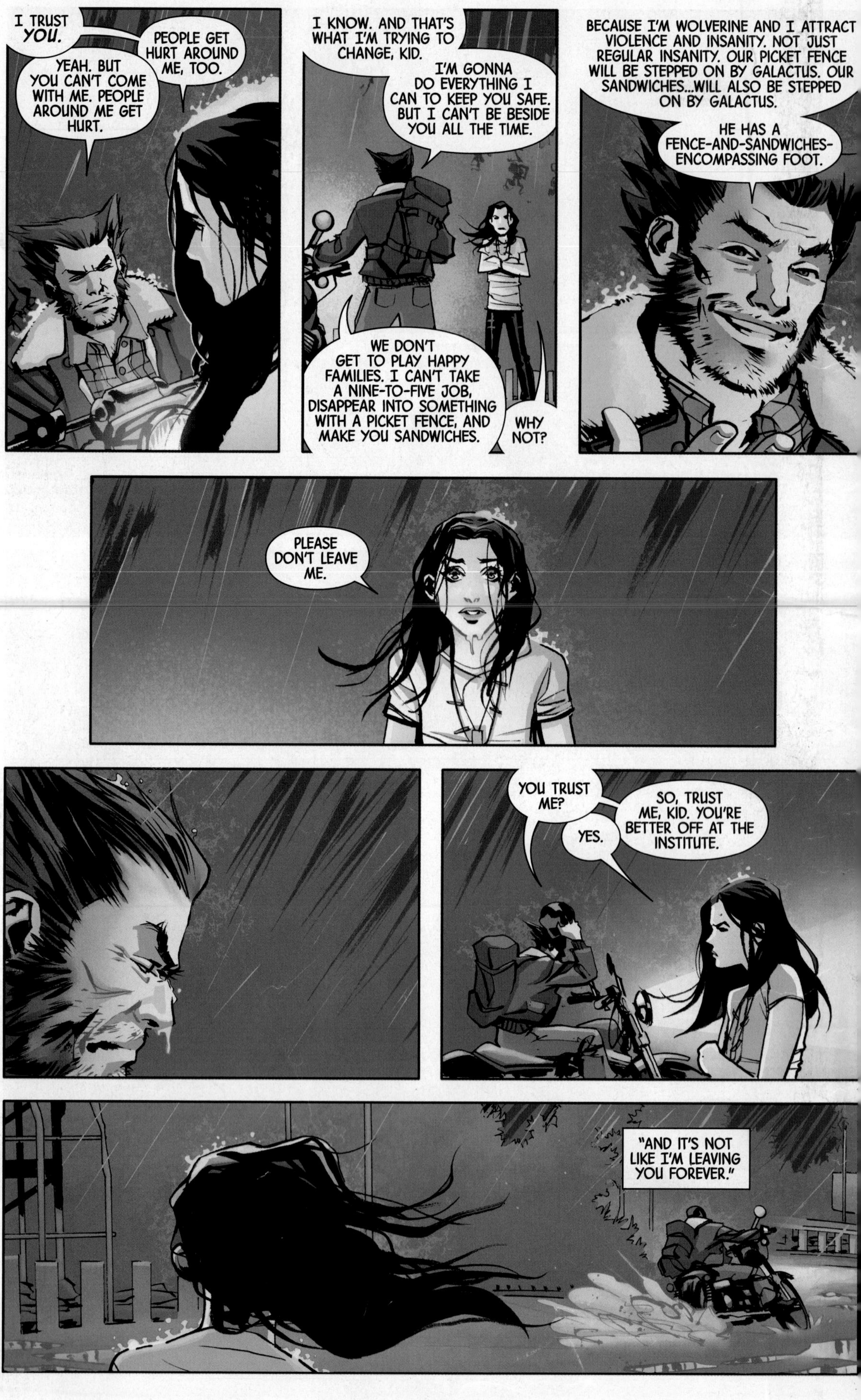

I TRUST *YOU.*
PEOPLE GET HURT AROUND ME, TOO.
YEAH. BUT YOU CAN'T COME WITH ME. PEOPLE AROUND ME GET HURT.
I KNOW. AND THAT'S WHAT I'M TRYING TO CHANGE, KID.
I'M GONNA DO EVERYTHING I CAN TO KEEP YOU SAFE. BUT I CAN'T BE BESIDE YOU ALL THE TIME.
WE DON'T GET TO PLAY HAPPY FAMILIES. I CAN'T TAKE A NINE-TO-FIVE JOB, DISAPPEAR INTO SOMETHING WITH A PICKET FENCE, AND MAKE YOU SANDWICHES.
WHY NOT?
BECAUSE I'M WOLVERINE AND I ATTRACT VIOLENCE AND INSANITY. NOT JUST REGULAR INSANITY. OUR PICKET FENCE WILL BE STEPPED ON BY GALACTUS. OUR SANDWICHES...WILL ALSO BE STEPPED ON BY GALACTUS.
HE HAS A FENCE-AND-SANDWICHES-ENCOMPASSING FOOT.
PLEASE DON'T LEAVE ME.
YOU TRUST ME?
YES.
SO, TRUST ME, KID. YOU'RE BETTER OFF AT THE INSTITUTE.
"AND IT'S NOT LIKE I'M LEAVING YOU FOREVER."

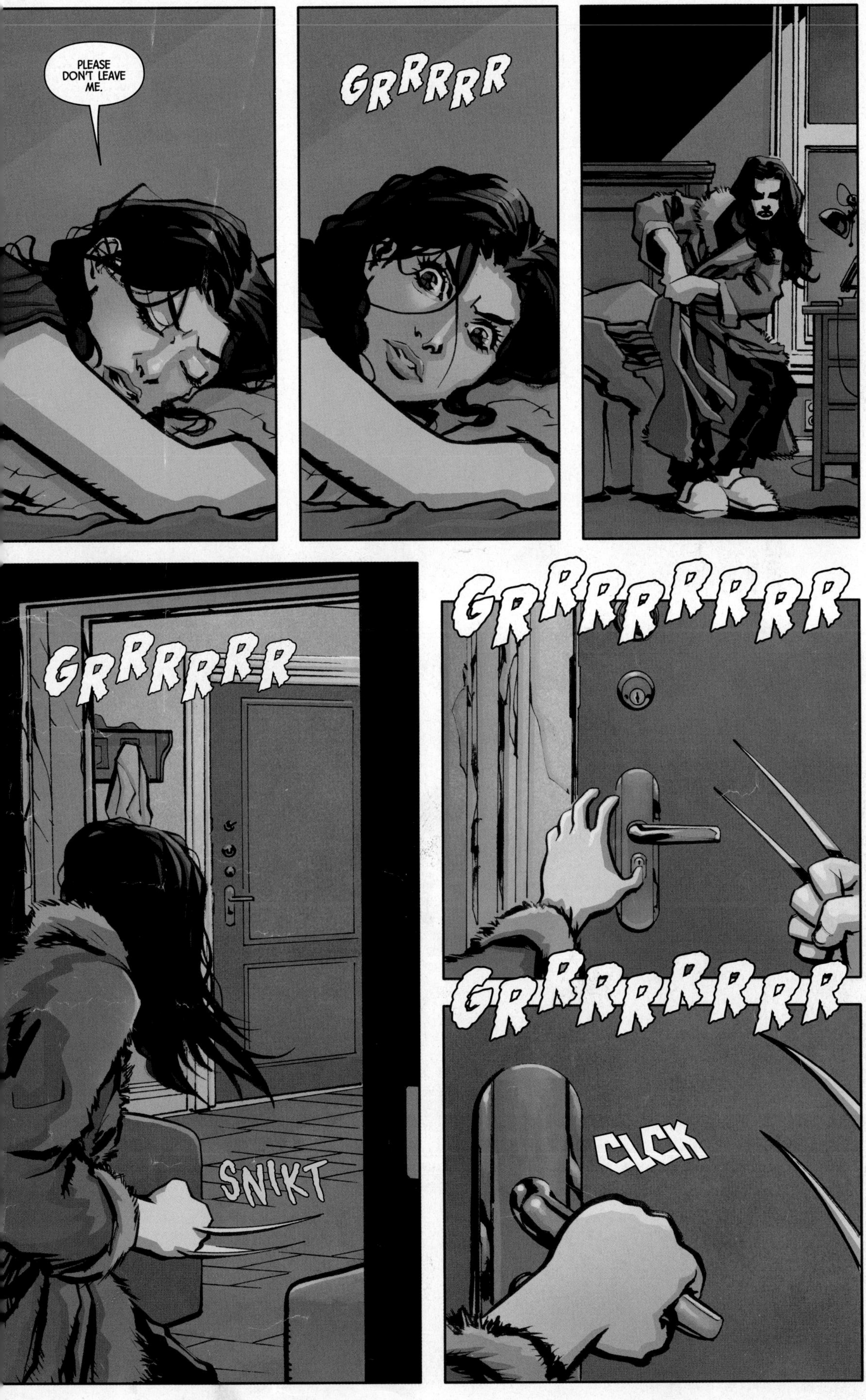
PLEASE DON'T LEAVE ME.
GRRRRR
GRRRRRR
GRRRRRRRRR
SNIKT
GRRRRRRRRR
CLCK

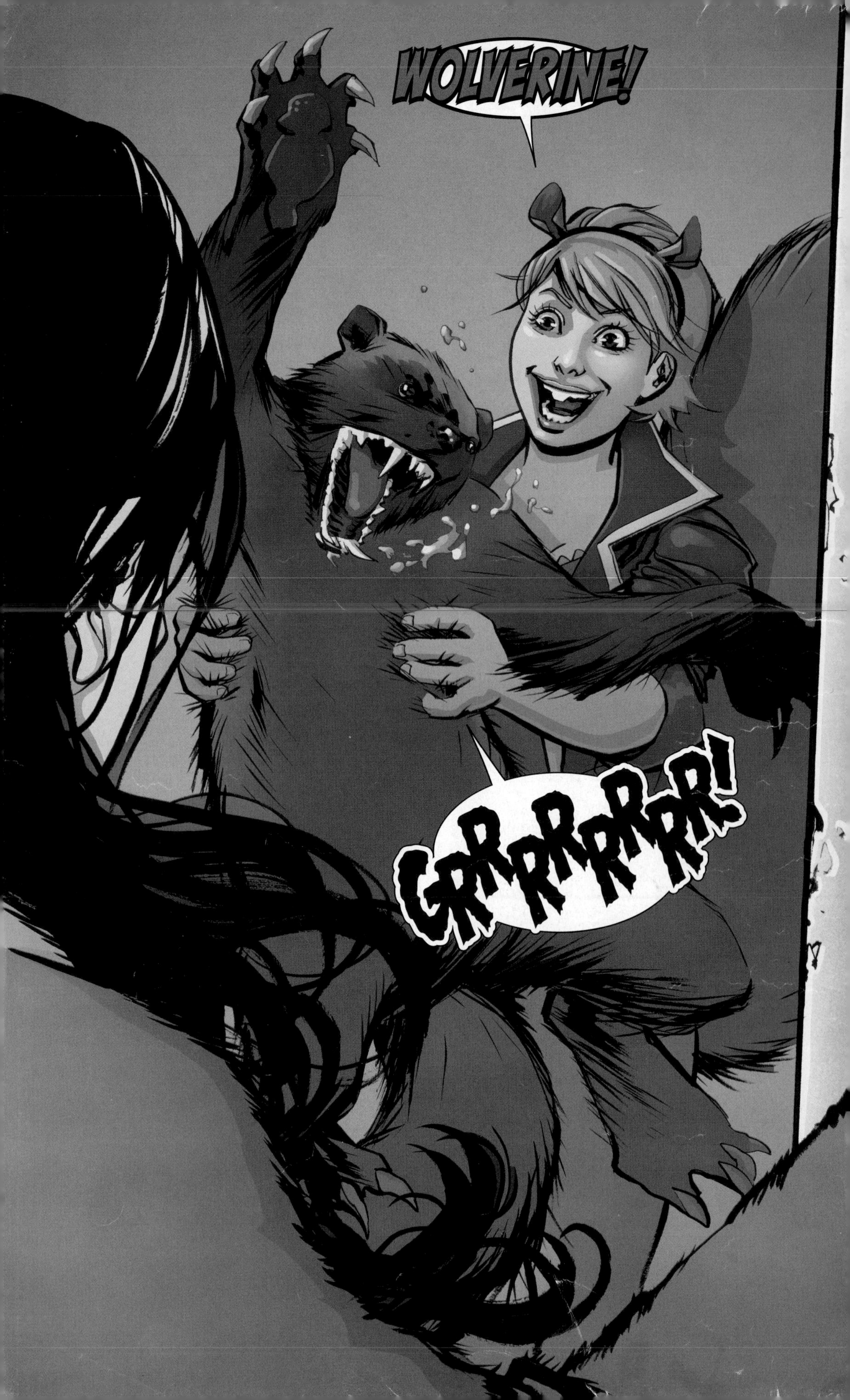
WOLVERINE!
GRRRRRRRR!

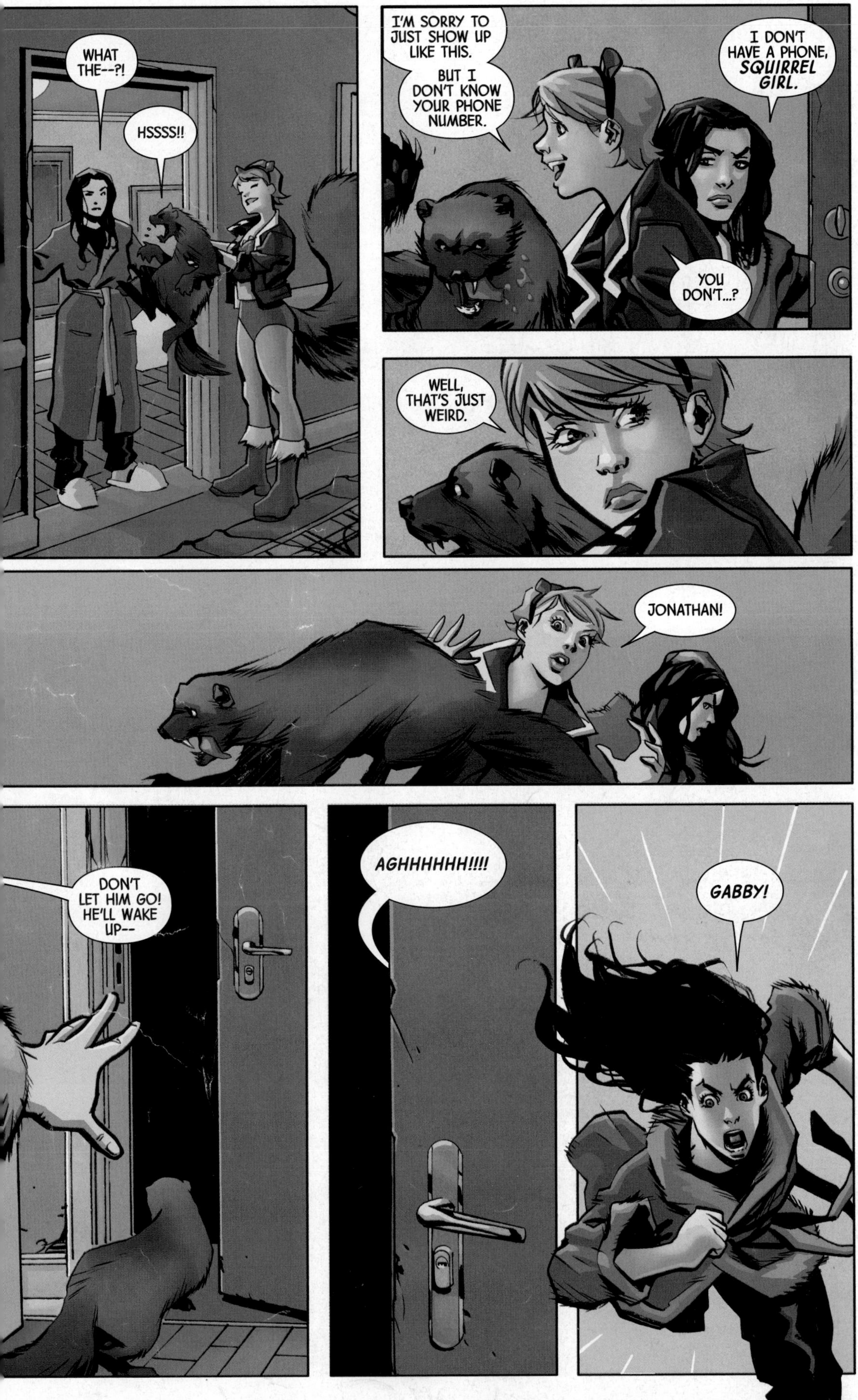

WHAT THE--?!
HSSSS!!
I'M SORRY TO JUST SHOW UP LIKE THIS.
BUT I DON'T KNOW YOUR PHONE NUMBER.
I DON'T HAVE A PHONE, SQUIRREL GIRL.
YOU DON'T...?
WELL, THAT'S JUST WEIRD.
JONATHAN!
DON'T LET HIM GO! HE'LL WAKE UP--
AGHHHHHH!!!!
GABBY!

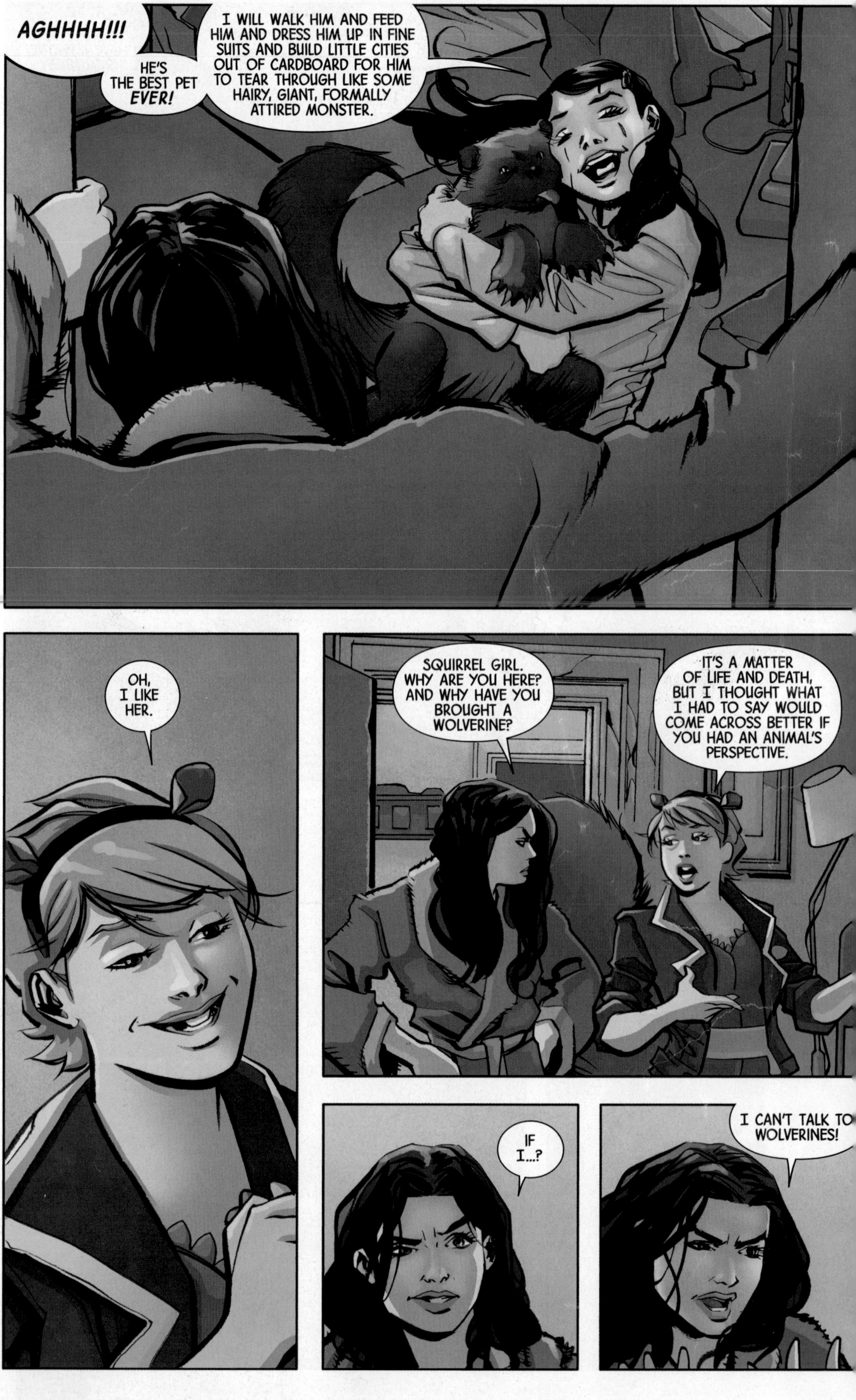
AGHHHH!!!
HE'S THE BEST PET EVER!
I WILL WALK HIM AND FEED HIM AND DRESS HIM UP IN FINE SUITS AND BUILD LITTLE CITIES OUT OF CARDBOARD FOR HIM TO TEAR THROUGH LIKE SOME HAIRY, GIANT, FORMALLY ATTIRED MONSTER.
OH, I LIKE HER.
SQUIRREL GIRL. WHY ARE YOU HERE? AND WHY HAVE YOU BROUGHT A WOLVERINE?
IT'S A MATTER OF LIFE AND DEATH, BUT I THOUGHT WHAT I HAD TO SAY WOULD COME ACROSS BETTER IF YOU HAD AN ANIMAL'S PERSPECTIVE.
IF I...?
I CAN'T TALK TO WOLVERINES!

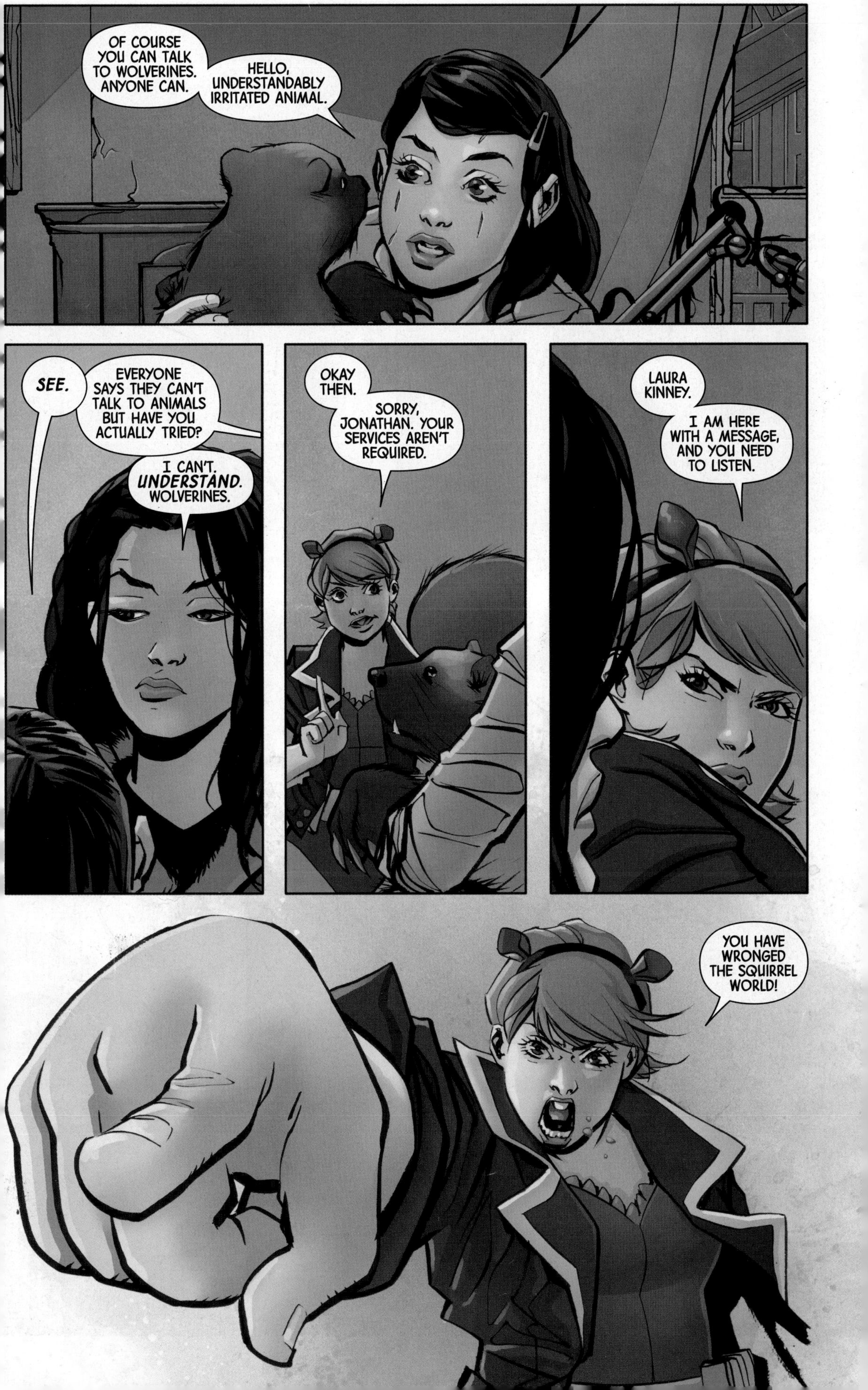
OF COURSE YOU CAN TALK TO WOLVERINES. ANYONE CAN.
HELLO, UNDERSTANDABLY IRRITATED ANIMAL.
SEE.
EVERYONE SAYS THEY CAN'T TALK TO ANIMALS BUT HAVE YOU ACTUALLY TRIED?
I CAN'T. UNDERSTAND. WOLVERINES.
OKAY THEN.
SORRY, JONATHAN. YOUR SERVICES AREN'T REQUIRED.
LAURA KINNEY.
I AM HERE WITH A MESSAGE, AND YOU NEED TO LISTEN.
YOU HAVE WRONGED THE SQUIRREL WORLD!

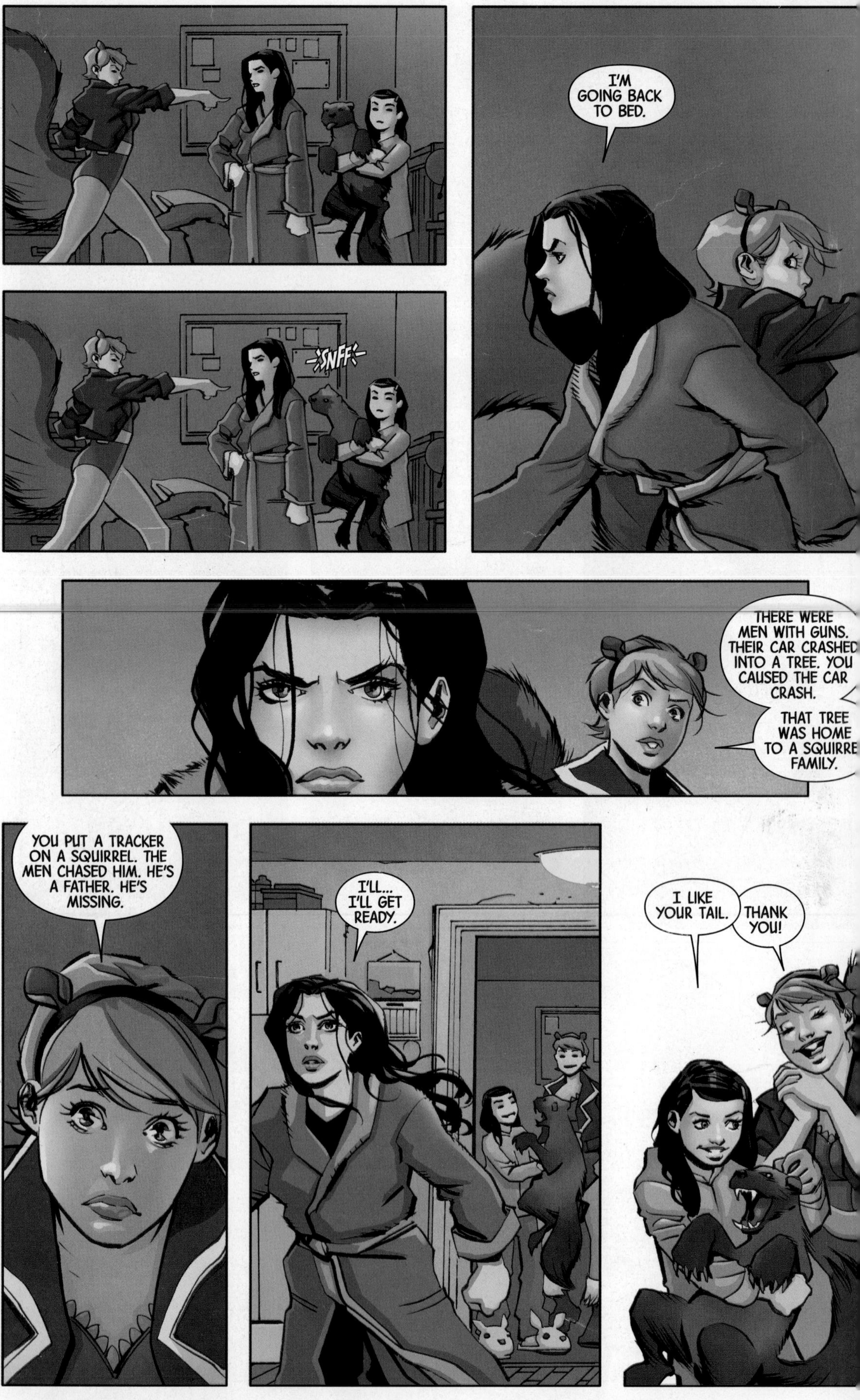
-SNFF-
I'M GOING BACK TO BED.
THERE WERE MEN WITH GUNS. THEIR CAR CRASHED INTO A TREE. YOU CAUSED THE CAR CRASH.
THAT TREE WAS HOME TO A SQUIRREL FAMILY.
YOU PUT A TRACKER ON A SQUIRREL. THE MEN CHASED HIM. HE'S A FATHER. HE'S MISSING.
I'LL... I'LL GET READY.
I LIKE YOUR TAIL.
THANK YOU!

240 – 1016 68 AVE SW

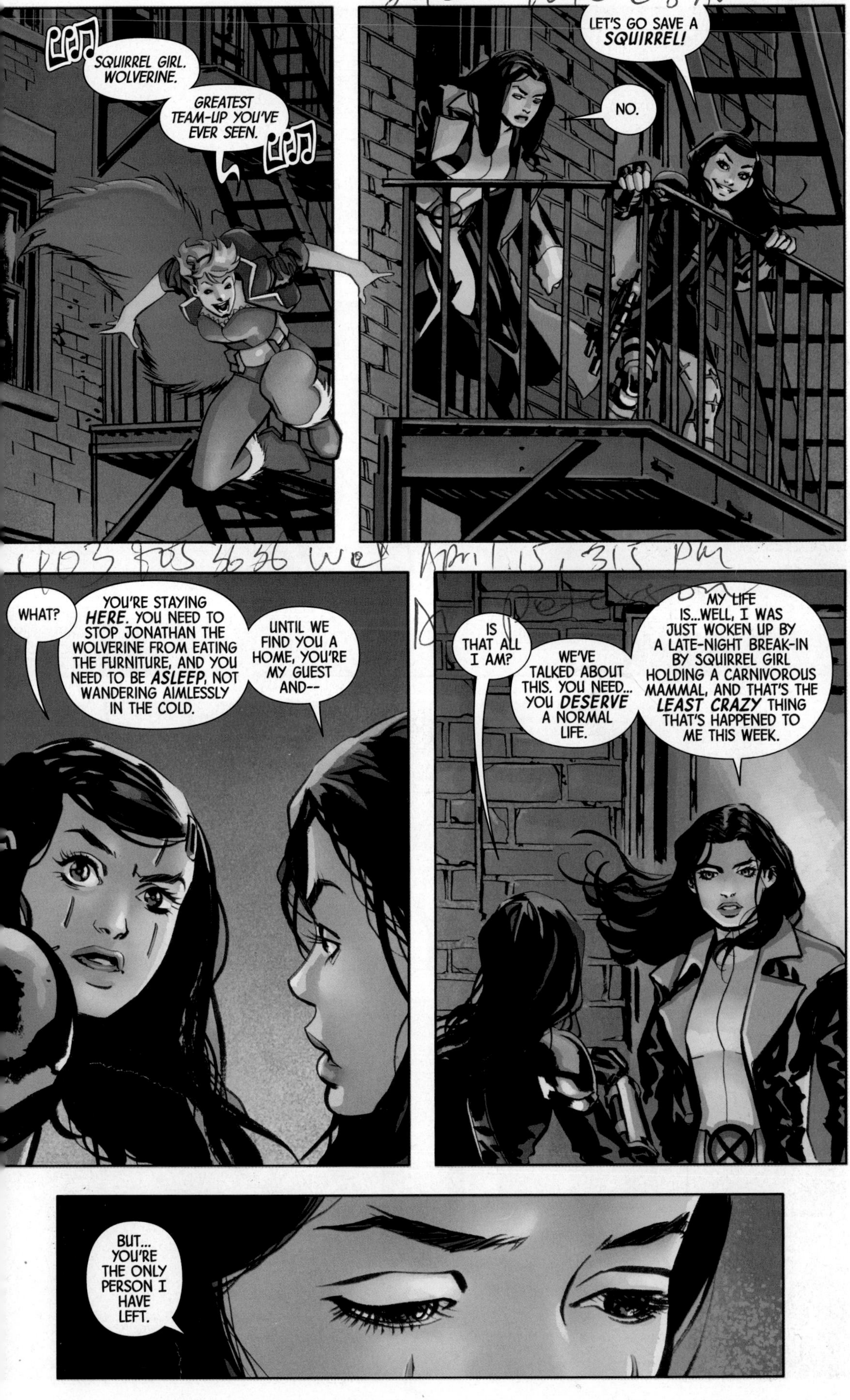
SQUIRREL GIRL. WOLVERINE.
GREATEST TEAM-UP YOU'VE EVER SEEN.
LET'S GO SAVE A SQUIRREL!
NO.
WHAT?
YOU'RE STAYING HERE. YOU NEED TO STOP JONATHAN THE WOLVERINE FROM EATING THE FURNITURE, AND YOU NEED TO BE ASLEEP, NOT WANDERING AIMLESSLY IN THE COLD.
UNTIL WE FIND YOU A HOME, YOU'RE MY GUEST AND--
IS THAT ALL I AM?
WE'VE TALKED ABOUT THIS. YOU NEED... YOU DESERVE A NORMAL LIFE.
MY LIFE IS...WELL, I WAS JUST WOKEN UP BY A LATE-NIGHT BREAK-IN BY SQUIRREL GIRL HOLDING A CARNIVOROUS MAMMAL, AND THAT'S THE LEAST CRAZY THING THAT'S HAPPENED TO ME THIS WEEK.
BUT... YOU'RE THE ONLY PERSON I HAVE LEFT.

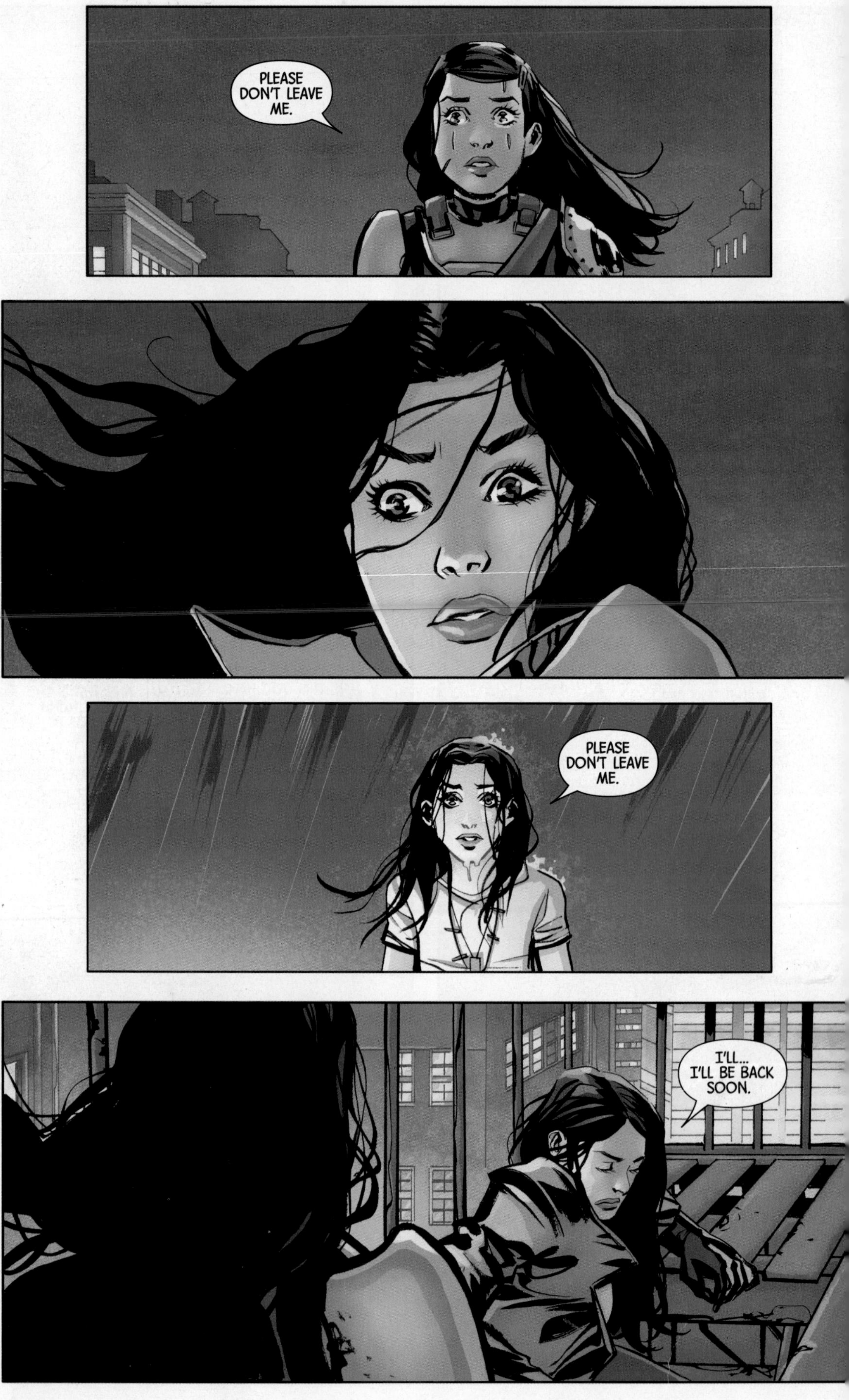
PLEASE DON'T LEAVE ME.
PLEASE DON'T LEAVE ME.
I'LL... I'LL BE BACK SOON.

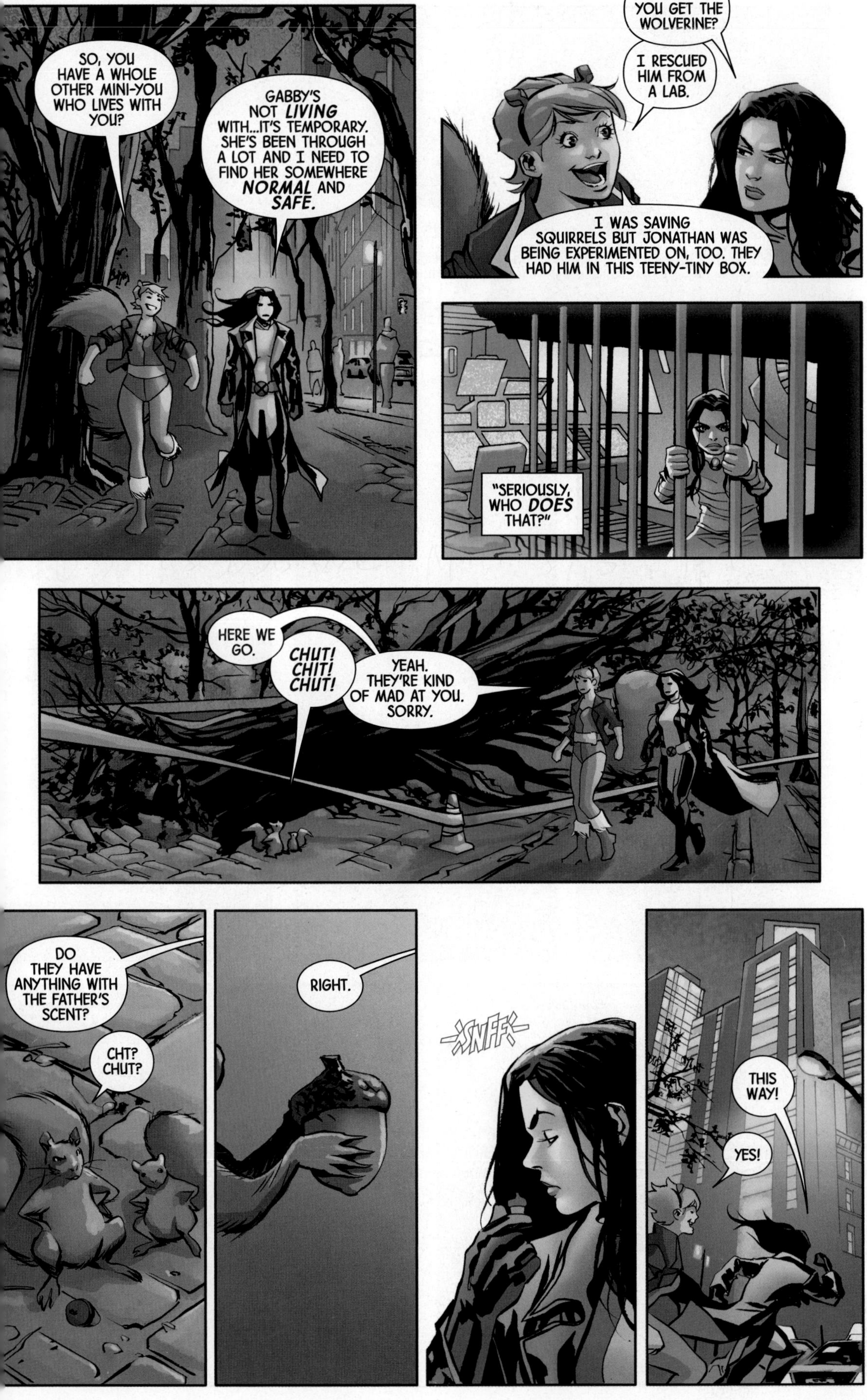
SO, YOU HAVE A WHOLE OTHER MINI-YOU WHO LIVES WITH YOU?
GABBY'S NOT LIVING WITH...IT'S TEMPORARY. SHE'S BEEN THROUGH A LOT AND I NEED TO FIND HER SOMEWHERE NORMAL AND SAFE.
WHERE DID YOU GET THE WOLVERINE?
I RESCUED HIM FROM A LAB.
I WAS SAVING SQUIRRELS BUT JONATHAN WAS BEING EXPERIMENTED ON, TOO. THEY HAD HIM IN THIS TEENY-TINY BOX.
"SERIOUSLY, WHO DOES THAT?"
HERE WE GO.
CHUT! CHIT! CHUT!
YEAH. THEY'RE KIND OF MAD AT YOU. SORRY.
DO THEY HAVE ANYTHING WITH THE FATHER'S SCENT?
CHT? CHUT?
RIGHT.
SNFF
THIS WAY!
YES!

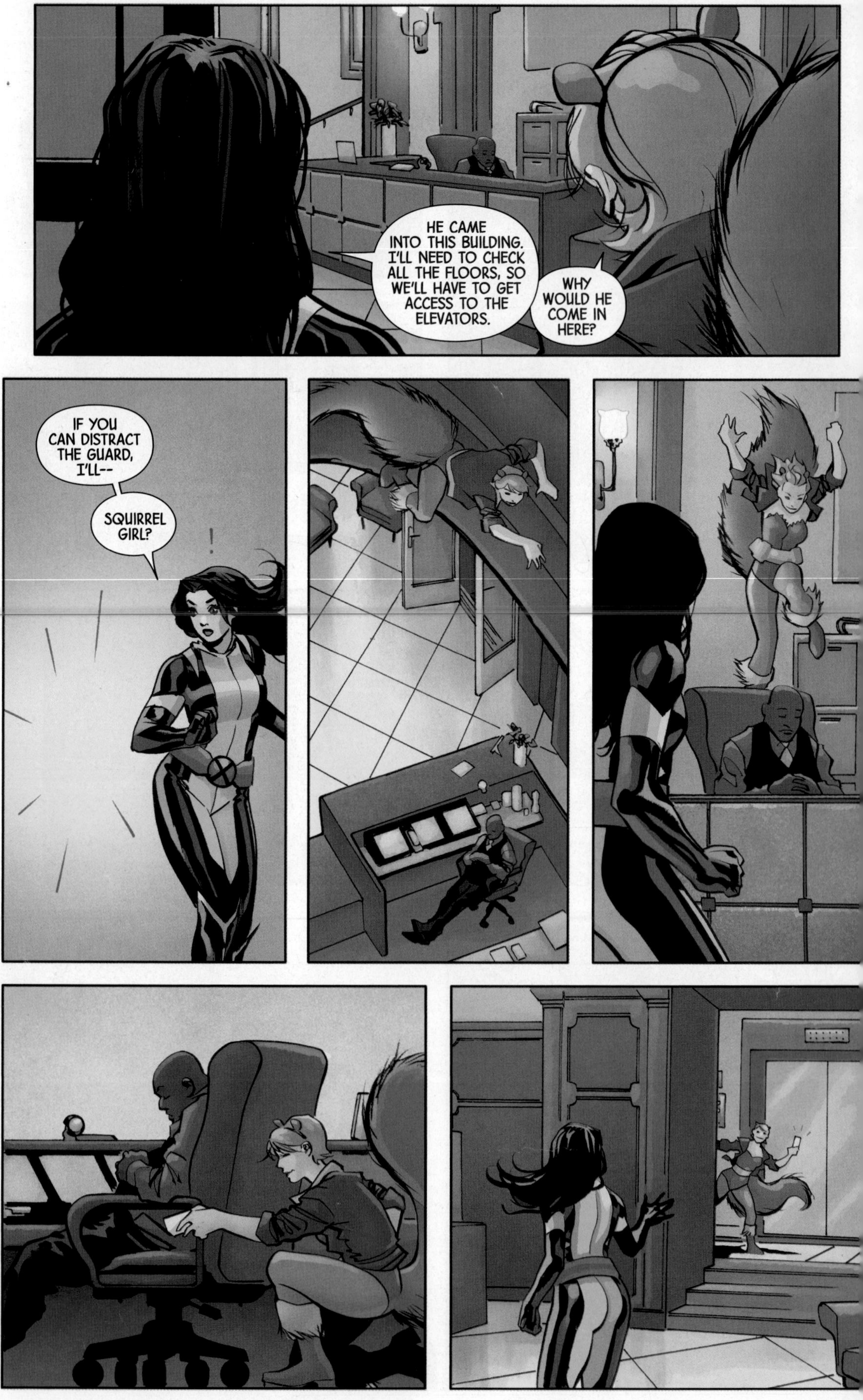
HE CAME INTO THIS BUILDING. I'LL NEED TO CHECK ALL THE FLOORS, SO WE'LL HAVE TO GET ACCESS TO THE ELEVATORS.
WHY WOULD HE COME IN HERE?
IF YOU CAN DISTRACT THE GUARD, I'LL--
SQUIRREL GIRL?
!

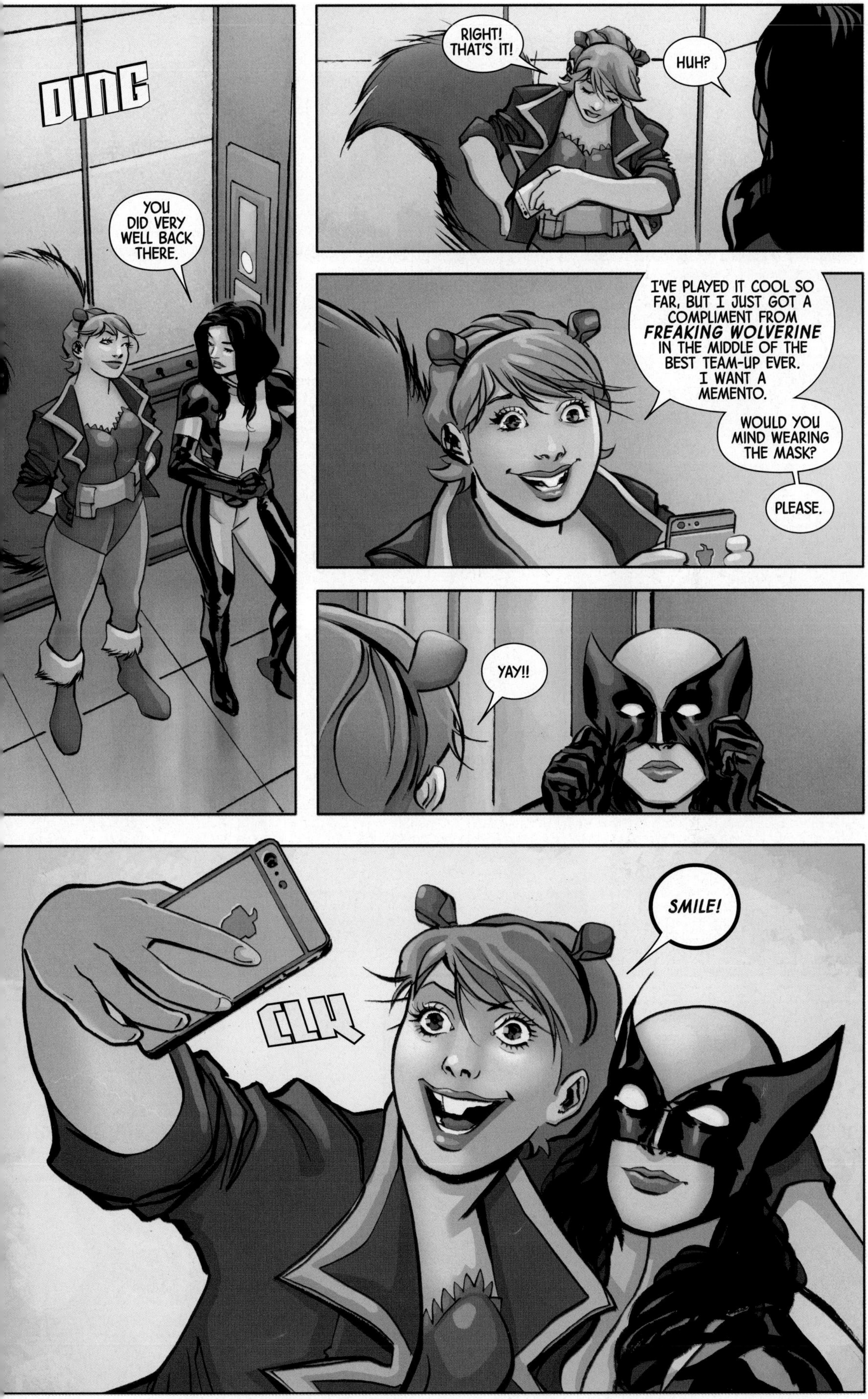
DING
YOU DID VERY WELL BACK THERE.
RIGHT! THAT'S IT!
HUH?
I'VE PLAYED IT COOL SO FAR, BUT I JUST GOT A COMPLIMENT FROM FREAKING WOLVERINE IN THE MIDDLE OF THE BEST TEAM-UP EVER. I WANT A MEMENTO.
WOULD YOU MIND WEARING THE MASK?
PLEASE.
YAY!!
SMILE!
CLK

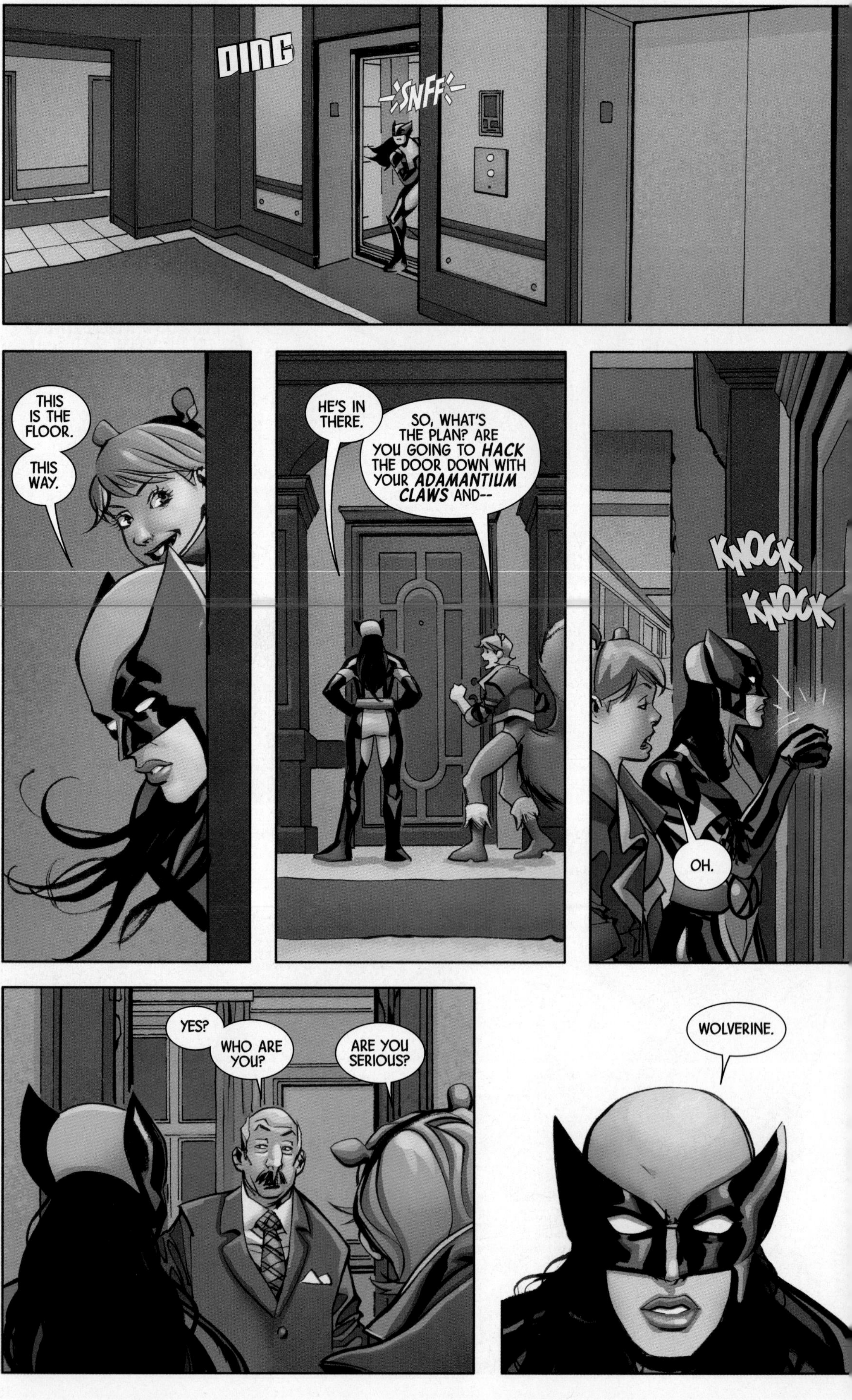
DING
SNFF
THIS IS THE FLOOR.
THIS WAY.
HE'S IN THERE.
SO, WHAT'S THE PLAN? ARE YOU GOING TO HACK THE DOOR DOWN WITH YOUR ADAMANTIUM CLAWS AND--
KNOCK
KNOCK
OH.
YES?
WHO ARE YOU?
ARE YOU SERIOUS?
WOLVERINE.

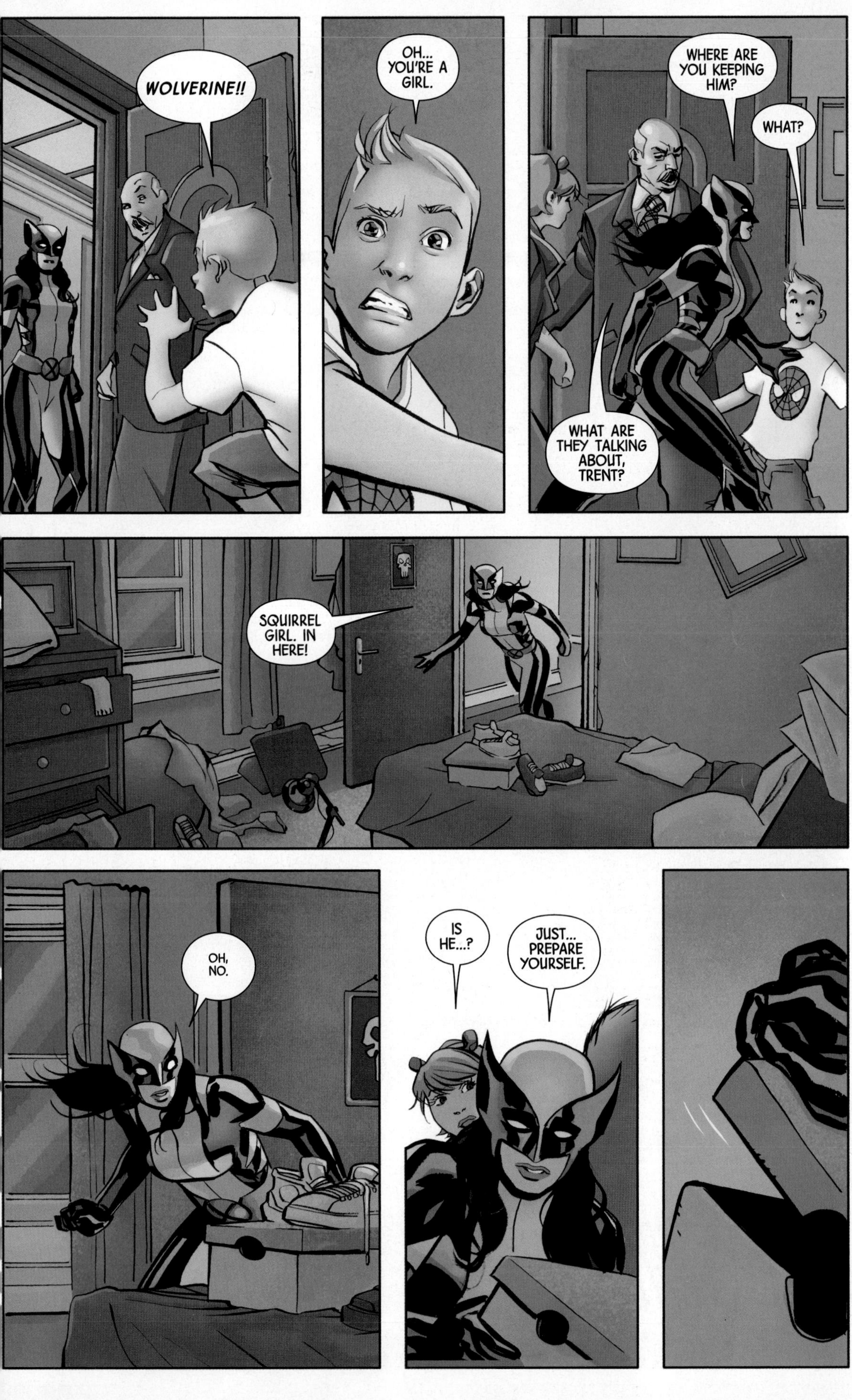
WOLVERINE!!
OH... YOU'RE A GIRL.
WHERE ARE YOU KEEPING HIM?
WHAT?
WHAT ARE THEY TALKING ABOUT, TRENT?
SQUIRREL GIRL. IN HERE!
OH, NO.
IS HE...?
JUST... PREPARE YOURSELF.

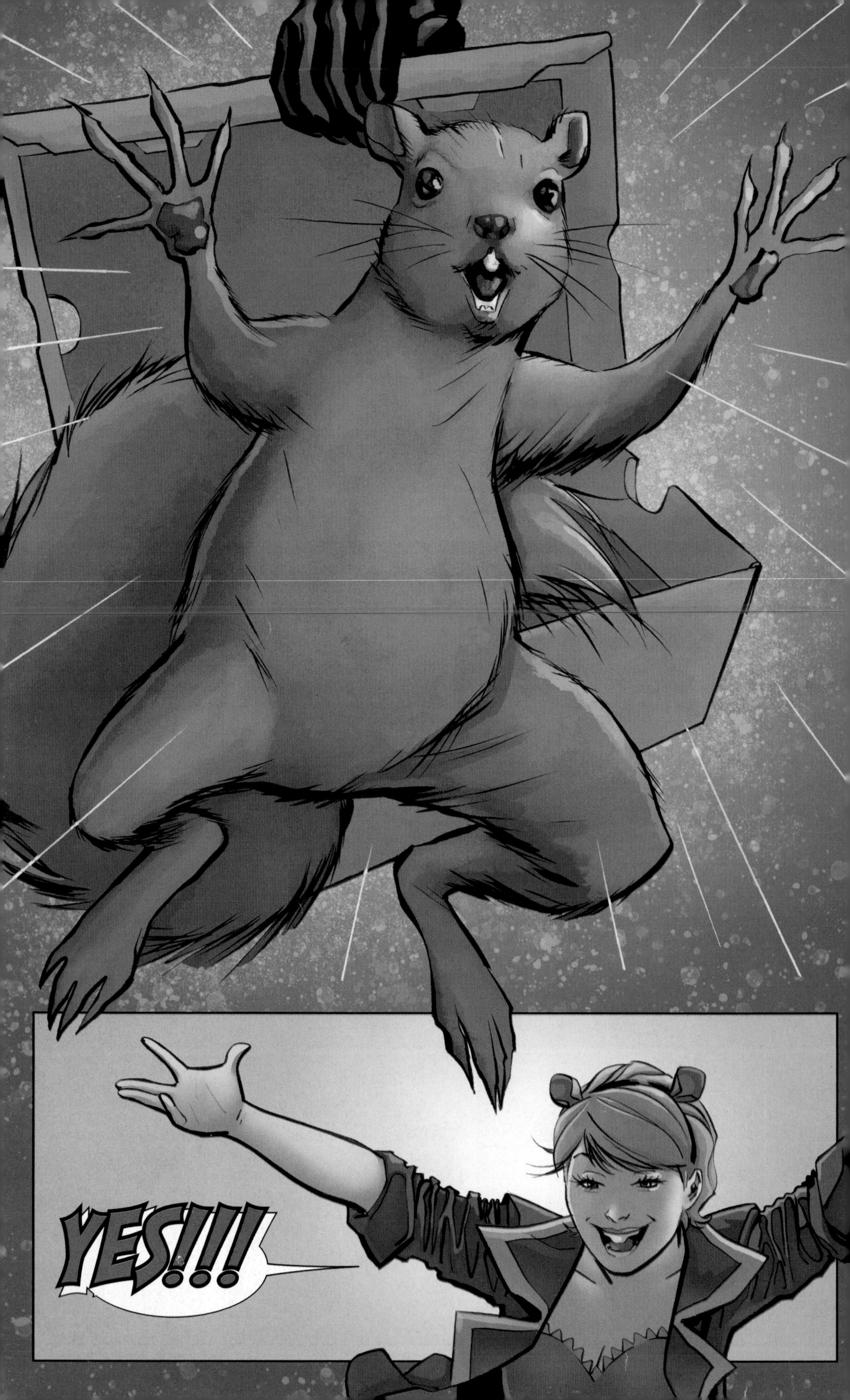
YES!!!

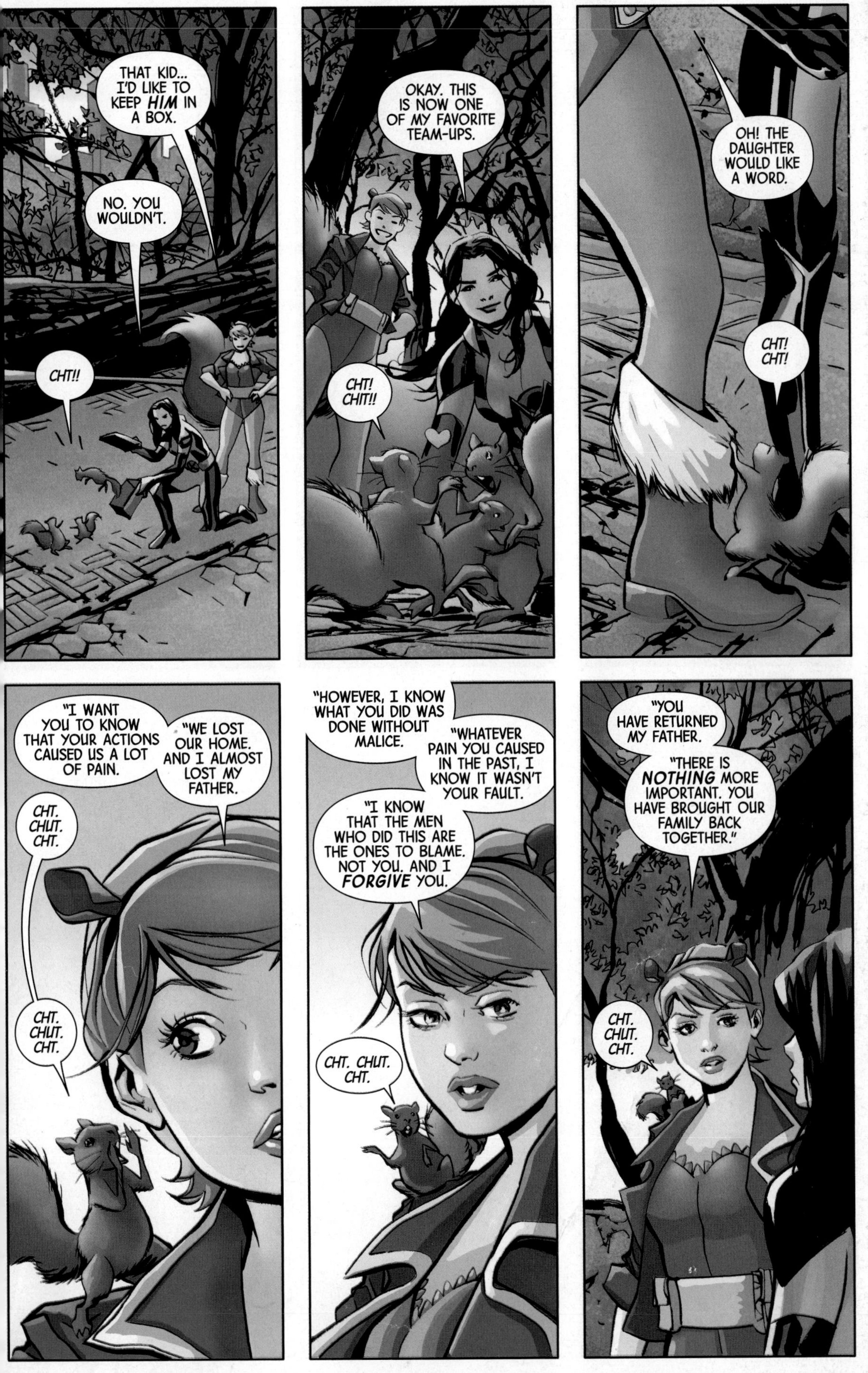
THAT KID... I'D LIKE TO KEEP HIM IN A BOX.
NO. YOU WOULDN'T.
CHT!!
OKAY. THIS IS NOW ONE OF MY FAVORITE TEAM-UPS.
CHT! CHIT!!
OH! THE DAUGHTER WOULD LIKE A WORD.
CHT! CHT!
"I WANT YOU TO KNOW THAT YOUR ACTIONS CAUSED US A LOT OF PAIN.
"WE LOST OUR HOME. AND I ALMOST LOST MY FATHER.
CHT. CHUT. CHT.
CHT. CHUT. CHT.
"HOWEVER, I KNOW WHAT YOU DID WAS DONE WITHOUT MALICE.
"WHATEVER PAIN YOU CAUSED IN THE PAST, I KNOW IT WASN'T YOUR FAULT.
"I KNOW THAT THE MEN WHO DID THIS ARE THE ONES TO BLAME. NOT YOU. AND I FORGIVE YOU.
CHT. CHUT. CHT.
"YOU HAVE RETURNED MY FATHER.
"THERE IS NOTHING MORE IMPORTANT. YOU HAVE BROUGHT OUR FAMILY BACK TOGETHER."
CHT. CHUT. CHT.

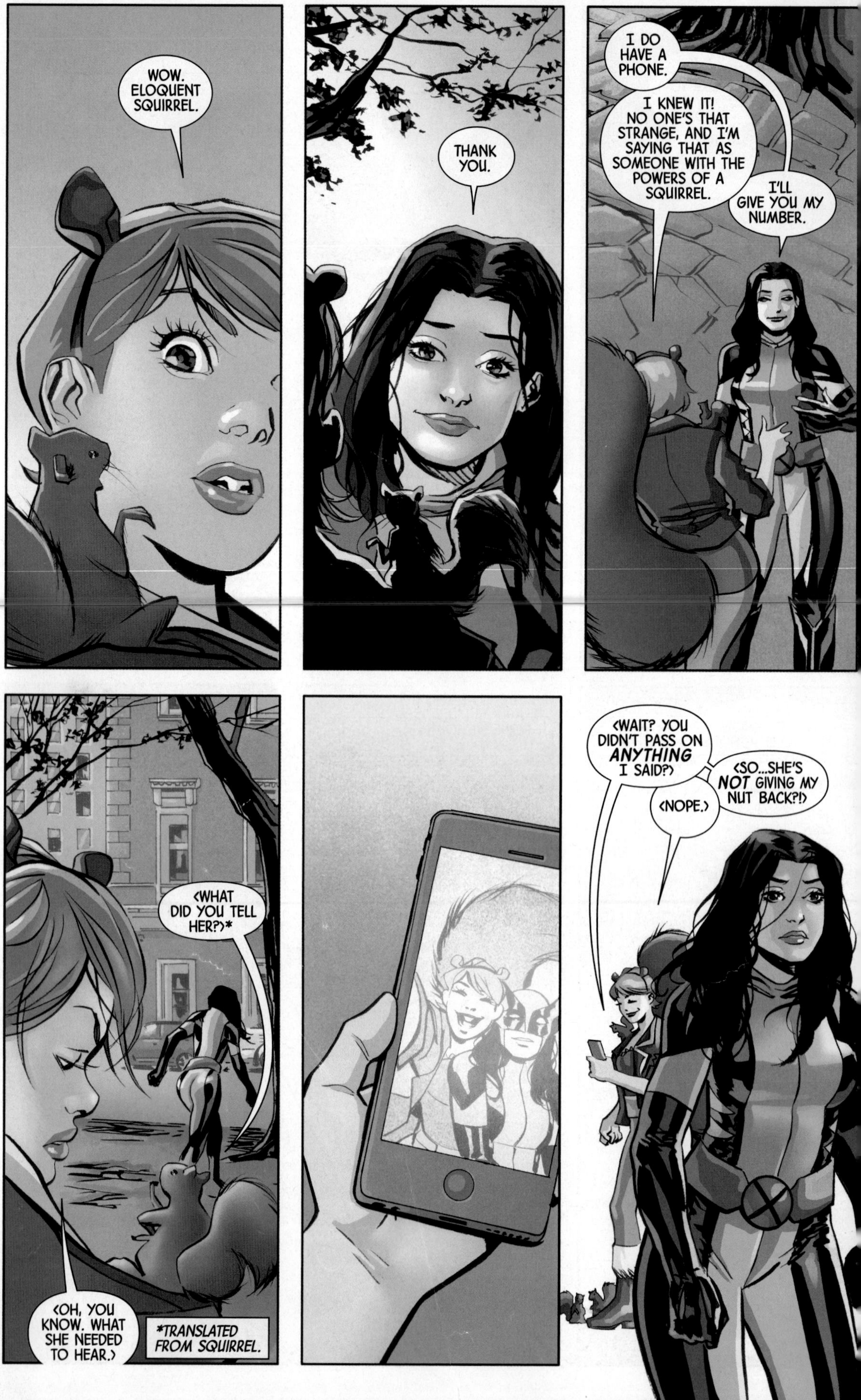
WOW. ELOQUENT SQUIRREL.
THANK YOU.
I DO HAVE A PHONE.
I KNEW IT! NO ONE'S THAT STRANGE, AND I'M SAYING THAT AS SOMEONE WITH THE POWERS OF A SQUIRREL.
I'LL GIVE YOU MY NUMBER.
<WHAT DID YOU TELL HER?>*
<OH, YOU KNOW. WHAT SHE NEEDED TO HEAR.>
*TRANSLATED FROM SQUIRREL.
<WAIT? YOU DIDN'T PASS ON *ANYTHING* I SAID?>
<NOPE.>
<SO...SHE'S **NOT** GIVING MY NUT BACK?!>

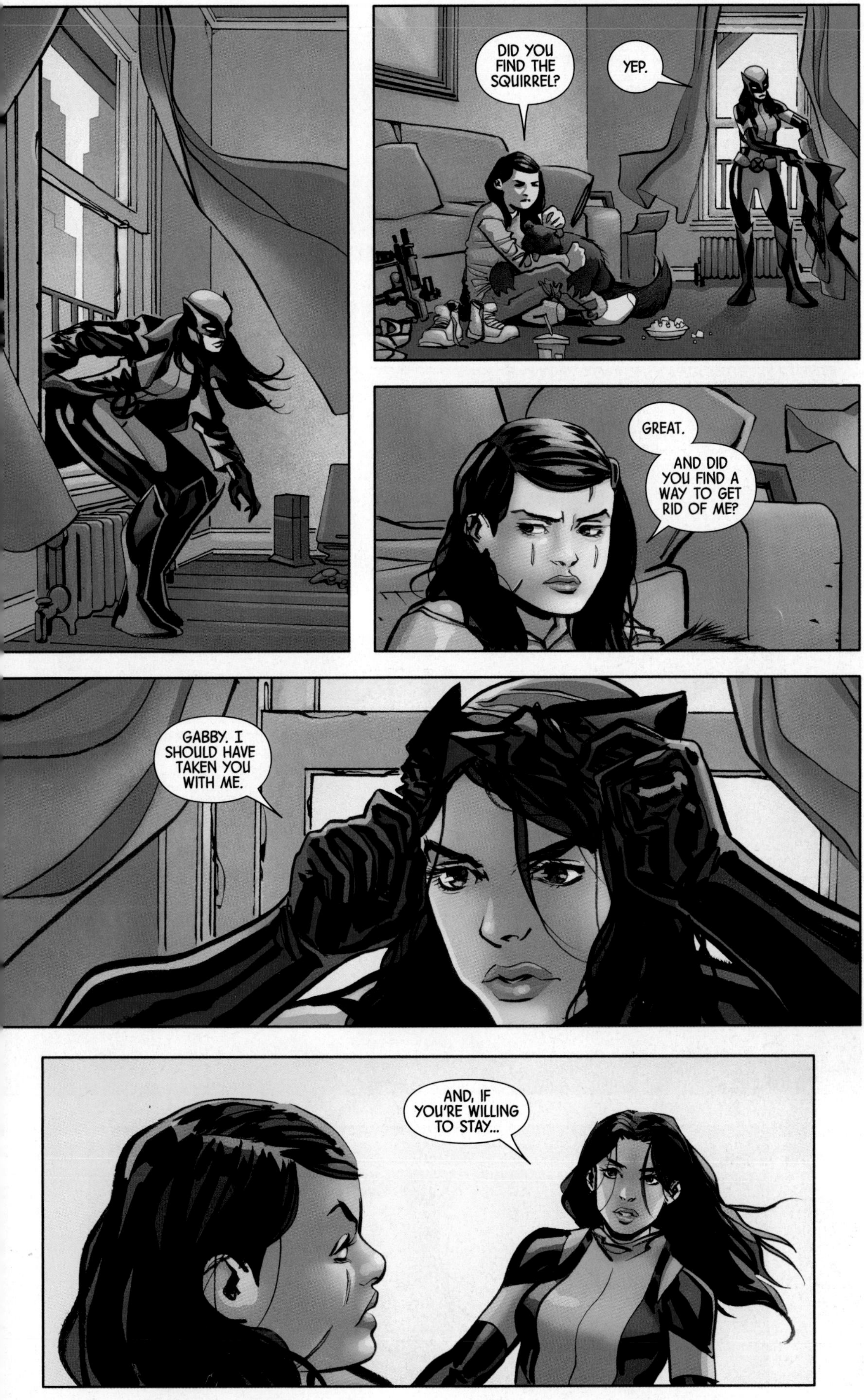
DID YOU FIND THE SQUIRREL?
YEP.
GREAT.
AND DID YOU FIND A WAY TO GET RID OF ME?
GABBY. I SHOULD HAVE TAKEN YOU WITH ME.
AND, IF YOU'RE WILLING TO STAY...

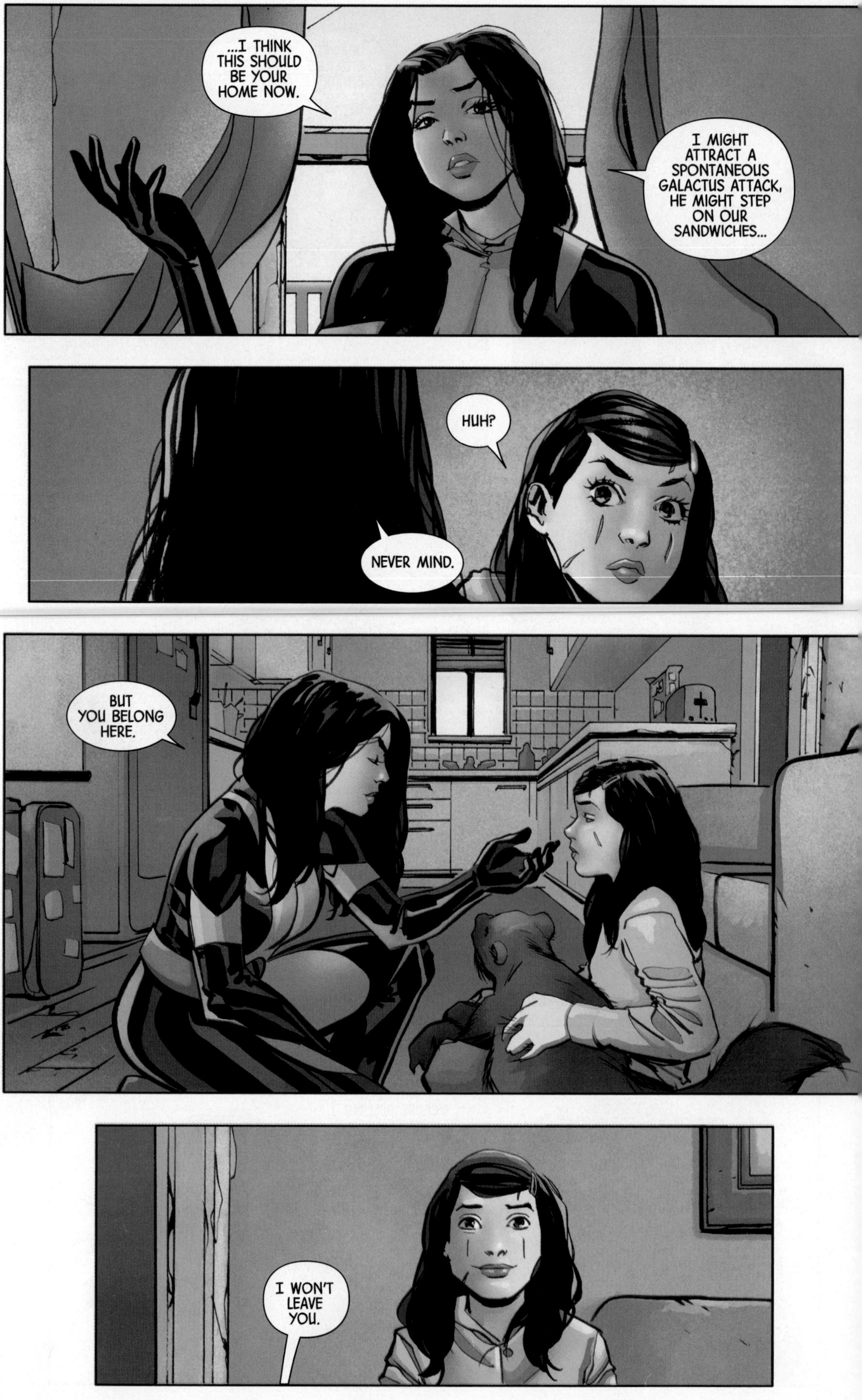

...I THINK THIS SHOULD BE YOUR HOME NOW.
I MIGHT ATTRACT A SPONTANEOUS GALACTUS ATTACK, HE MIGHT STEP ON OUR SANDWICHES...
HUH?
NEVER MIND.
BUT YOU BELONG HERE.
I WON'T LEAVE YOU.

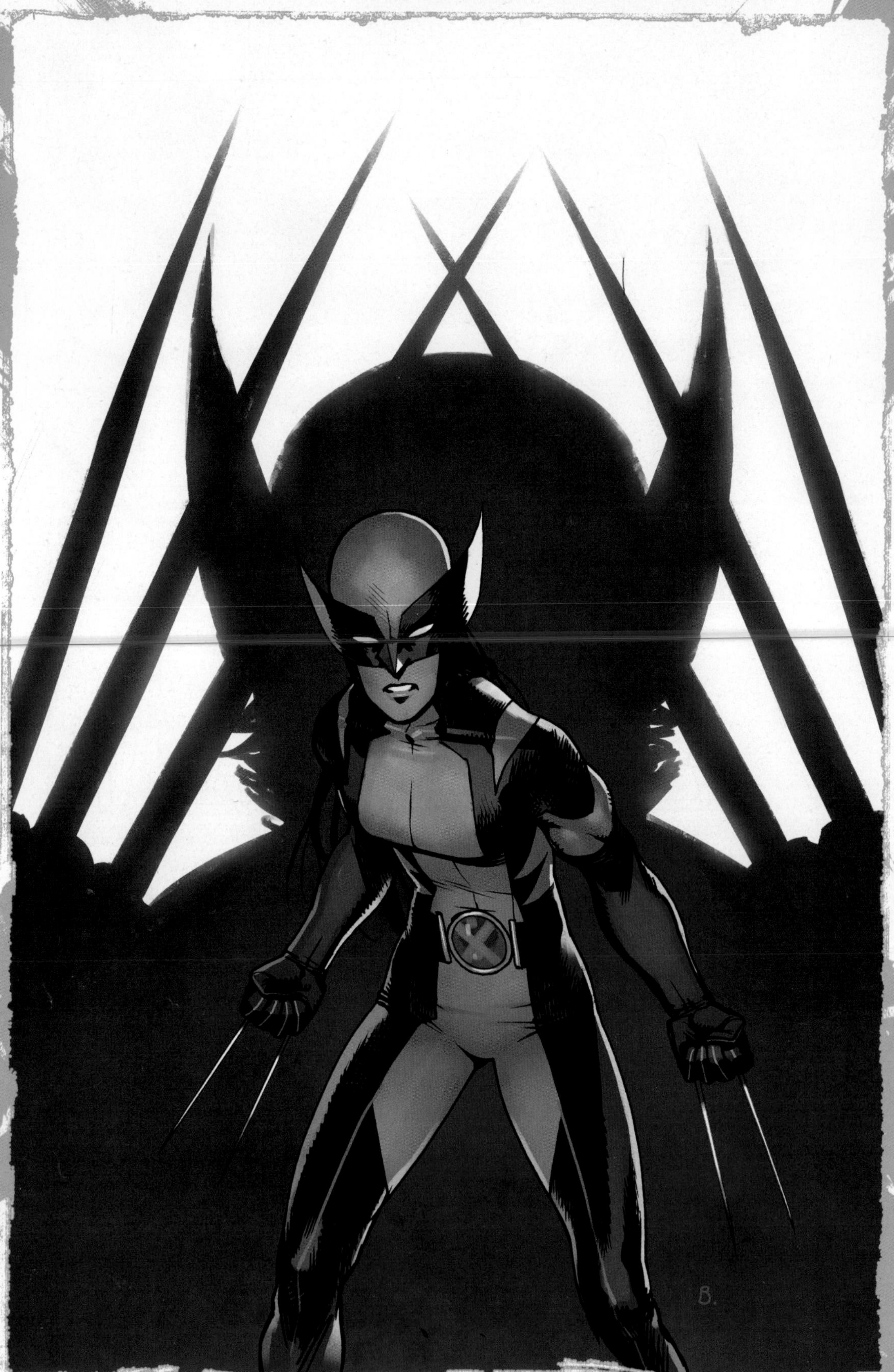
B.

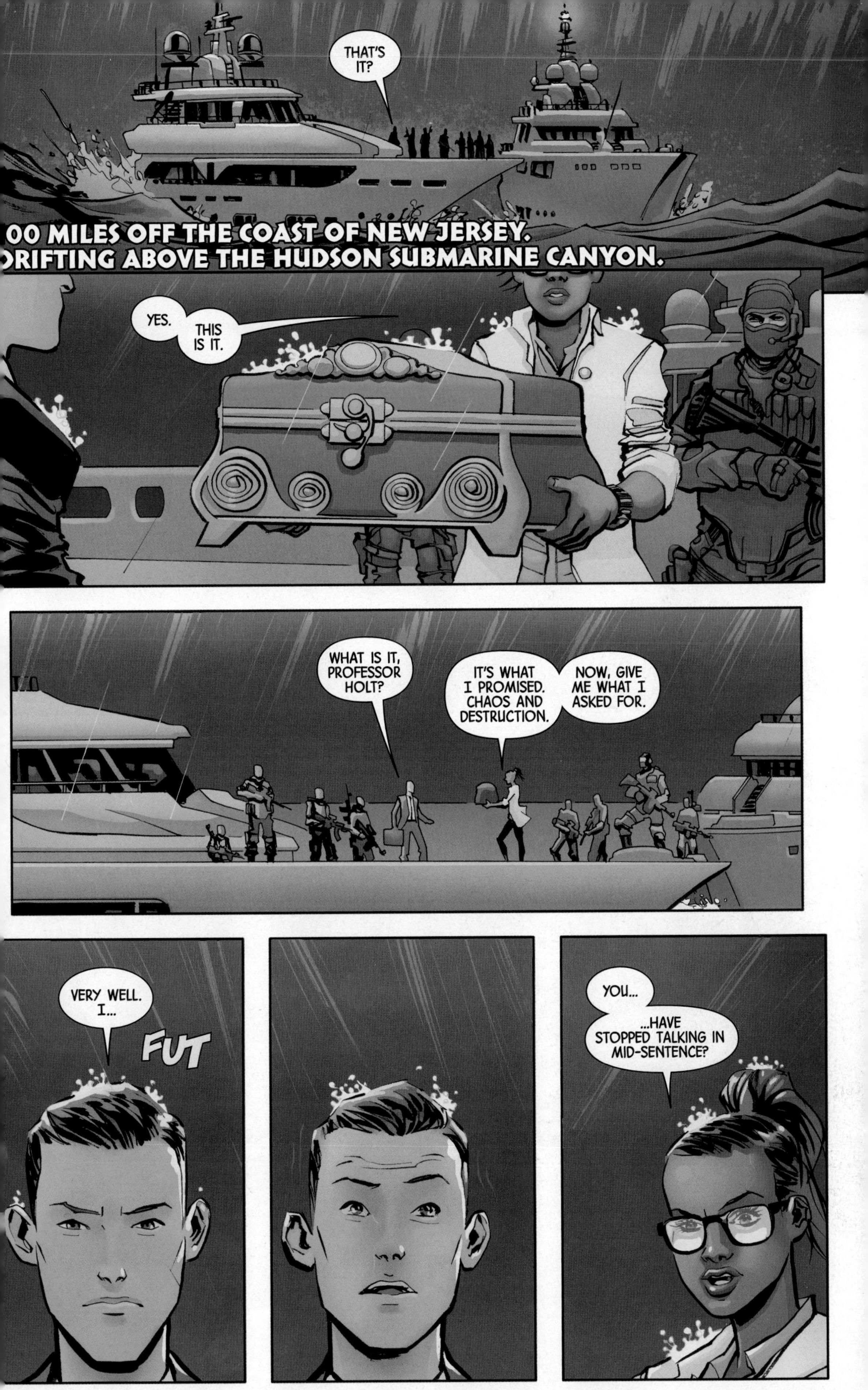
THAT'S IT?
00 MILES OFF THE COAST OF NEW JERSEY.
ORIFTING ABOVE THE HUDSON SUBMARINE CANYON.
YES.
THIS IS IT.
WHAT IS IT, PROFESSOR HOLT?
IT'S WHAT I PROMISED. CHAOS AND DESTRUCTION.
NOW, GIVE ME WHAT I ASKED FOR.
VERY WELL. I...
FUT
YOU...
...HAVE STOPPED TALKING IN MID-SENTENCE?

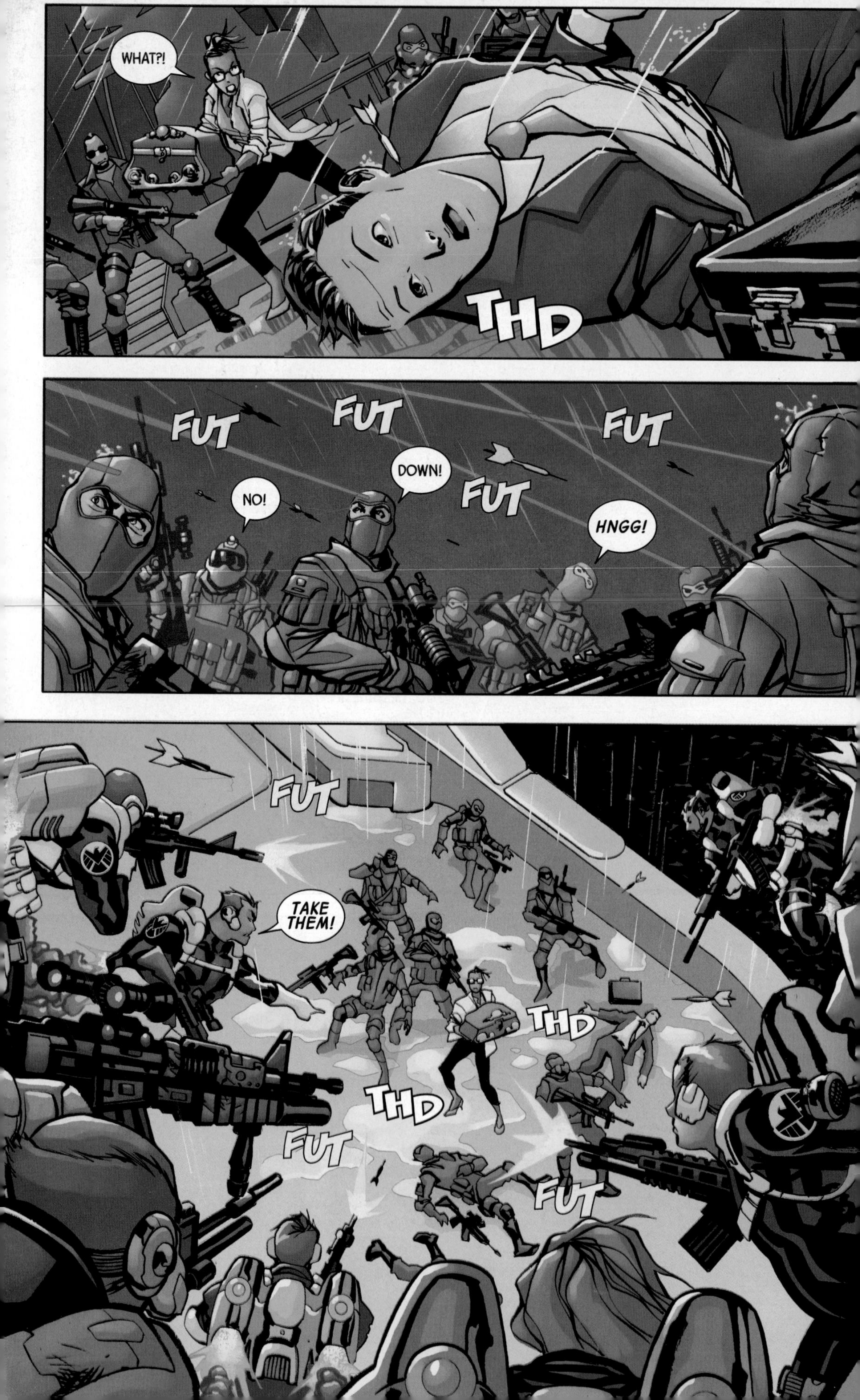
WHAT?!
THD
FUT
FUT
FUT
NO!
DOWN!
FUT
HNGG!
FUT
TAKE THEM!
THD
THD
FUT
FUT

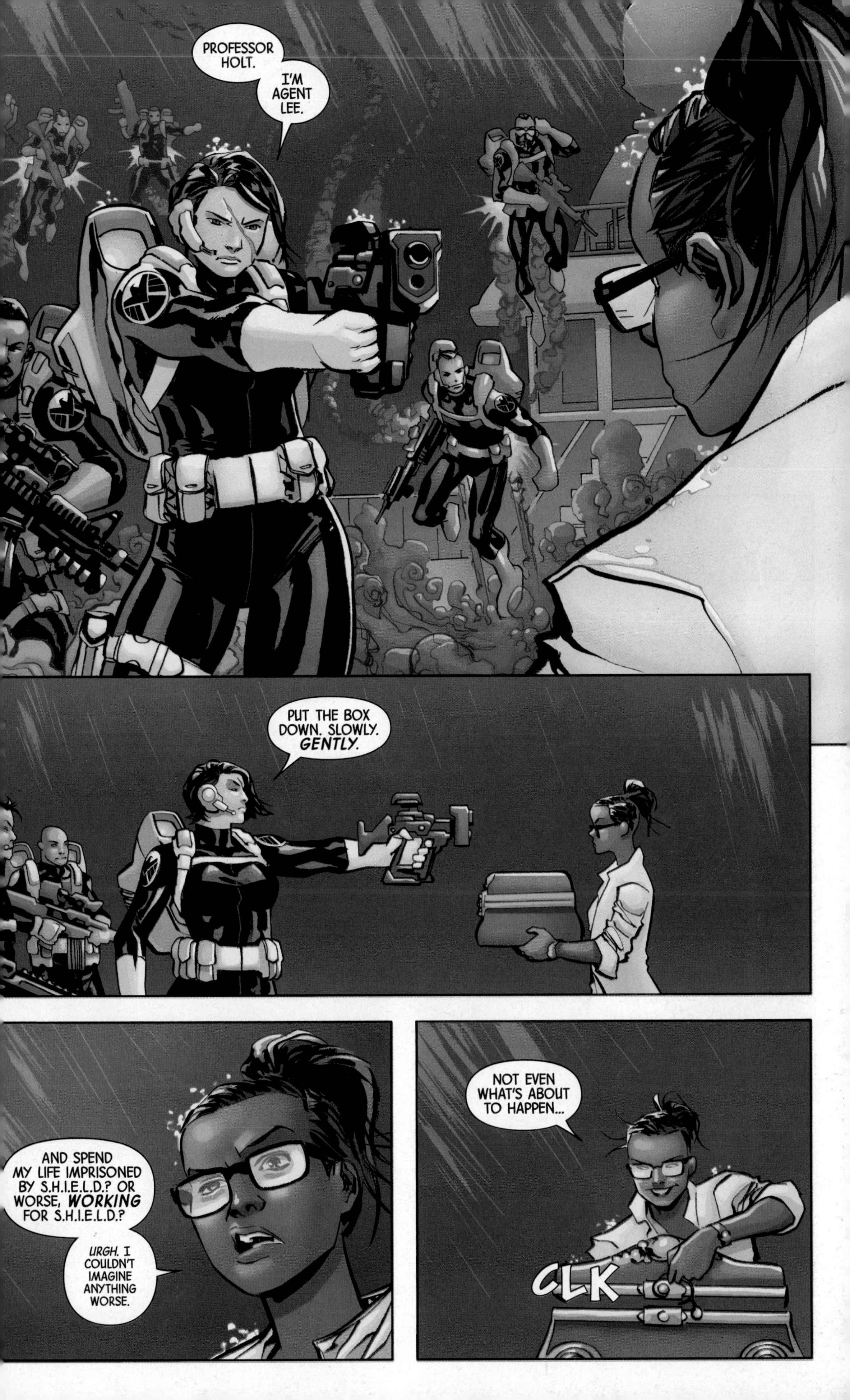
PROFESSOR HOLT.
I'M AGENT LEE.
PUT THE BOX DOWN. SLOWLY. *GENTLY.*
AND SPEND MY LIFE IMPRISONED BY S.H.I.E.L.D.? OR WORSE, ***WORKING*** FOR S.H.I.E.L.D.?
URGH. I COULDN'T IMAGINE ANYTHING WORSE.
NOT EVEN WHAT'S ABOUT TO HAPPEN...
CLK

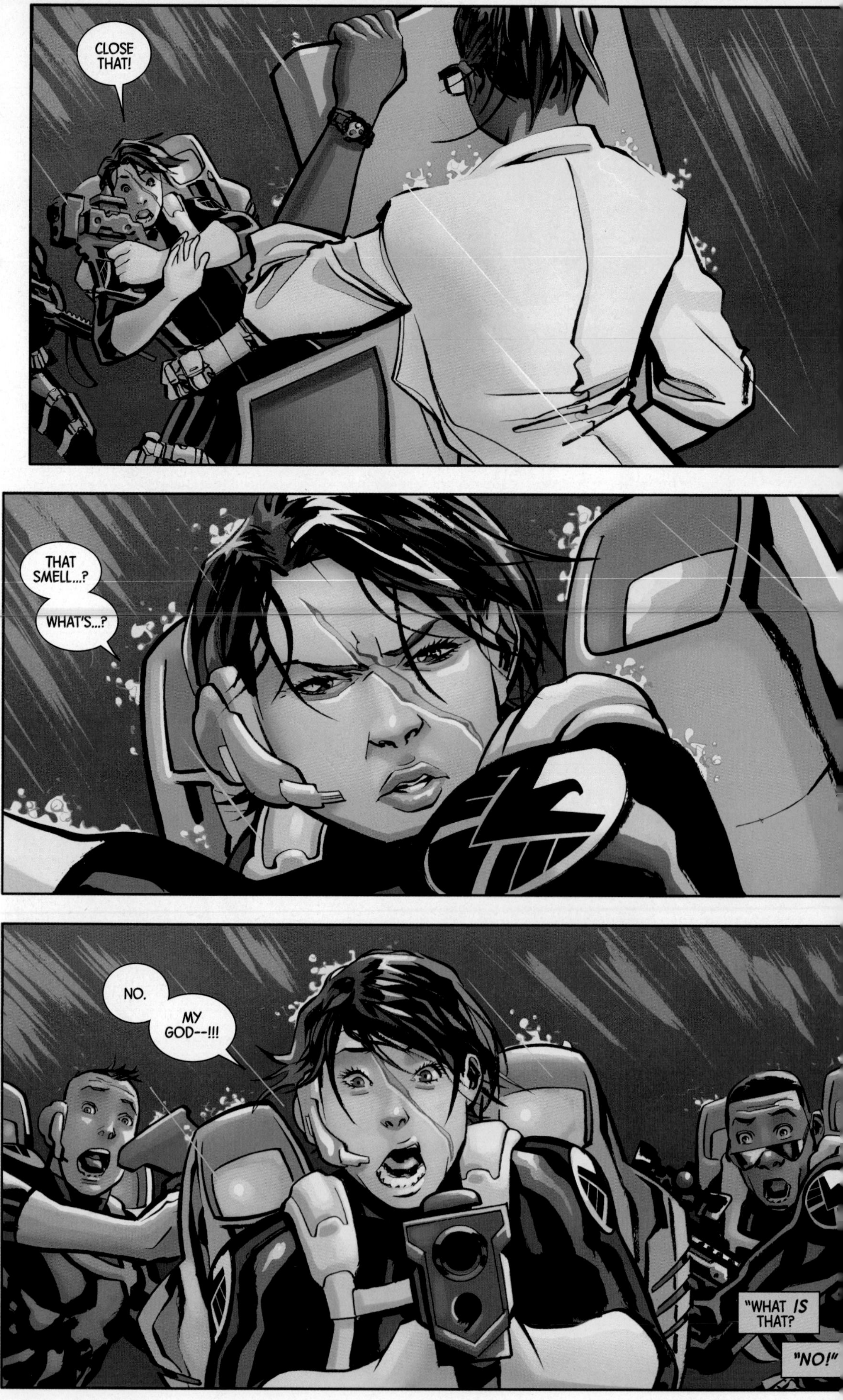
CLOSE THAT!
THAT SMELL...?
WHAT'S...?
NO.
MY GOD--!!!
"WHAT IS THAT?
"NO!"

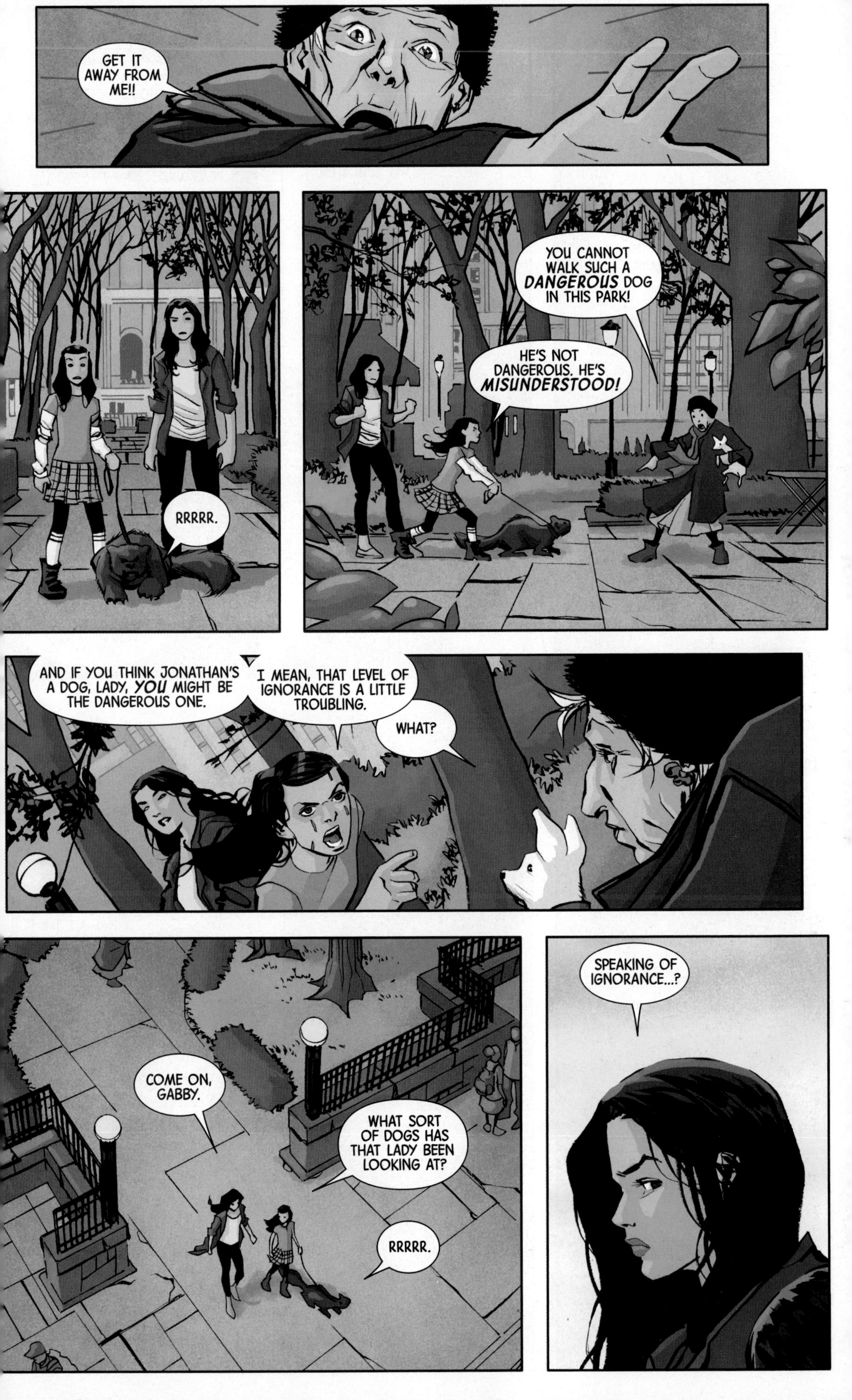
GET IT AWAY FROM ME!!
RRRRR.
YOU CANNOT WALK SUCH A DANGEROUS DOG IN THIS PARK!
HE'S NOT DANGEROUS. HE'S MISUNDERSTOOD!
AND IF YOU THINK JONATHAN'S A DOG, LADY, YOU MIGHT BE THE DANGEROUS ONE.
I MEAN, THAT LEVEL OF IGNORANCE IS A LITTLE TROUBLING.
WHAT?
COME ON, GABBY.
WHAT SORT OF DOGS HAS THAT LADY BEEN LOOKING AT?
RRRRR.
SPEAKING OF IGNORANCE...?

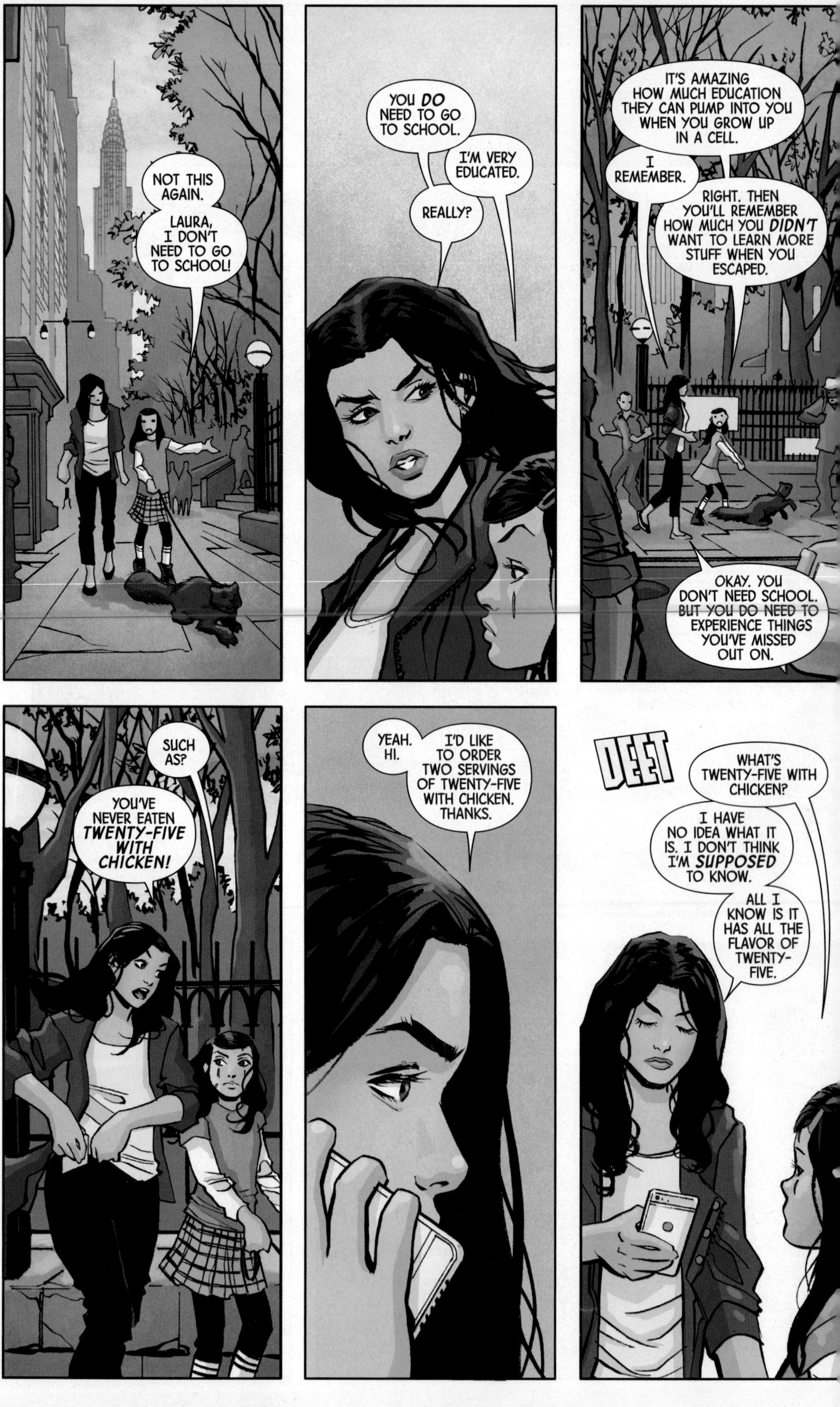

NOT THIS AGAIN.
LAURA, I DON'T NEED TO GO TO SCHOOL!
YOU DO NEED TO GO TO SCHOOL.
I'M VERY EDUCATED.
REALLY?
IT'S AMAZING HOW MUCH EDUCATION THEY CAN PUMP INTO YOU WHEN YOU GROW UP IN A CELL.
I REMEMBER.
RIGHT. THEN YOU'LL REMEMBER HOW MUCH YOU DIDN'T WANT TO LEARN MORE STUFF WHEN YOU ESCAPED.
OKAY. YOU DON'T NEED SCHOOL. BUT YOU DO NEED TO EXPERIENCE THINGS YOU'VE MISSED OUT ON.
SUCH AS?
YOU'VE NEVER EATEN TWENTY-FIVE WITH CHICKEN!
YEAH. HI.
I'D LIKE TO ORDER TWO SERVINGS OF TWENTY-FIVE WITH CHICKEN. THANKS.
DEET
WHAT'S TWENTY-FIVE WITH CHICKEN?
I HAVE NO IDEA WHAT IT IS. I DON'T THINK I'M SUPPOSED TO KNOW.
ALL I KNOW IS IT HAS ALL THE FLAVOR OF TWENTY-FIVE.

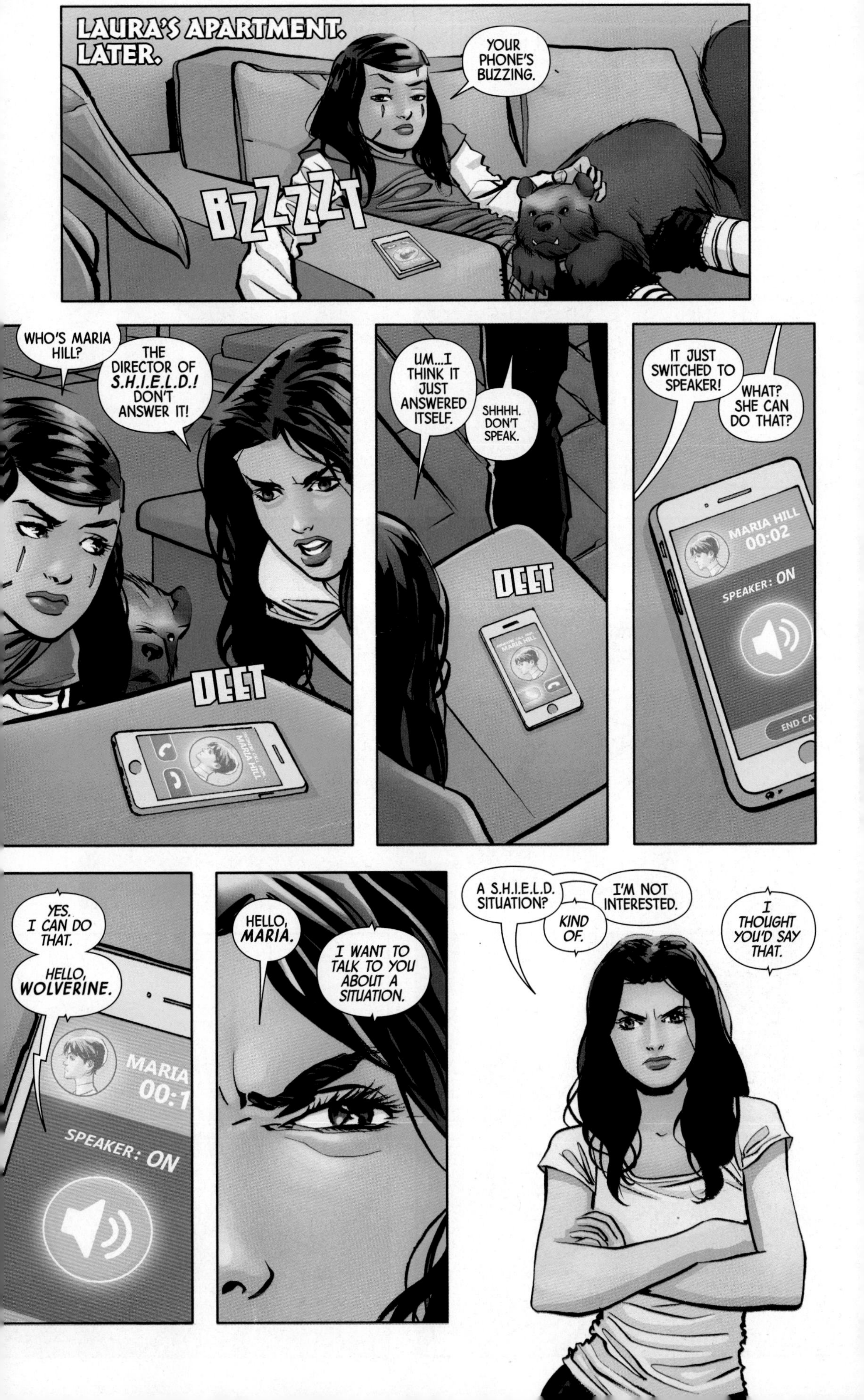
LAURA'S APARTMENT. LATER.
YOUR PHONE'S BUZZING.
BZZZZZT
WHO'S MARIA HILL?
THE DIRECTOR OF S.H.I.E.L.D.! DON'T ANSWER IT!
DEET
MARIA HILL
UM...I THINK IT JUST ANSWERED ITSELF.
SHHHH. DON'T SPEAK.
DEET
MARIA HILL
IT JUST SWITCHED TO SPEAKER!
WHAT? SHE CAN DO THAT?
MARIA HILL
00:02
SPEAKER: ON
YES. I CAN DO THAT.
HELLO, WOLVERINE.
SPEAKER: ON
HELLO, MARIA.
I WANT TO TALK TO YOU ABOUT A SITUATION.
A S.H.I.E.L.D. SITUATION?
KIND OF.
I'M NOT INTERESTED.
I THOUGHT YOU'D SAY THAT.

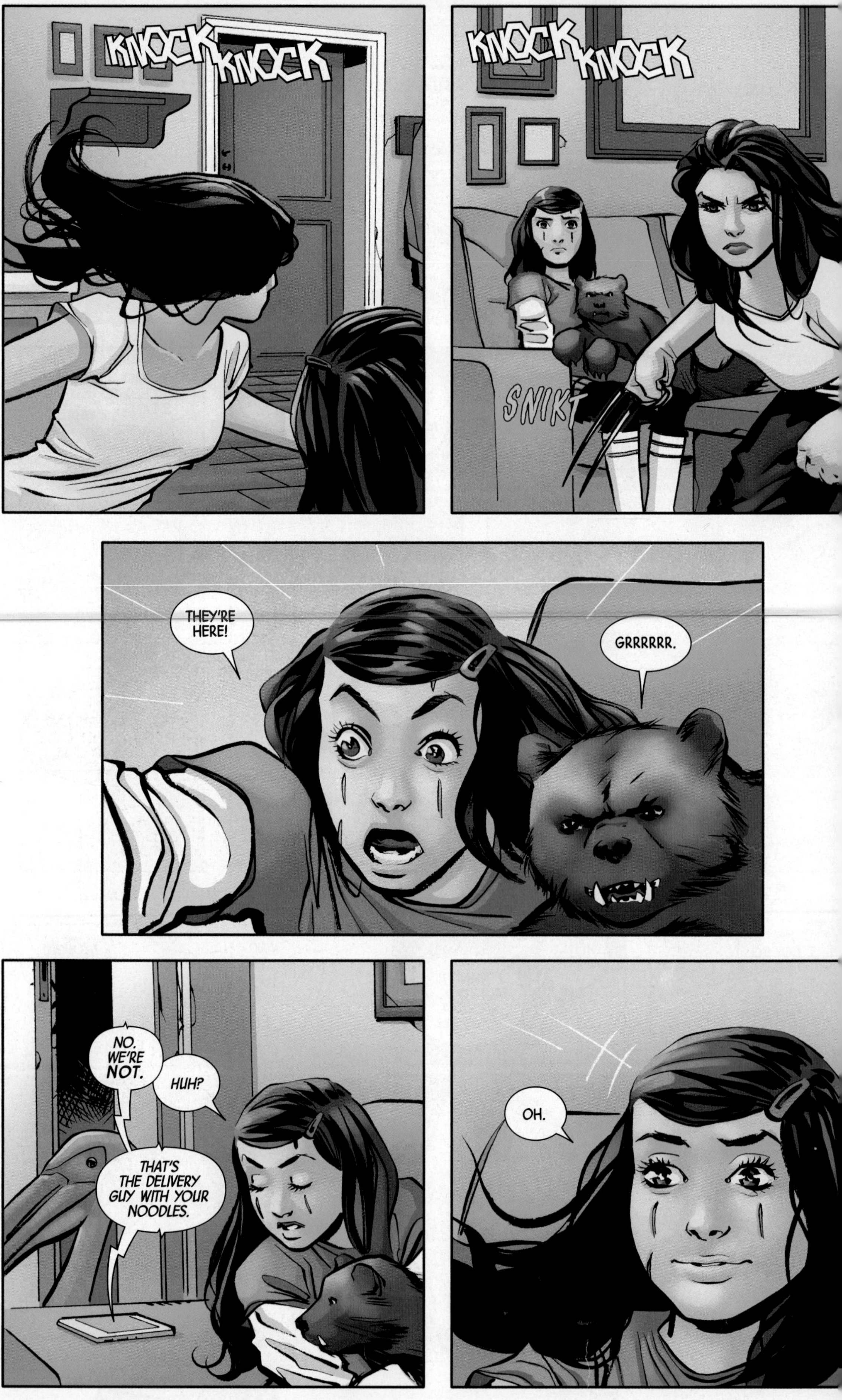
KNOCK KNOCK
KNOCK KNOCK
SNIKT
THEY'RE HERE!
GRRRRRR.
NO. WE'RE NOT.
HUH?
THAT'S THE DELIVERY GUY WITH YOUR NOODLES.
OH.

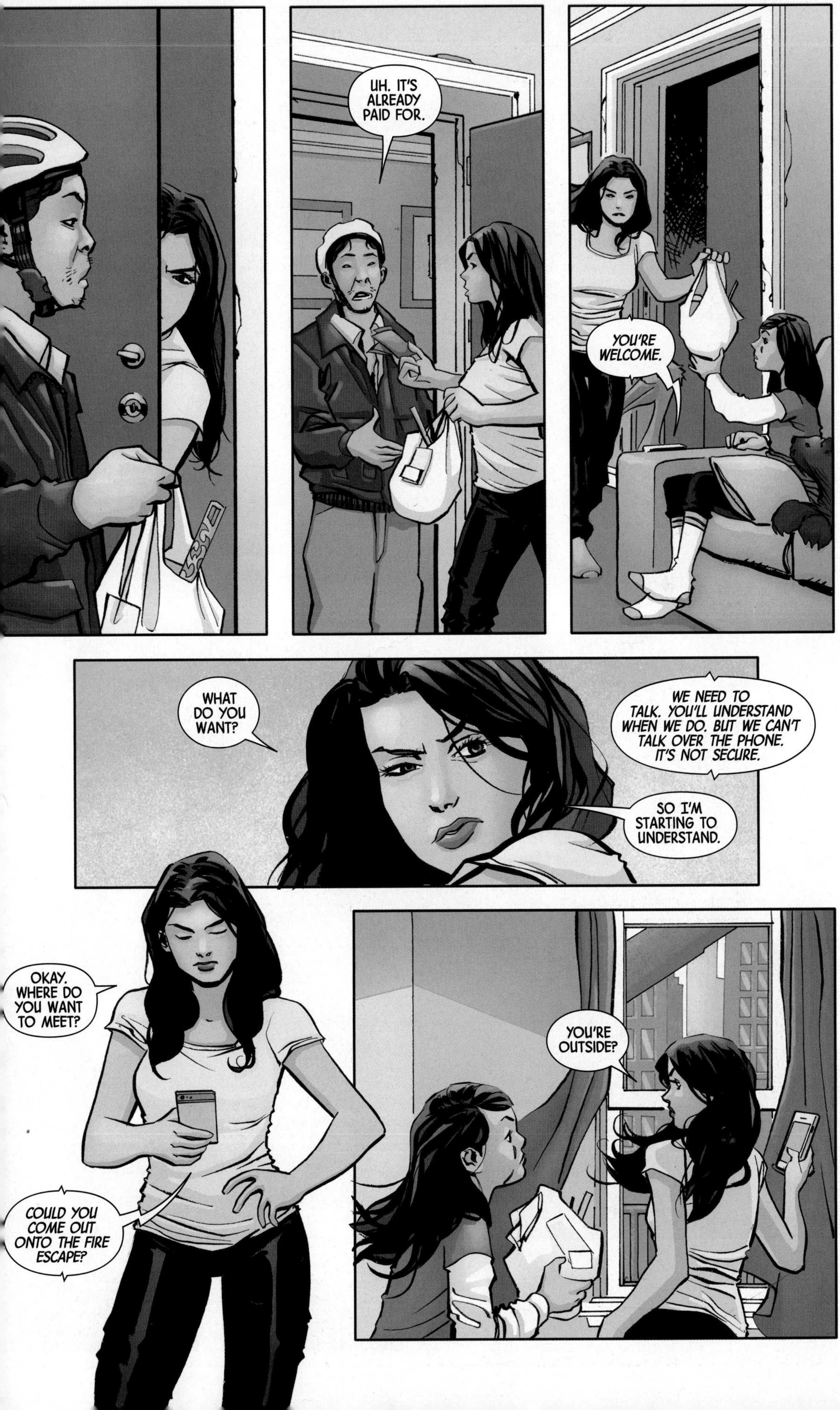

UH. IT'S ALREADY PAID FOR.
YOU'RE WELCOME.
WHAT DO YOU WANT?
WE NEED TO TALK. YOU'LL UNDERSTAND WHEN WE DO. BUT WE CAN'T TALK OVER THE PHONE. IT'S NOT SECURE.
SO I'M STARTING TO UNDERSTAND.
OKAY. WHERE DO YOU WANT TO MEET?
COULD YOU COME OUT ONTO THE FIRE ESCAPE?
YOU'RE OUTSIDE?

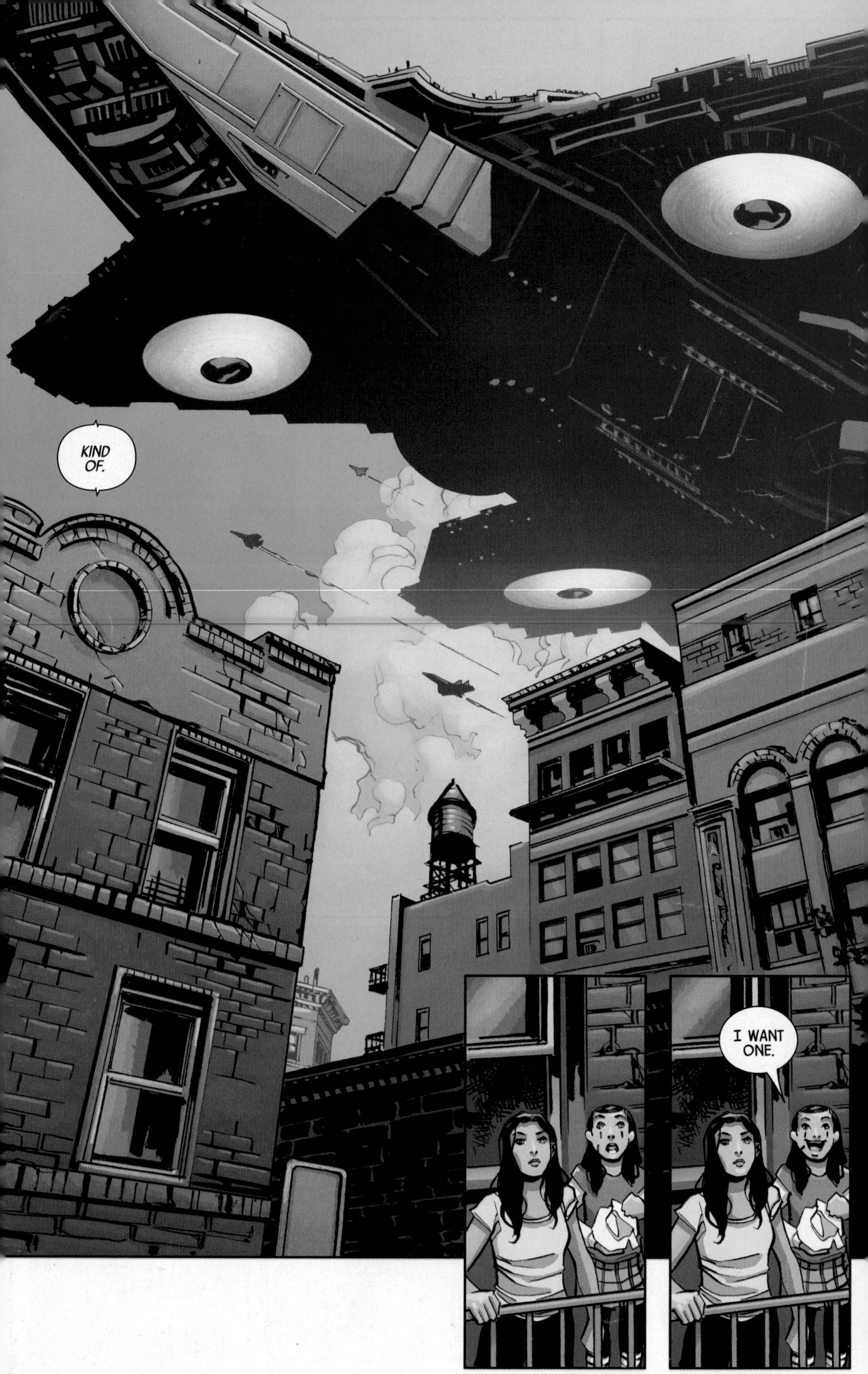
KIND OF.
I WANT ONE.

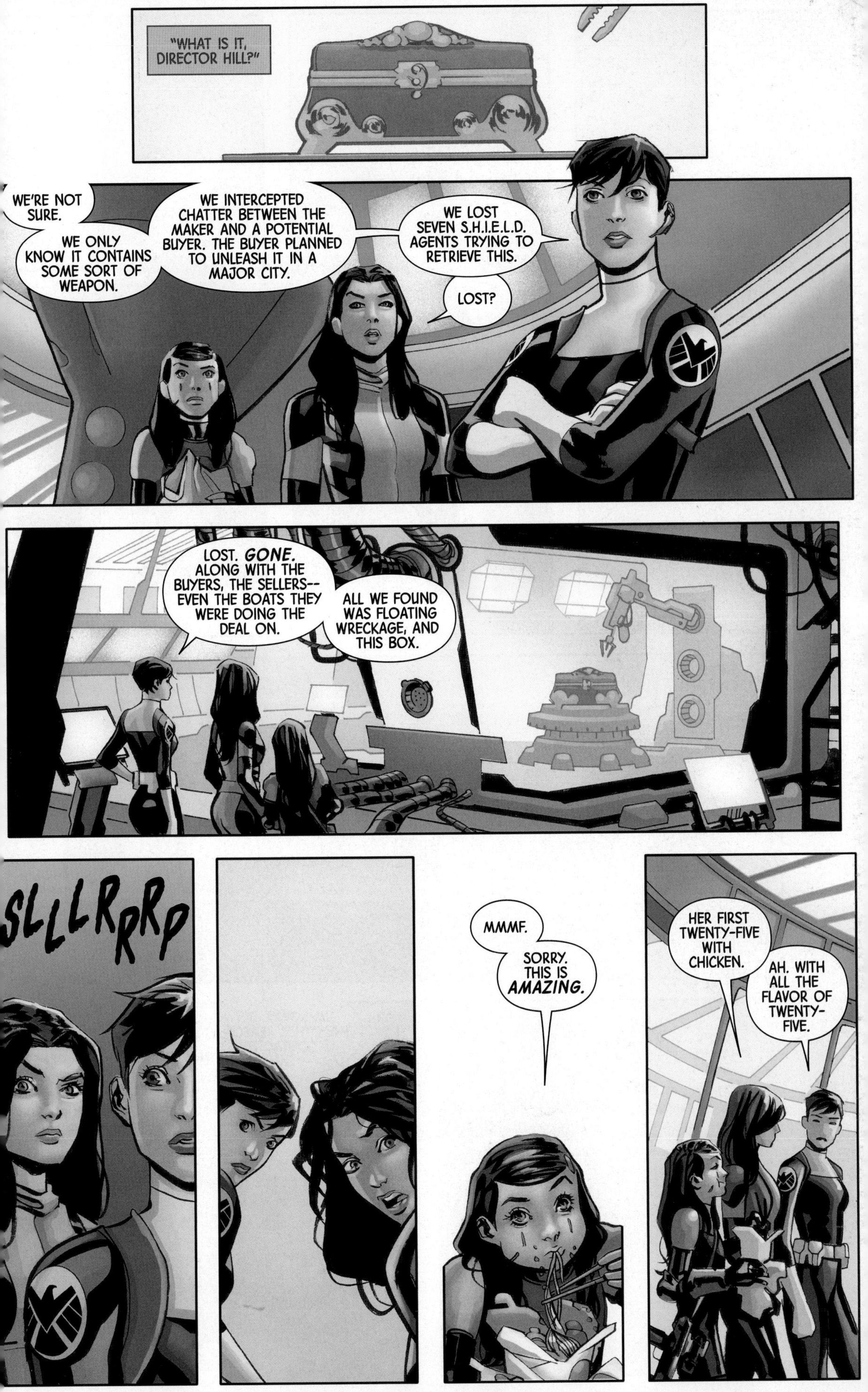
"WHAT IS IT, DIRECTOR HILL?"
WE'RE NOT SURE.
WE ONLY KNOW IT CONTAINS SOME SORT OF WEAPON.
WE INTERCEPTED CHATTER BETWEEN THE MAKER AND A POTENTIAL BUYER. THE BUYER PLANNED TO UNLEASH IT IN A MAJOR CITY.
WE LOST SEVEN S.H.I.E.L.D. AGENTS TRYING TO RETRIEVE THIS.
LOST?
LOST. GONE. ALONG WITH THE BUYERS, THE SELLERS--EVEN THE BOATS THEY WERE DOING THE DEAL ON.
ALL WE FOUND WAS FLOATING WRECKAGE, AND THIS BOX.
SLLLRRRP
MMMF.
SORRY. THIS IS AMAZING.
HER FIRST TWENTY-FIVE WITH CHICKEN.
AH. WITH ALL THE FLAVOR OF TWENTY-FIVE.

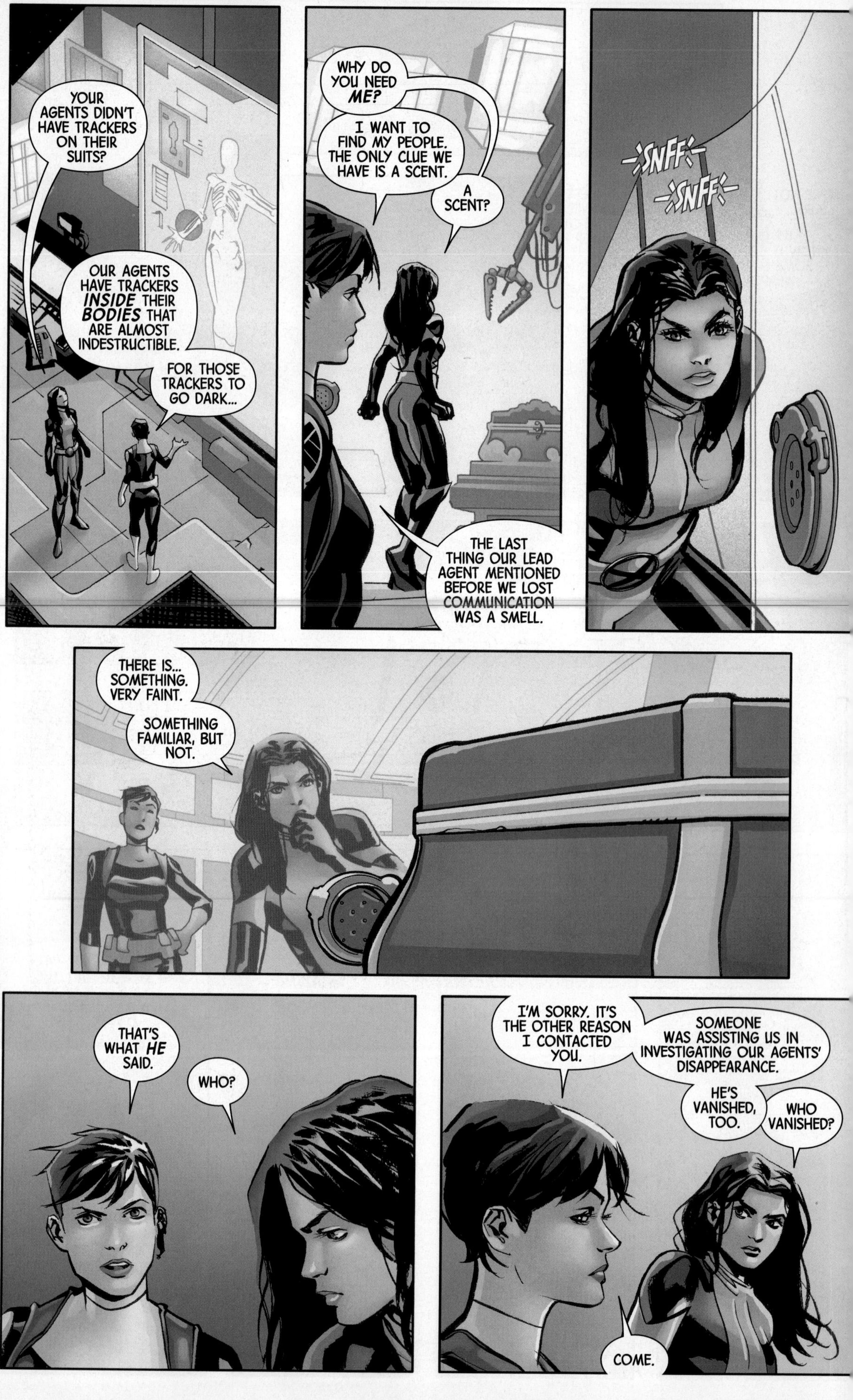
YOUR AGENTS DIDN'T HAVE TRACKERS ON THEIR SUITS?
OUR AGENTS HAVE TRACKERS *INSIDE* THEIR *BODIES* THAT ARE ALMOST INDESTRUCTIBLE.
FOR THOSE TRACKERS TO GO DARK...
WHY DO YOU NEED *ME?*
I WANT TO FIND MY PEOPLE. THE ONLY CLUE WE HAVE IS A SCENT.
A SCENT?
THE LAST THING OUR LEAD AGENT MENTIONED BEFORE WE LOST COMMUNICATION WAS A SMELL.
SNFF
SNFF
THERE IS... SOMETHING. VERY FAINT.
SOMETHING FAMILIAR, BUT NOT.
THAT'S WHAT *HE* SAID.
WHO?
I'M SORRY. IT'S THE OTHER REASON I CONTACTED YOU.
SOMEONE WAS ASSISTING US IN INVESTIGATING OUR AGENTS' DISAPPEARANCE.
HE'S VANISHED, TOO.
WHO VANISHED?
COME.

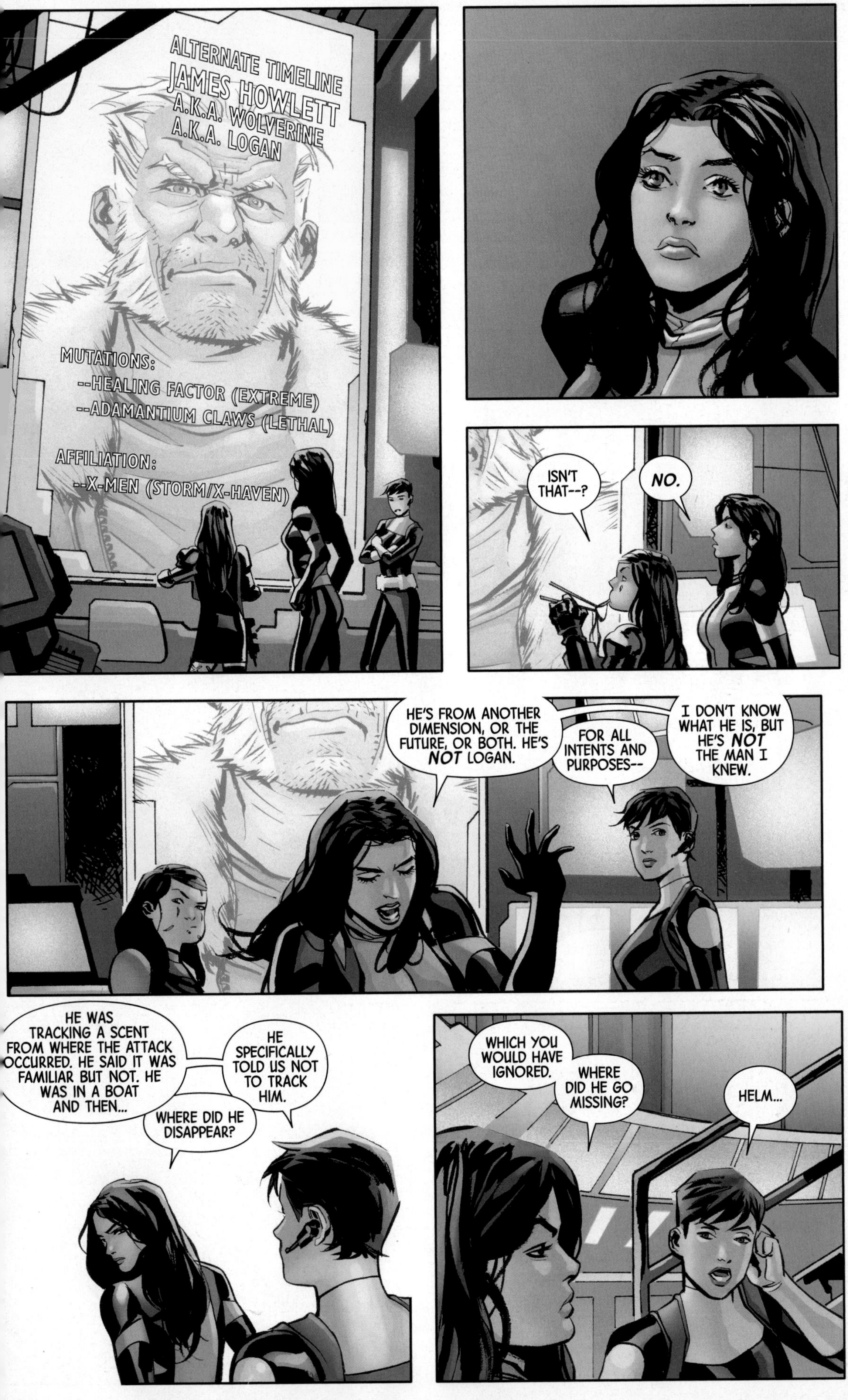
ALTERNATE TIMELINE
JAMES HOWLETT
A.K.A. WOLVERINE
A.K.A. LOGAN
MUTATIONS:
--HEALING FACTOR (EXTREME)
--ADAMANTIUM CLAWS (LETHAL)
AFFILIATION:
--X-MEN (STORM/X-HAVEN)
ISN'T THAT--?
NO.
HE'S FROM ANOTHER DIMENSION, OR THE FUTURE, OR BOTH. HE'S NOT LOGAN.
FOR ALL INTENTS AND PURPOSES--
I DON'T KNOW WHAT HE IS, BUT HE'S NOT THE MAN I KNEW.
HE WAS TRACKING A SCENT FROM WHERE THE ATTACK OCCURRED. HE SAID IT WAS FAMILIAR BUT NOT. HE WAS IN A BOAT AND THEN...
HE SPECIFICALLY TOLD US NOT TO TRACK HIM.
WHERE DID HE DISAPPEAR?
WHICH YOU WOULD HAVE IGNORED.
WHERE DID HE GO MISSING?
HELM...

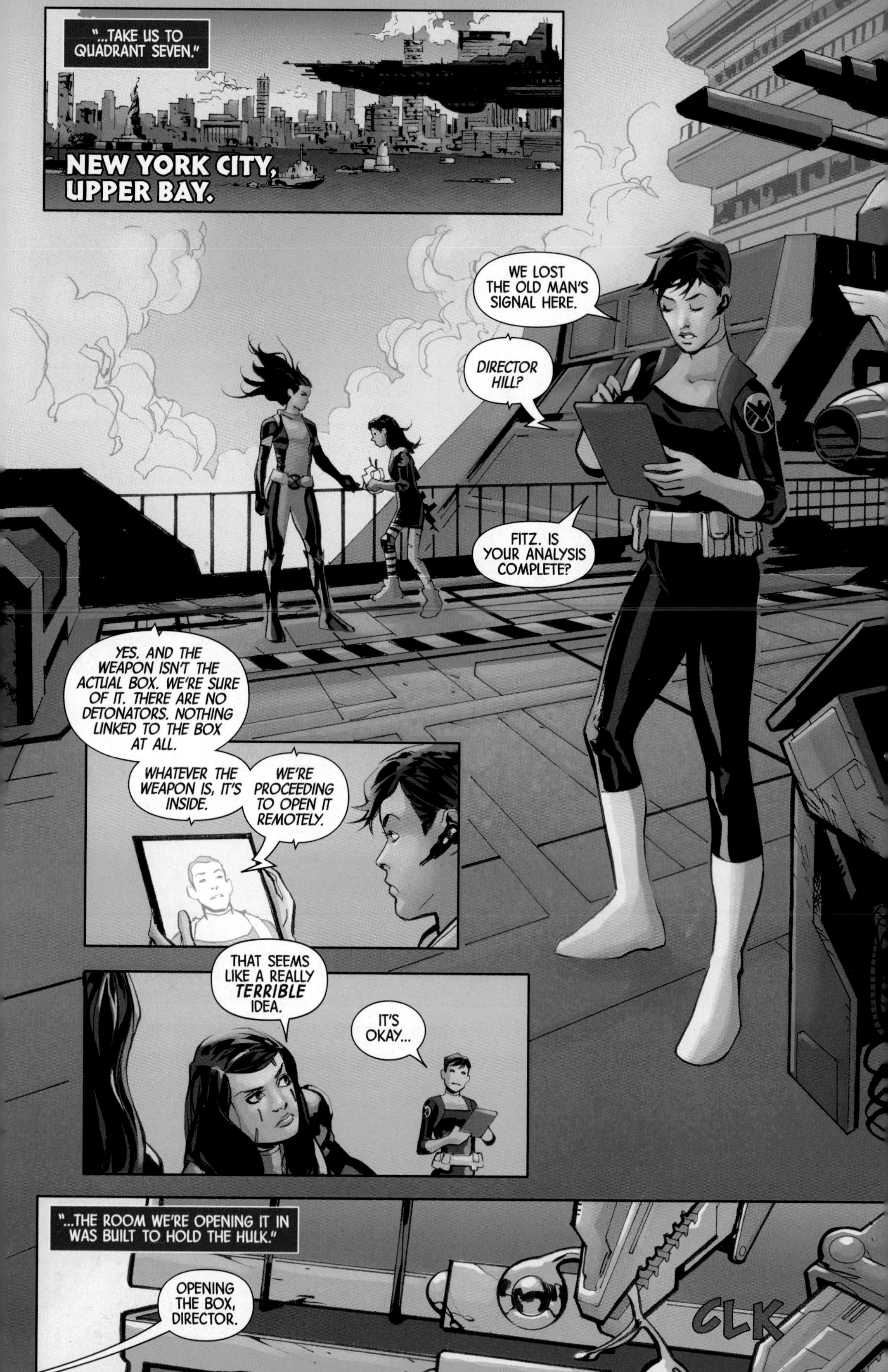
"...TAKE US TO QUADRANT SEVEN."
NEW YORK CITY, UPPER BAY.
WE LOST THE OLD MAN'S SIGNAL HERE.
DIRECTOR HILL?
FITZ. IS YOUR ANALYSIS COMPLETE?
YES. AND THE WEAPON ISN'T THE ACTUAL BOX. WE'RE SURE OF IT. THERE ARE NO DETONATORS. NOTHING LINKED TO THE BOX AT ALL.
WHATEVER THE WEAPON IS, IT'S INSIDE.
WE'RE PROCEEDING TO OPEN IT REMOTELY.
THAT SEEMS LIKE A REALLY TERRIBLE IDEA.
IT'S OKAY...
"...THE ROOM WE'RE OPENING IT IN WAS BUILT TO HOLD THE HULK."
OPENING THE BOX, DIRECTOR.
CLK

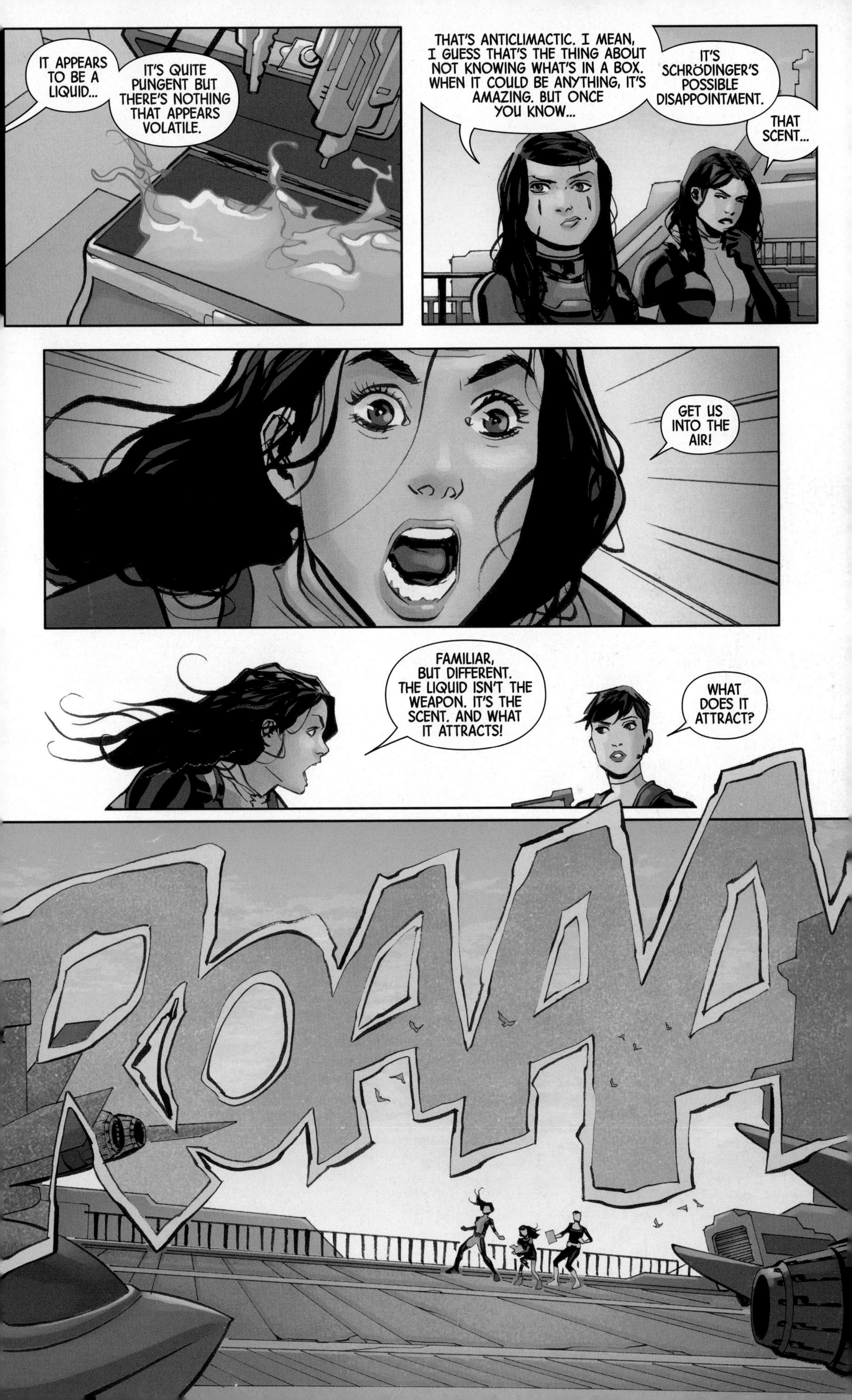
IT APPEARS TO BE A LIQUID...
IT'S QUITE PUNGENT BUT THERE'S NOTHING THAT APPEARS VOLATILE.
THAT'S ANTICLIMACTIC. I MEAN, I GUESS THAT'S THE THING ABOUT NOT KNOWING WHAT'S IN A BOX. WHEN IT COULD BE ANYTHING, IT'S AMAZING. BUT ONCE YOU KNOW...
IT'S SCHRÖDINGER'S POSSIBLE DISAPPOINTMENT.
THAT SCENT...
GET US INTO THE AIR!
FAMILIAR, BUT DIFFERENT. THE LIQUID ISN'T THE WEAPON. IT'S THE SCENT. AND WHAT IT ATTRACTS!
WHAT DOES IT ATTRACT?
ROAAAR

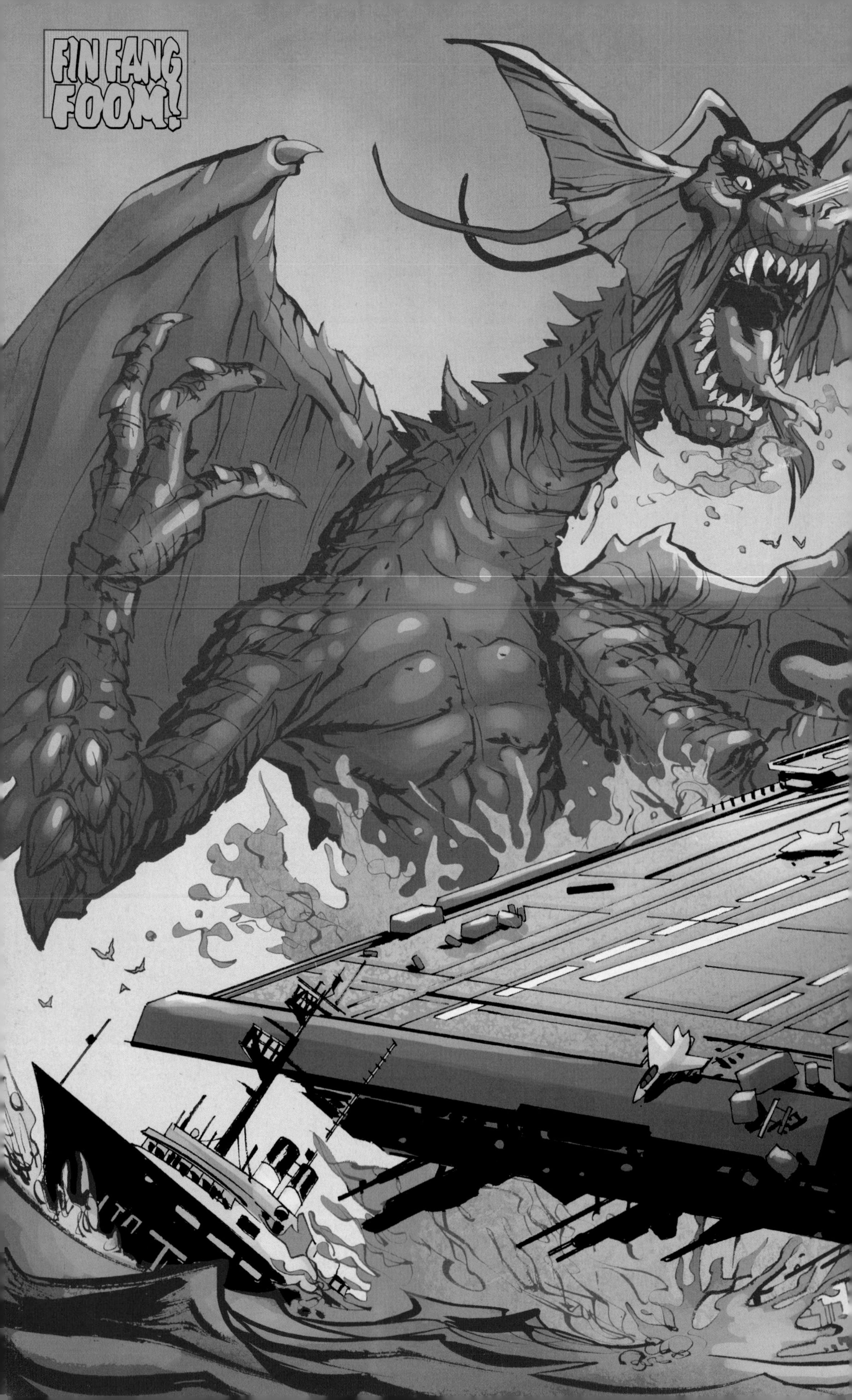
FIN FANG FOOM!

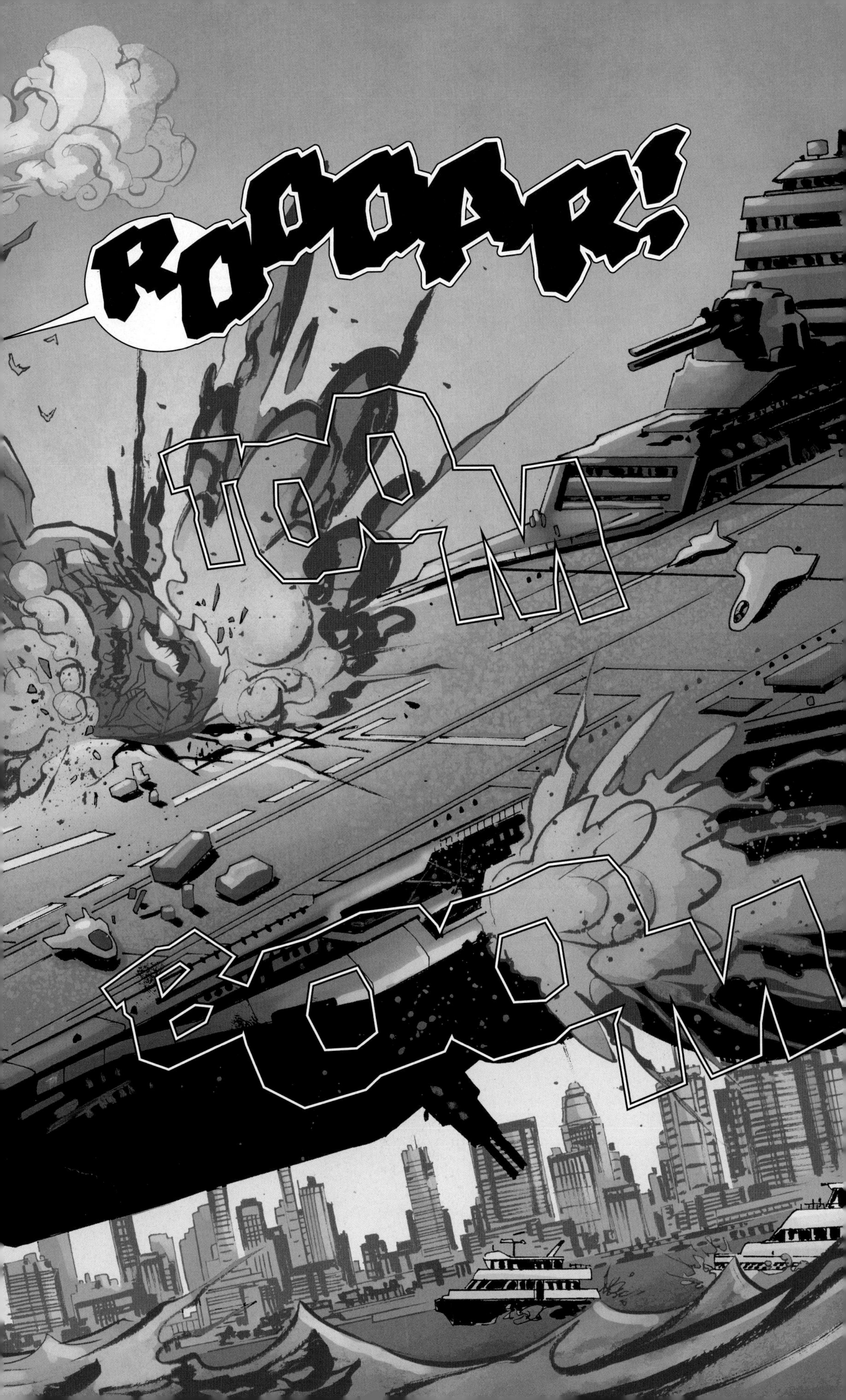
ROOOAR!
TOOM
BOOM

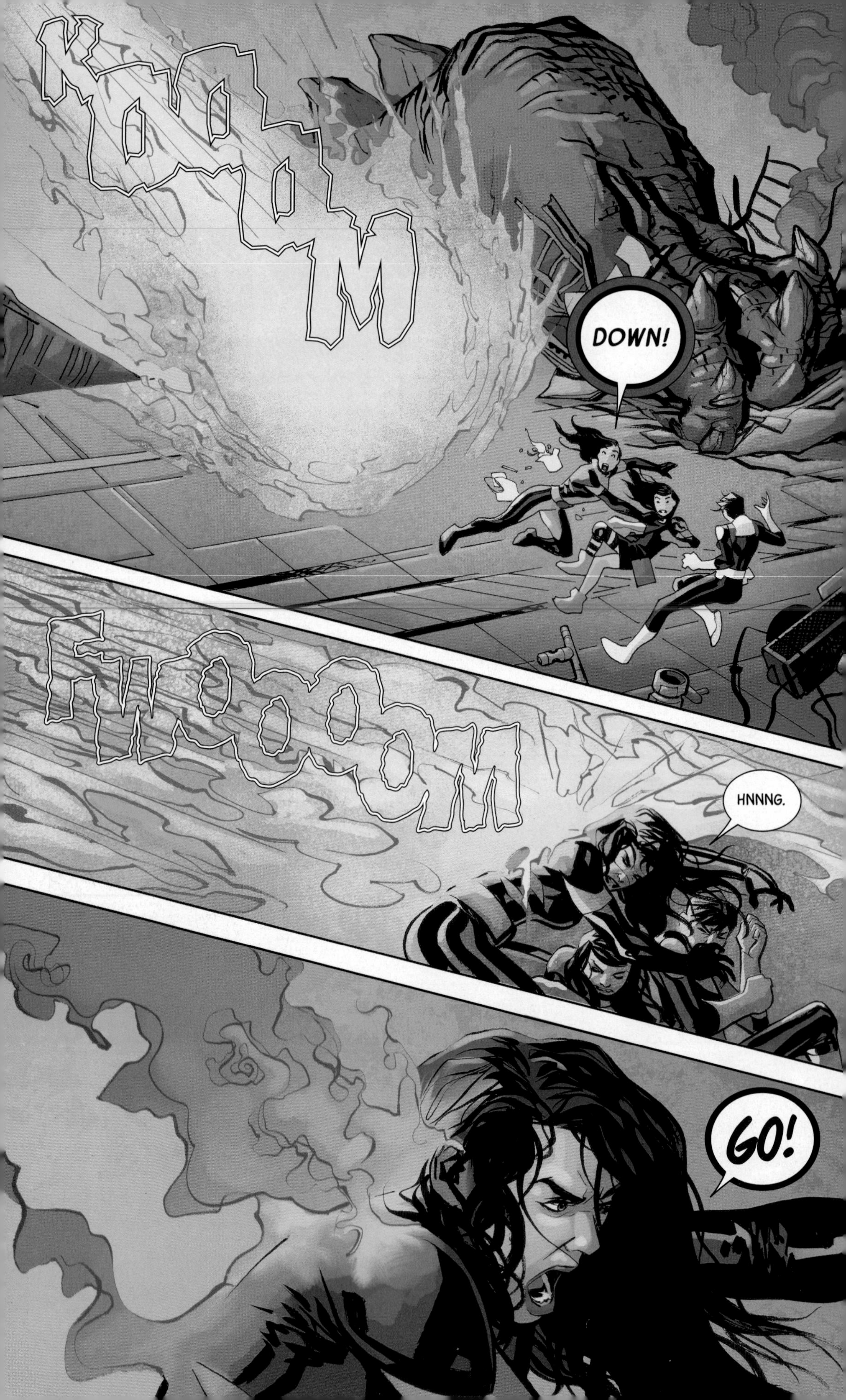
KOOOOM
DOWN!
FWOOOOOM
HNNNG.
GO!

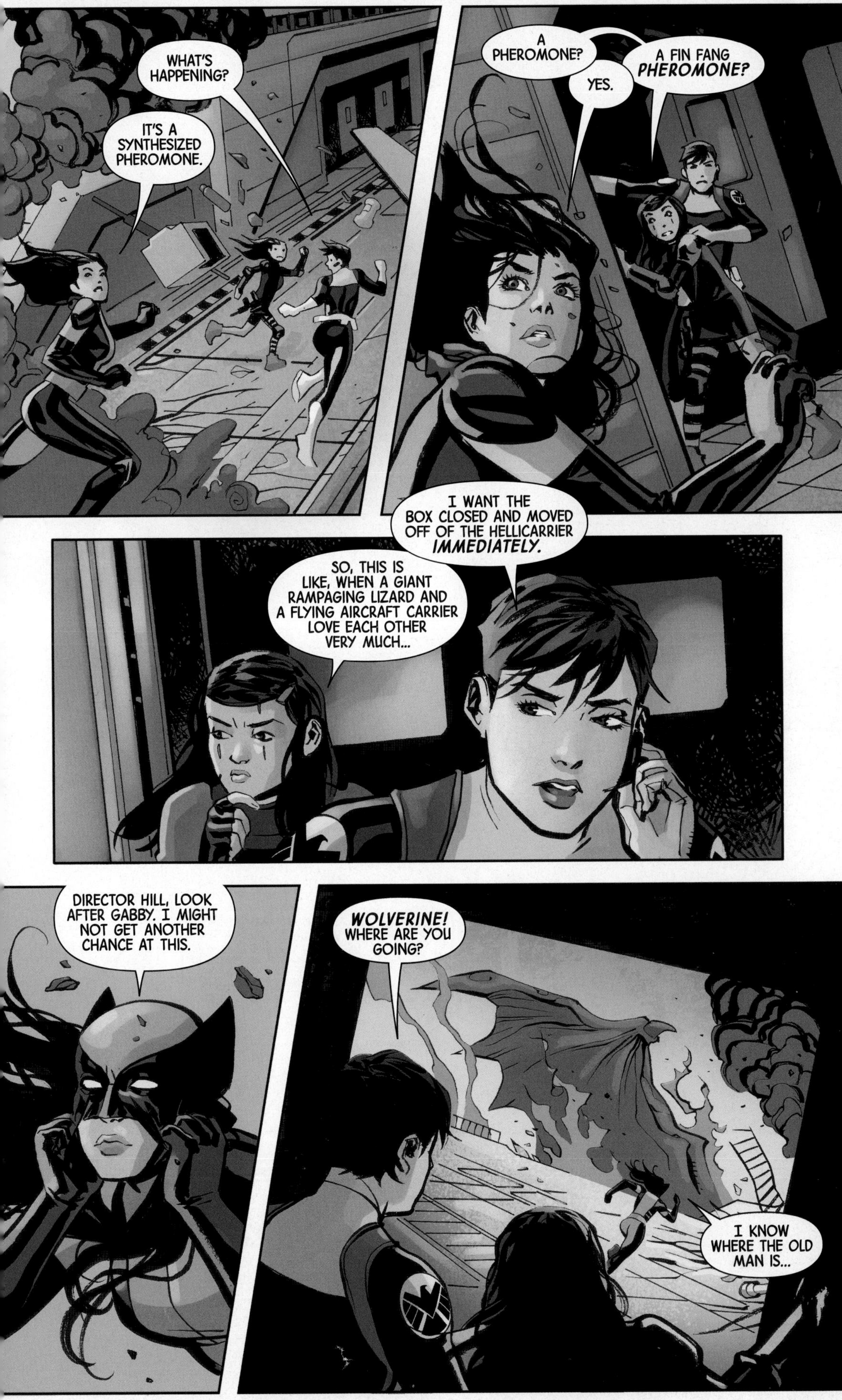
WHAT'S HAPPENING?
IT'S A SYNTHESIZED PHEROMONE.
A PHEROMONE?
YES.
A FIN FANG PHEROMONE?
I WANT THE BOX CLOSED AND MOVED OFF OF THE HELLICARRIER IMMEDIATELY.
SO, THIS IS LIKE, WHEN A GIANT RAMPAGING LIZARD AND A FLYING AIRCRAFT CARRIER LOVE EACH OTHER VERY MUCH...
DIRECTOR HILL, LOOK AFTER GABBY. I MIGHT NOT GET ANOTHER CHANCE AT THIS.
WOLVERINE! WHERE ARE YOU GOING?
I KNOW WHERE THE OLD MAN IS...

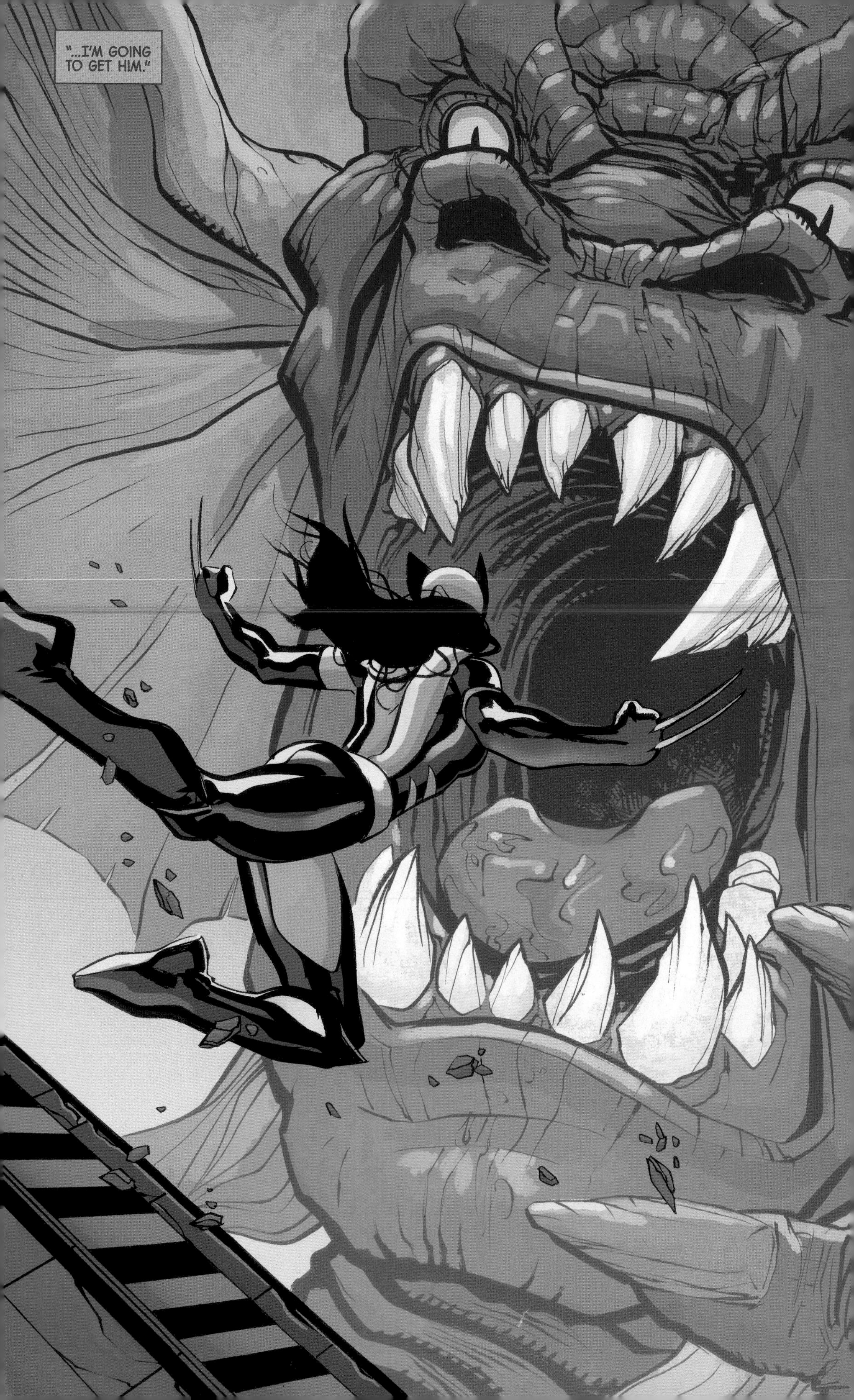
"...I'M GOING TO GET HIM."

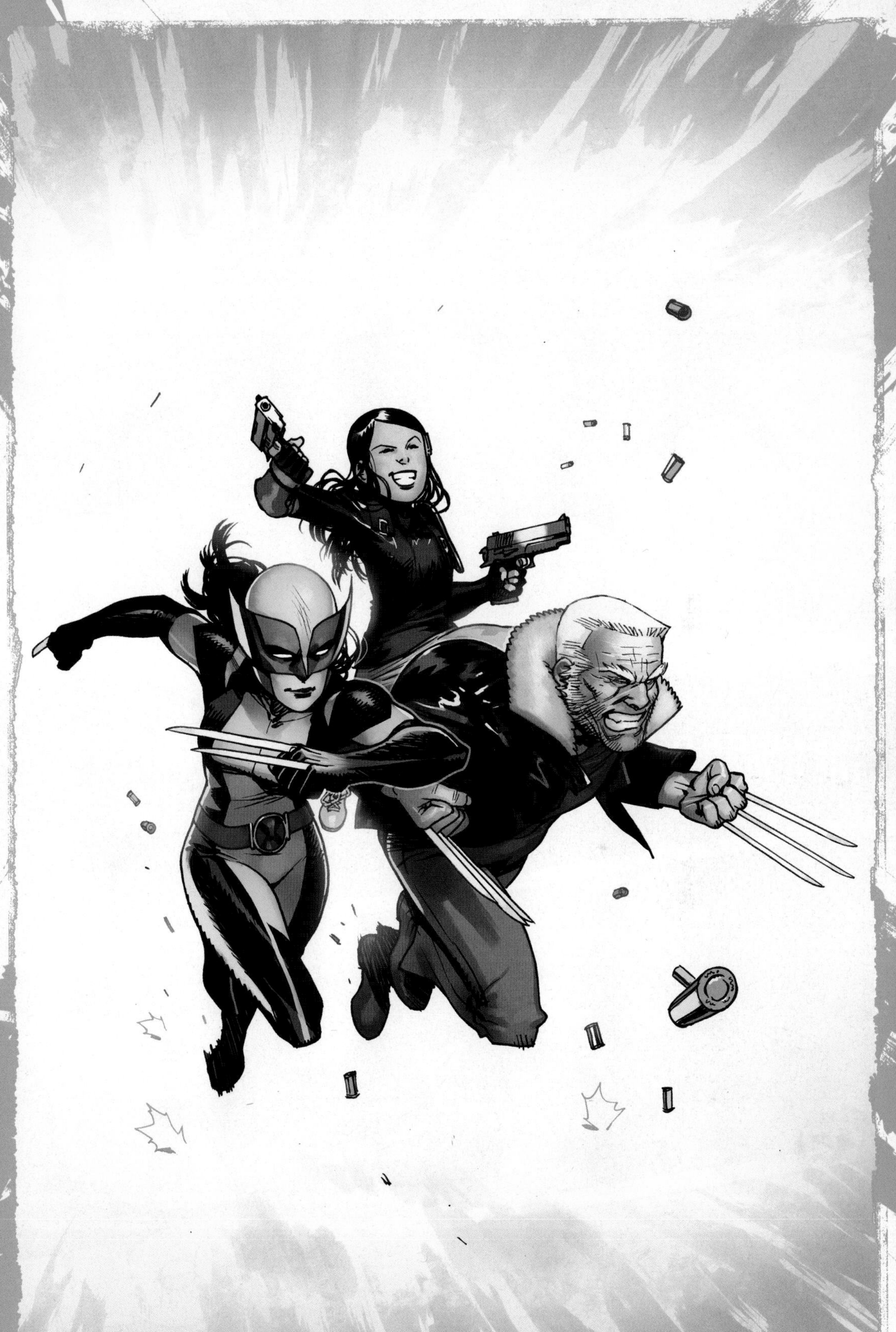

9

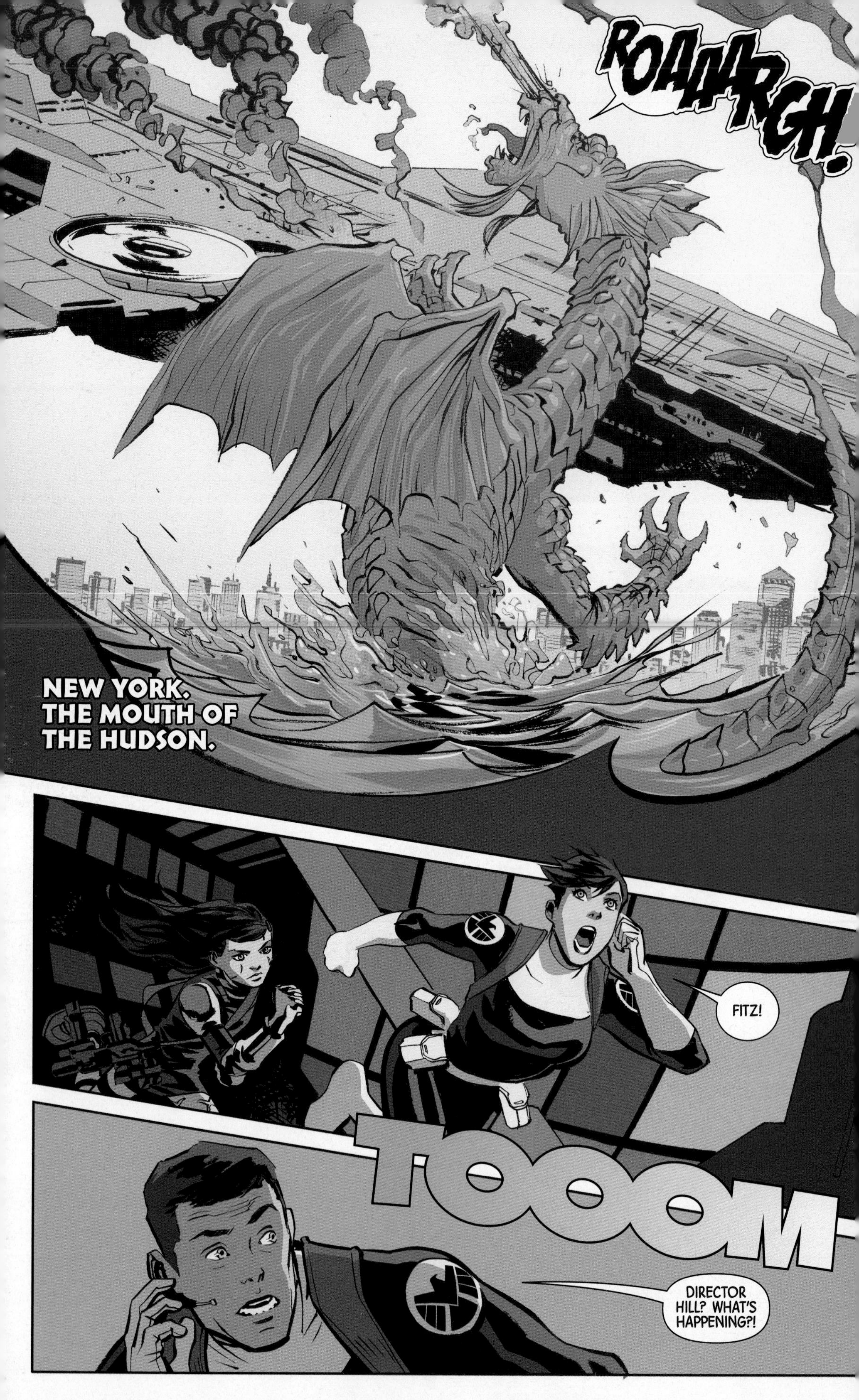
ROAAARGH!
NEW YORK. THE MOUTH OF THE HUDSON.
FITZ!
TOOOOM
DIRECTOR HILL? WHAT'S HAPPENING?!

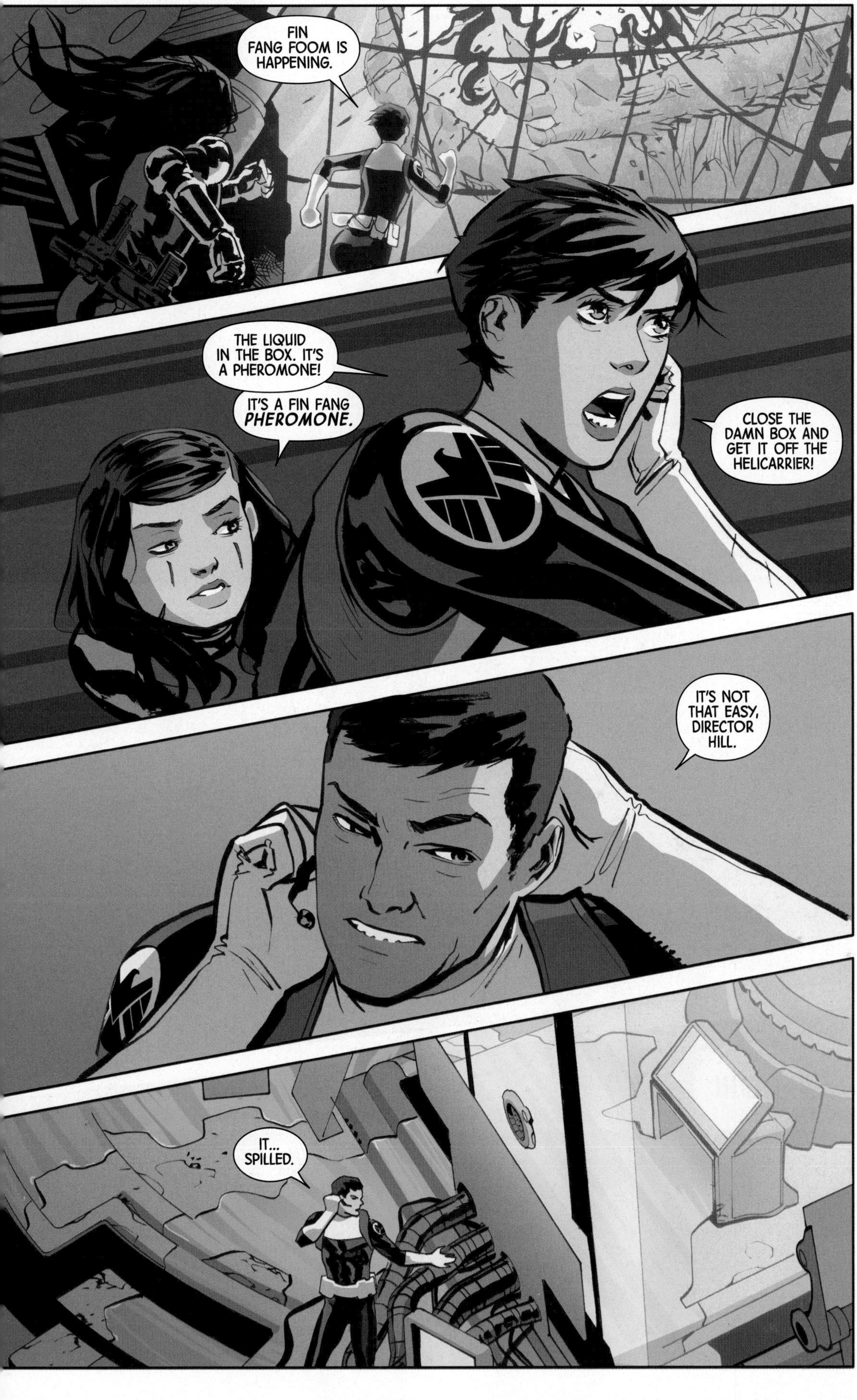
FIN FANG FOOM IS HAPPENING.
THE LIQUID IN THE BOX. IT'S A PHEROMONE!
IT'S A FIN FANG *PHEROMONE.*
CLOSE THE DAMN BOX AND GET IT OFF THE HELICARRIER!
IT'S NOT THAT EASY, DIRECTOR HILL.
IT... SPILLED.

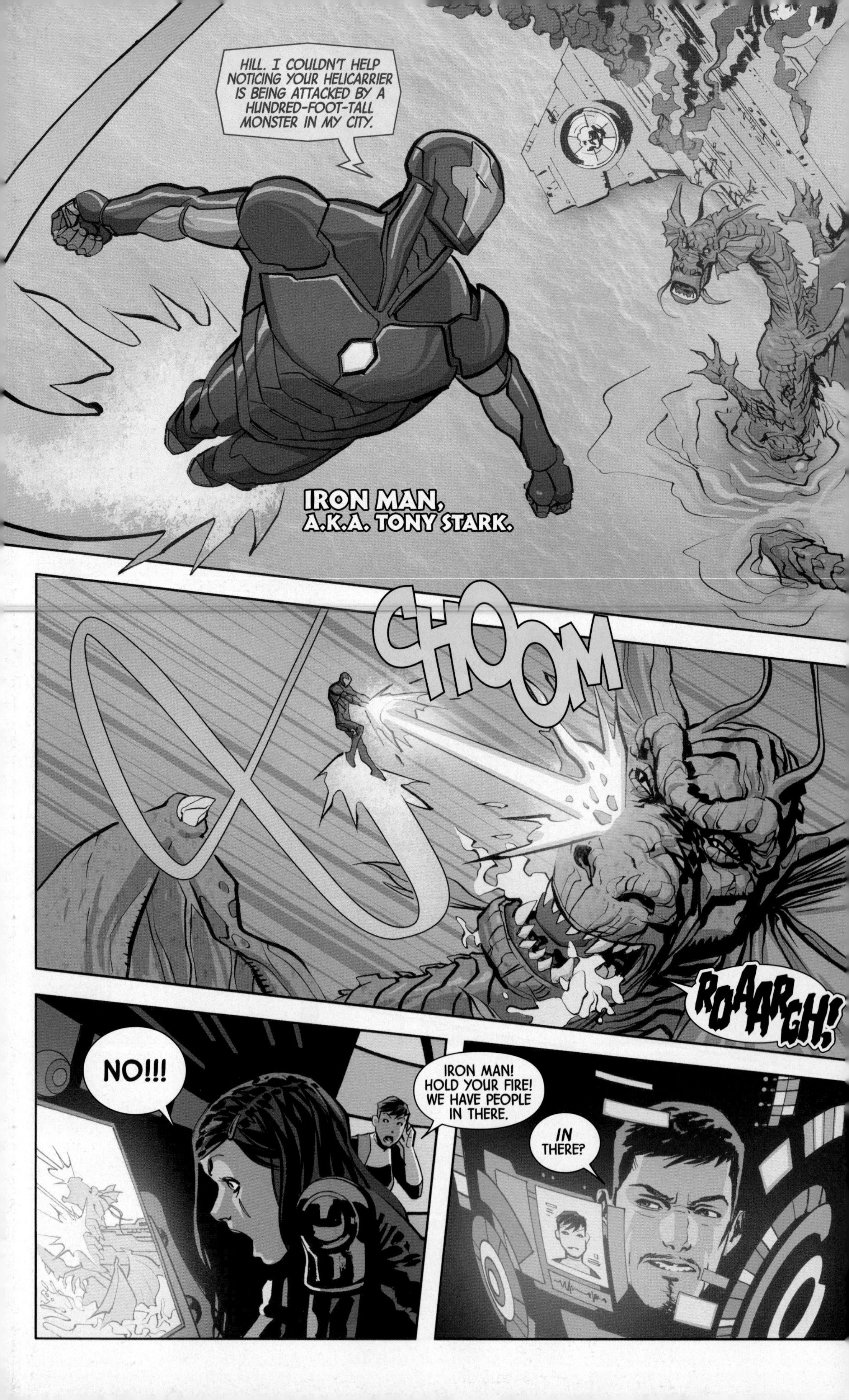
HILL. I COULDN'T HELP NOTICING YOUR HELICARRIER IS BEING ATTACKED BY A HUNDRED-FOOT-TALL MONSTER IN MY CITY.
IRON MAN, A.K.A. TONY STARK.
CHOOM
ROAAARGH!
NO!!!
IRON MAN! HOLD YOUR FIRE! WE HAVE PEOPLE IN THERE.
IN THERE?

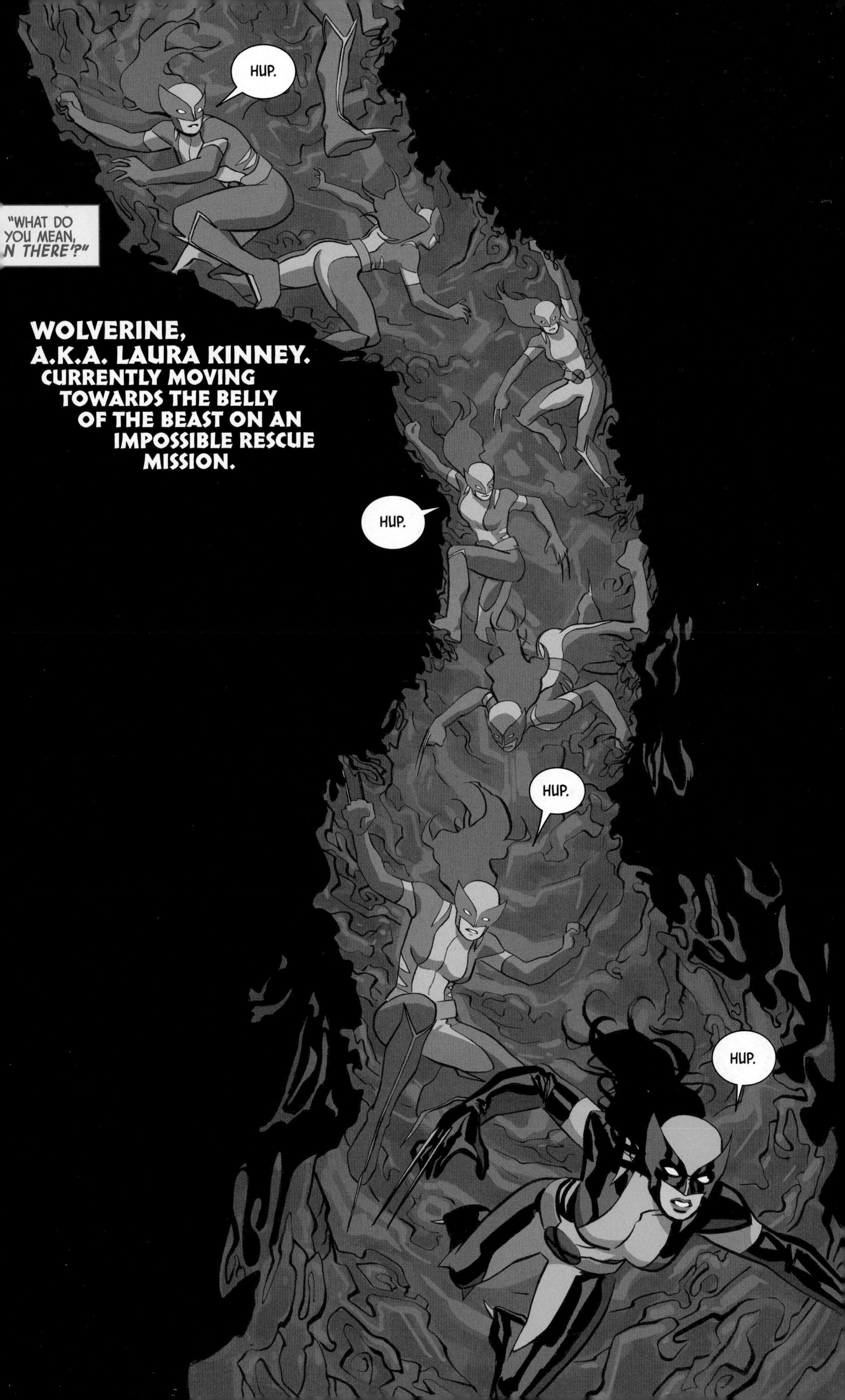

"WHAT DO
YOU MEAN,
N THERE'?"
HUP.
WOLVERINE,
A.K.A. LAURA KINNEY.
CURRENTLY MOVING
TOWARDS THE BELLY
OF THE BEAST ON AN
IMPOSSIBLE RESCUE
MISSION.
HUP.
HUP.
HUP.

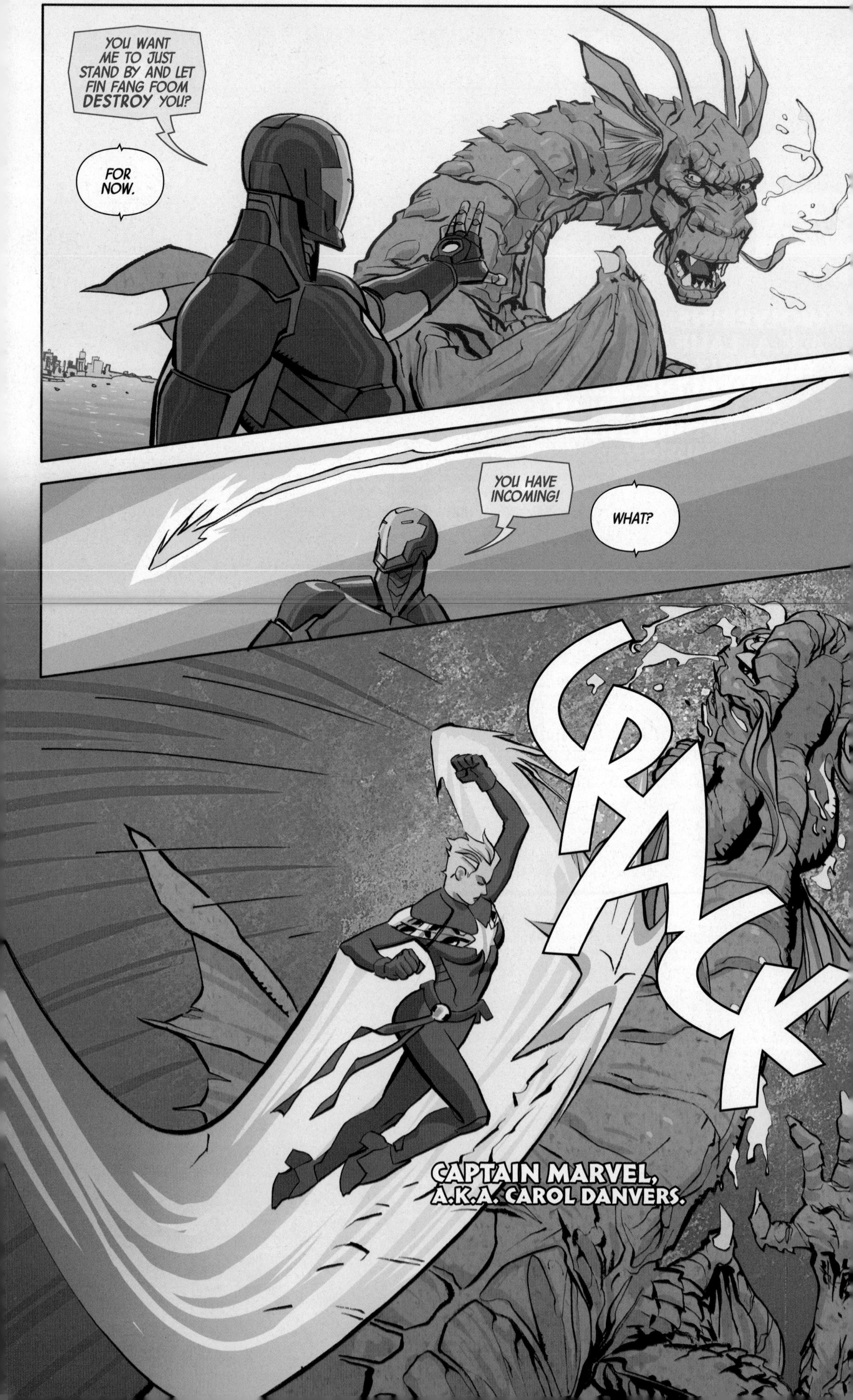
YOU WANT ME TO JUST STAND BY AND LET FIN FANG FOOM DESTROY YOU?
FOR NOW.
YOU HAVE INCOMING!
WHAT?
CRACK
CAPTAIN MARVEL, A.K.A. CAROL DANVERS.

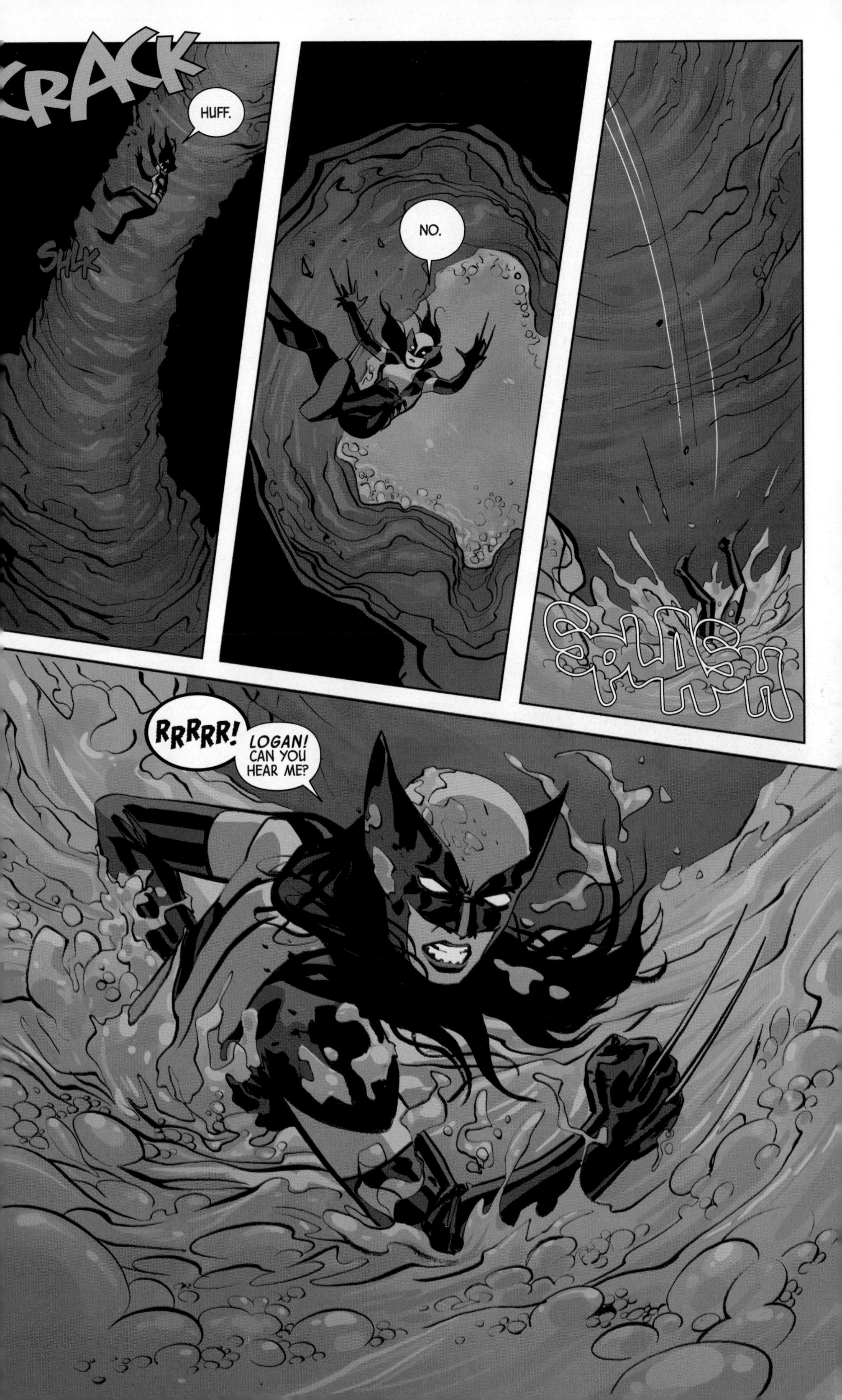
CRACK
HUFF.
SHLK
NO.
SPLASH
RRRRR!
LOGAN! CAN YOU HEAR ME?

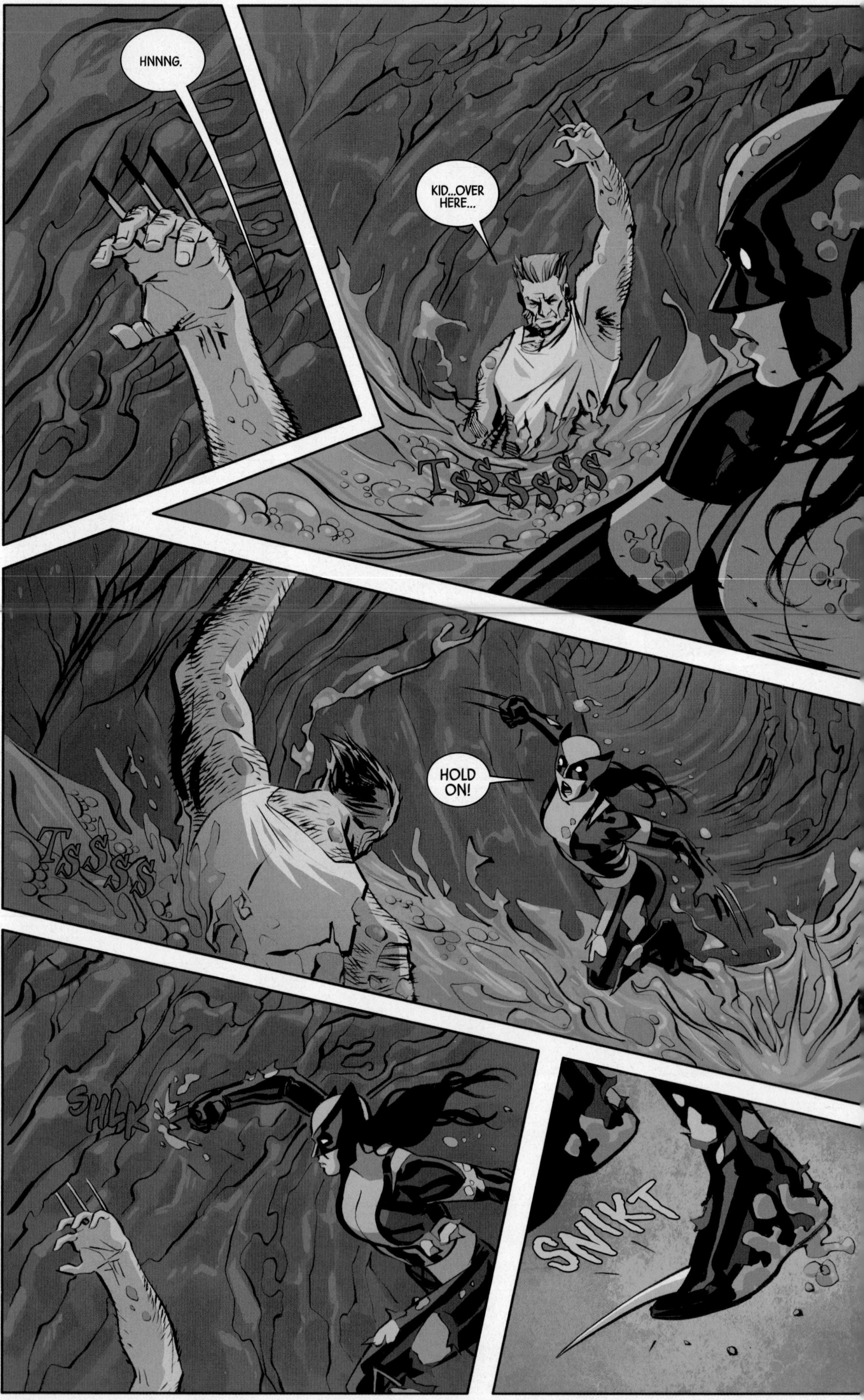
HNNNG.
KID...OVER HERE...
TSSSSSS
HOLD ON!
TSSSS
SHLK
SNIKT

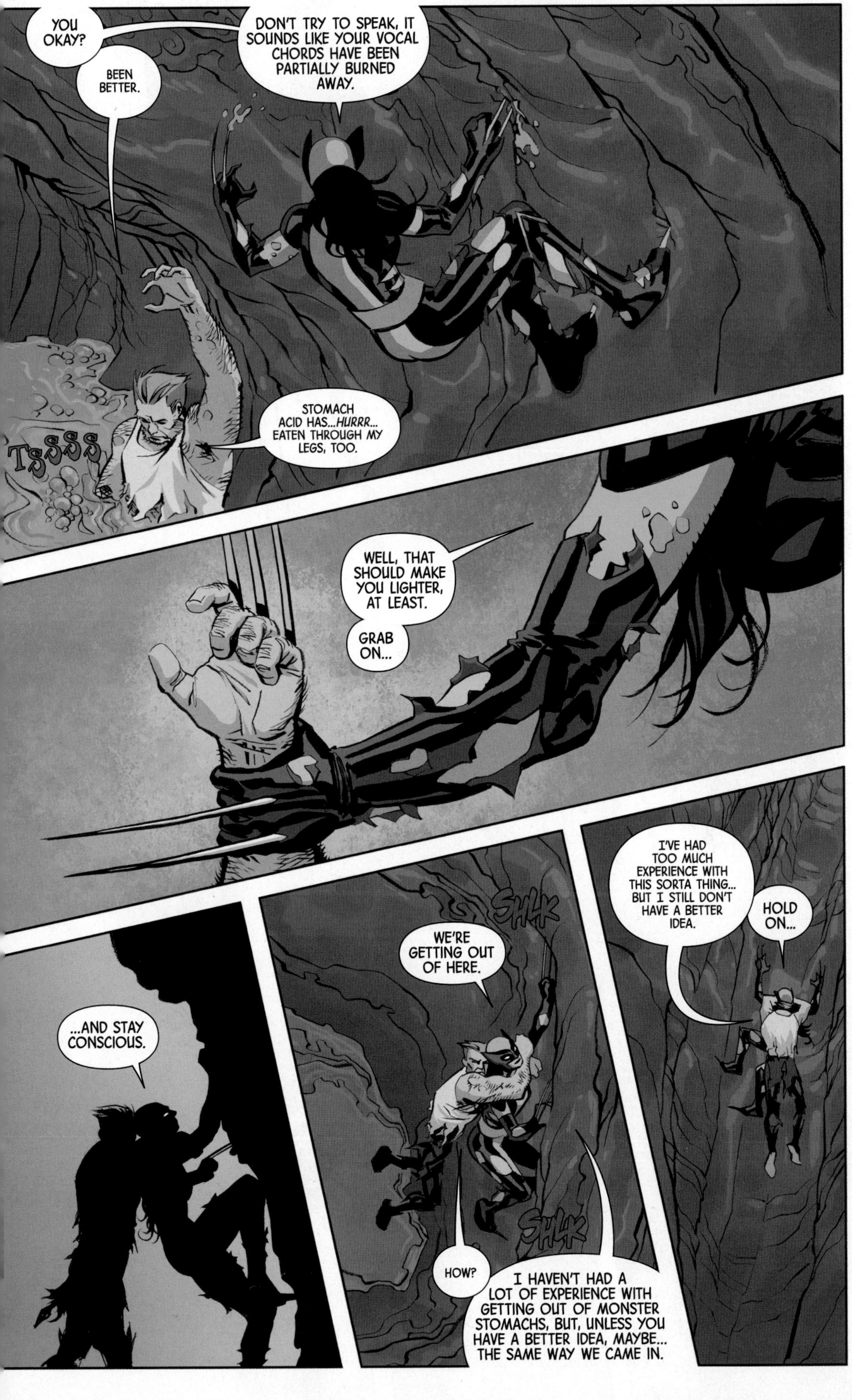
YOU OKAY?
DON'T TRY TO SPEAK, IT SOUNDS LIKE YOUR VOCAL CHORDS HAVE BEEN PARTIALLY BURNED AWAY.
BEEN BETTER.
TSSSS
STOMACH ACID HAS...*HURRR*... EATEN THROUGH MY LEGS, TOO.
WELL, THAT SHOULD MAKE YOU LIGHTER, AT LEAST.
GRAB ON...
...AND STAY CONSCIOUS.
SHLK
WE'RE GETTING OUT OF HERE.
SHLK
HOW?
I HAVEN'T HAD A LOT OF EXPERIENCE WITH GETTING OUT OF MONSTER STOMACHS, BUT, UNLESS YOU HAVE A BETTER IDEA, MAYBE... THE SAME WAY WE CAME IN.
I'VE HAD TOO MUCH EXPERIENCE WITH THIS SORTA THING... BUT I STILL DON'T HAVE A BETTER IDEA.
HOLD ON...

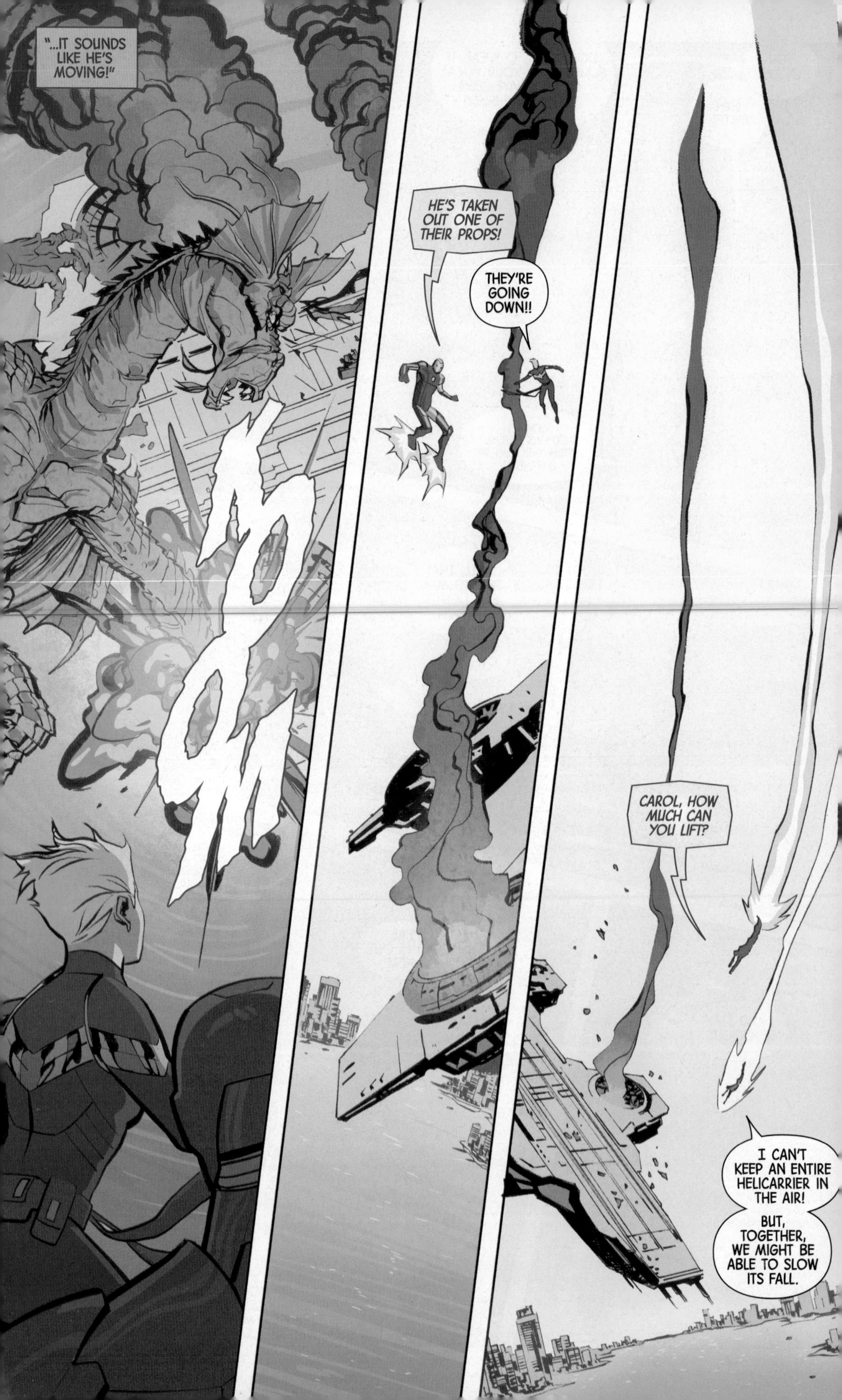

"...IT SOUNDS LIKE HE'S MOVING!"
HE'S TAKEN OUT ONE OF THEIR PROPS!
THEY'RE GOING DOWN!!
CAROL, HOW MUCH CAN YOU LIFT?
I CAN'T KEEP AN ENTIRE HELICARRIER IN THE AIR!
BUT, TOGETHER, WE MIGHT BE ABLE TO SLOW ITS FALL.

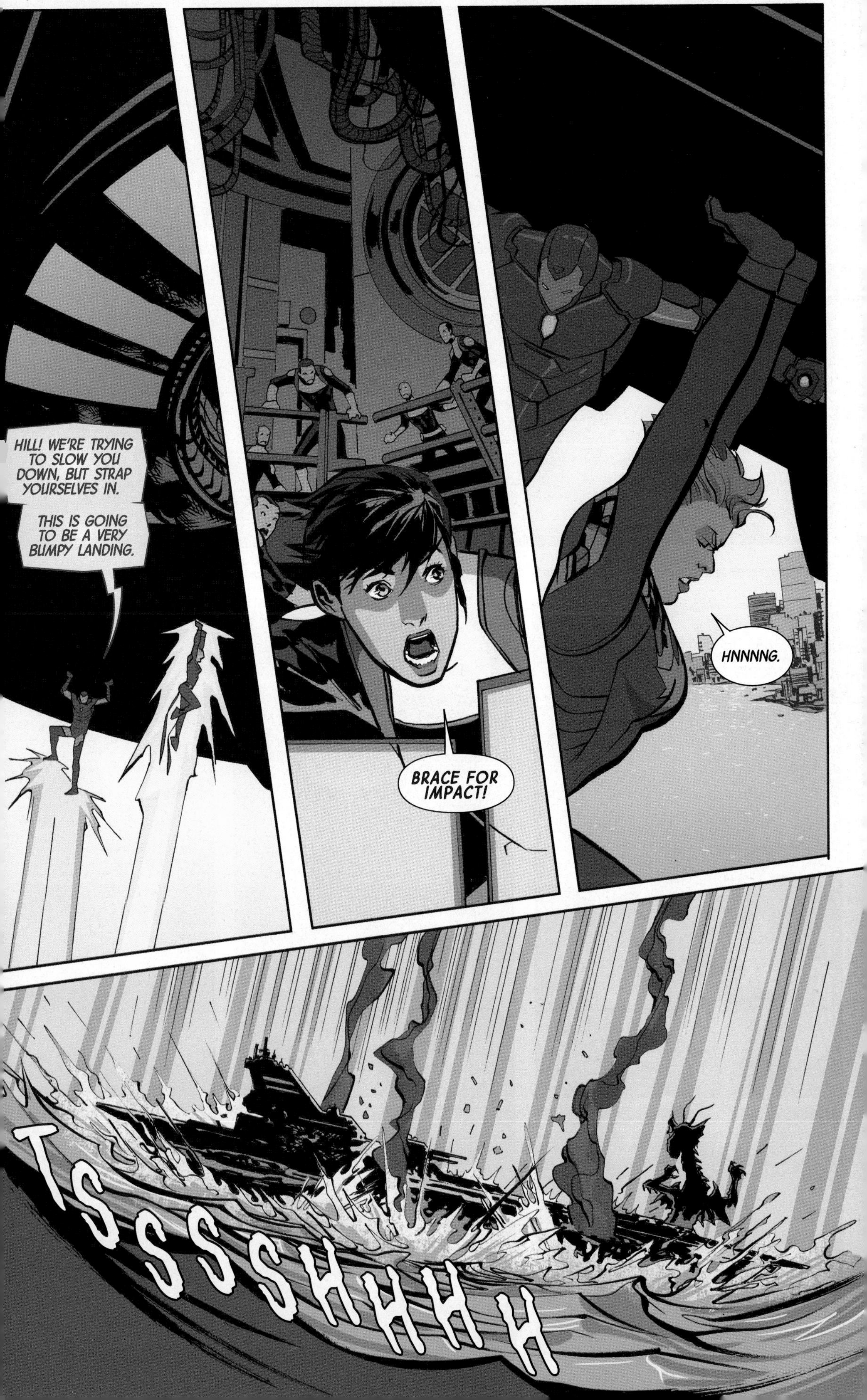
HILL! WE'RE TRYING TO SLOW YOU DOWN, BUT STRAP YOURSELVES IN.
THIS IS GOING TO BE A VERY BUMPY LANDING.
BRACE FOR IMPACT!
HNNNNG.
TSSSSHHHHH

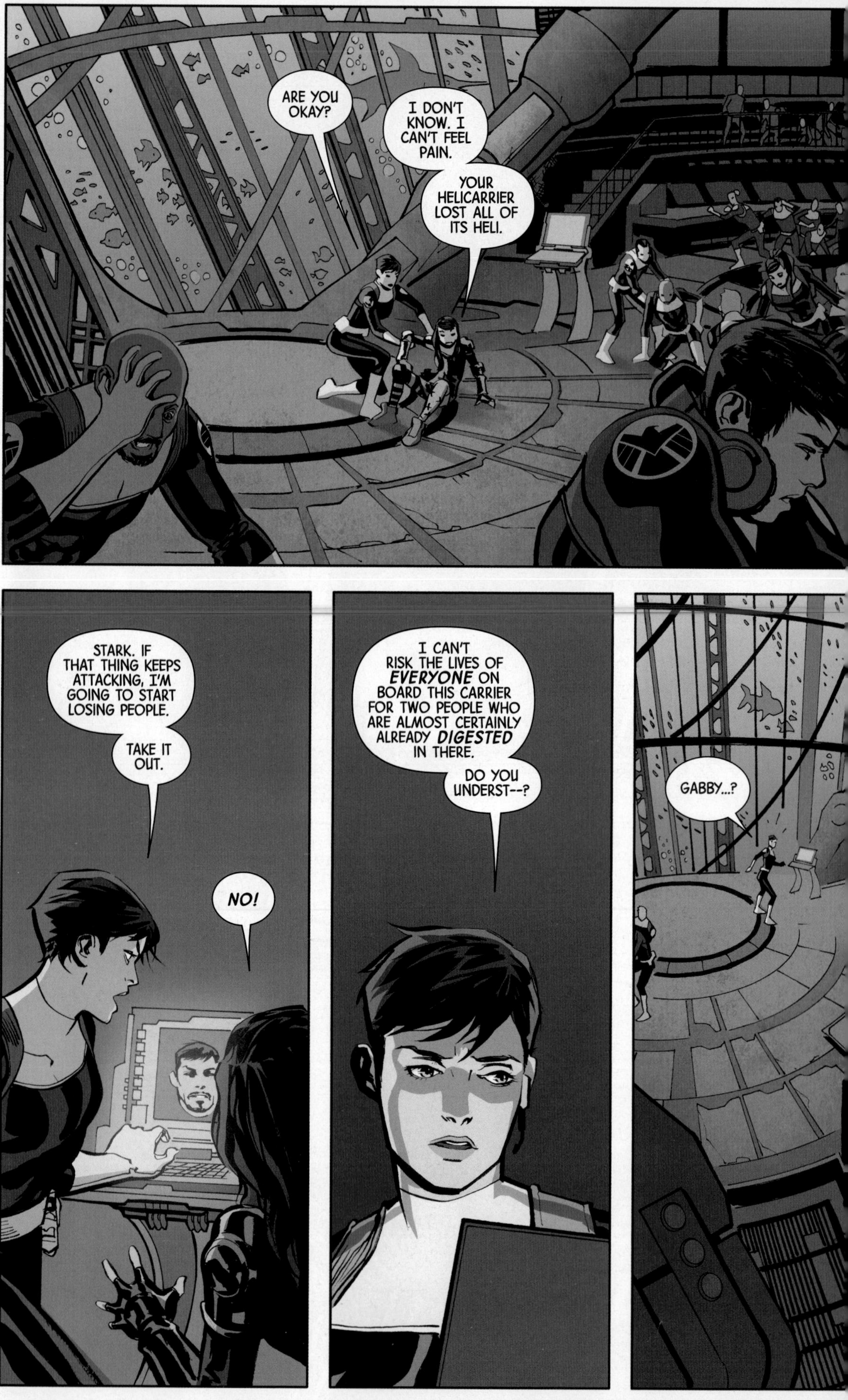
ARE YOU OKAY?
I DON'T KNOW. I CAN'T FEEL PAIN.
YOUR HELICARRIER LOST ALL OF ITS HELI.
STARK. IF THAT THING KEEPS ATTACKING, I'M GOING TO START LOSING PEOPLE.
TAKE IT OUT.
NO!
I CAN'T RISK THE LIVES OF EVERYONE ON BOARD THIS CARRIER FOR TWO PEOPLE WHO ARE ALMOST CERTAINLY ALREADY DIGESTED IN THERE.
DO YOU UNDERST--?
GABBY...?

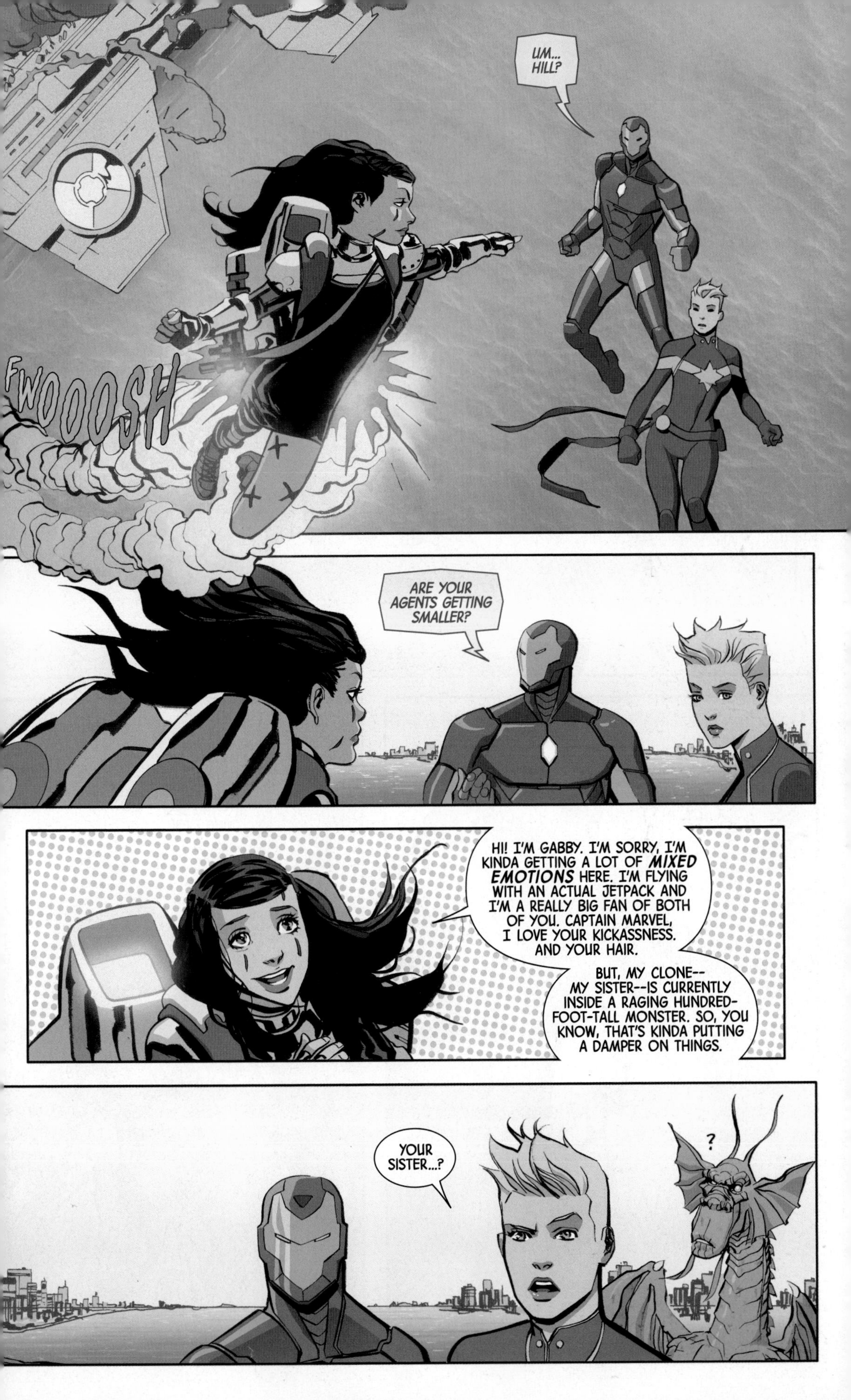
UM... HILL?
FWOOOSH
ARE YOUR AGENTS GETTING SMALLER?
HI! I'M GABBY. I'M SORRY, I'M KINDA GETTING A LOT OF *MIXED EMOTIONS* HERE. I'M FLYING WITH AN ACTUAL JETPACK AND I'M A REALLY BIG FAN OF BOTH OF YOU. CAPTAIN MARVEL, I LOVE YOUR KICKASSNESS. AND YOUR HAIR.
BUT, MY CLONE-- MY SISTER--IS CURRENTLY INSIDE A RAGING HUNDRED-FOOT-TALL MONSTER. SO, YOU KNOW, THAT'S KINDA PUTTING A DAMPER ON THINGS.
YOUR SISTER...?
?

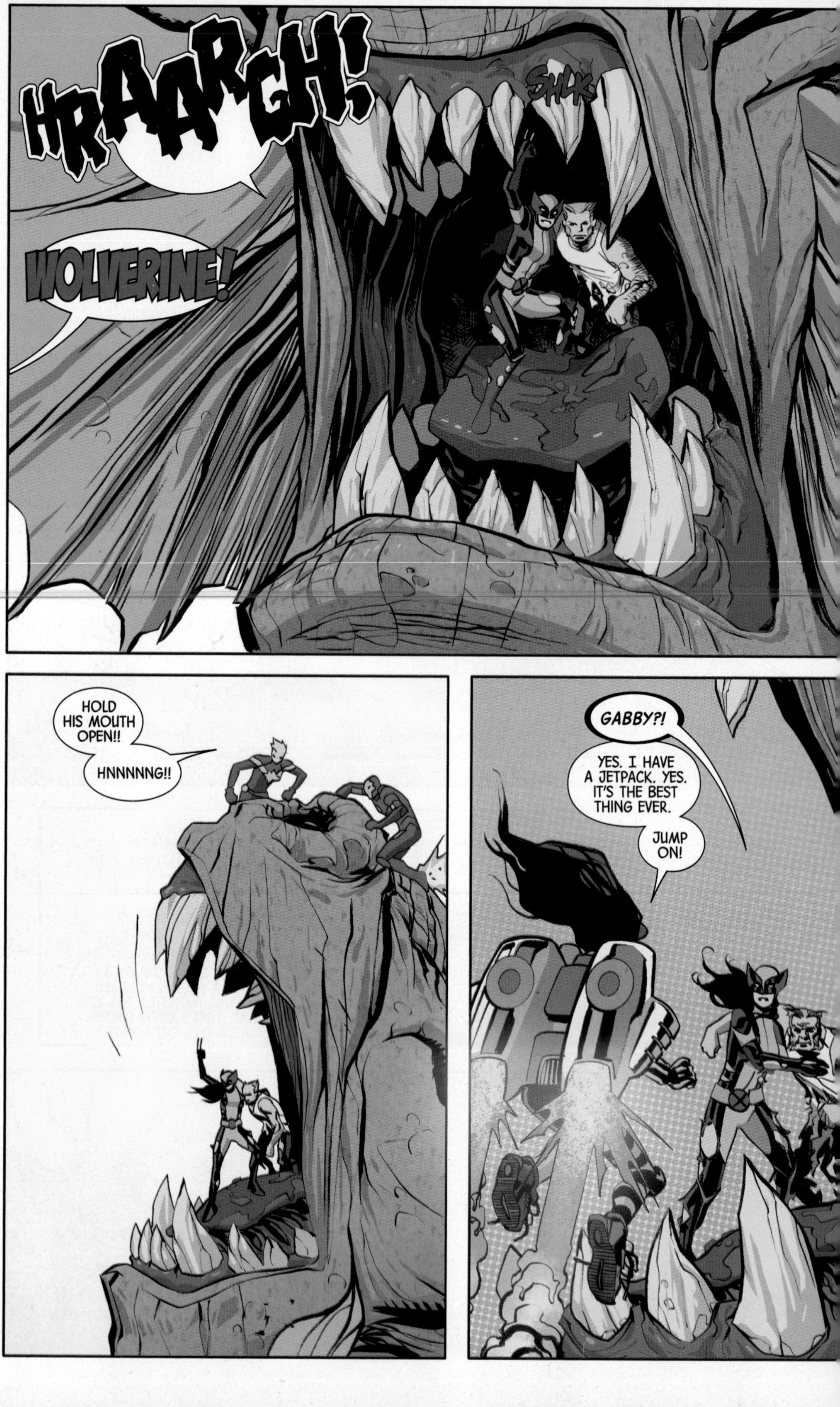
HRAARGH!
SHLK
WOLVERINE!
HOLD HIS MOUTH OPEN!!
HNNNNNG!!
GABBY?!
YES. I HAVE A JETPACK. YES. IT'S THE BEST THING EVER.
JUMP ON!

I THINK YOU'RE TOO HEAVY!

I KNOW. JUST TAKE THE OLD MAN...OR WHAT'S LEFT OF HIM...AND GET HIM TO SAFETY!

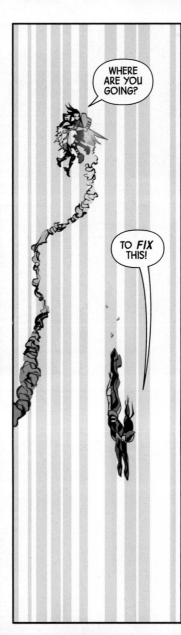

WHERE ARE YOU GOING?

TO *FIX* THIS!

FSSH

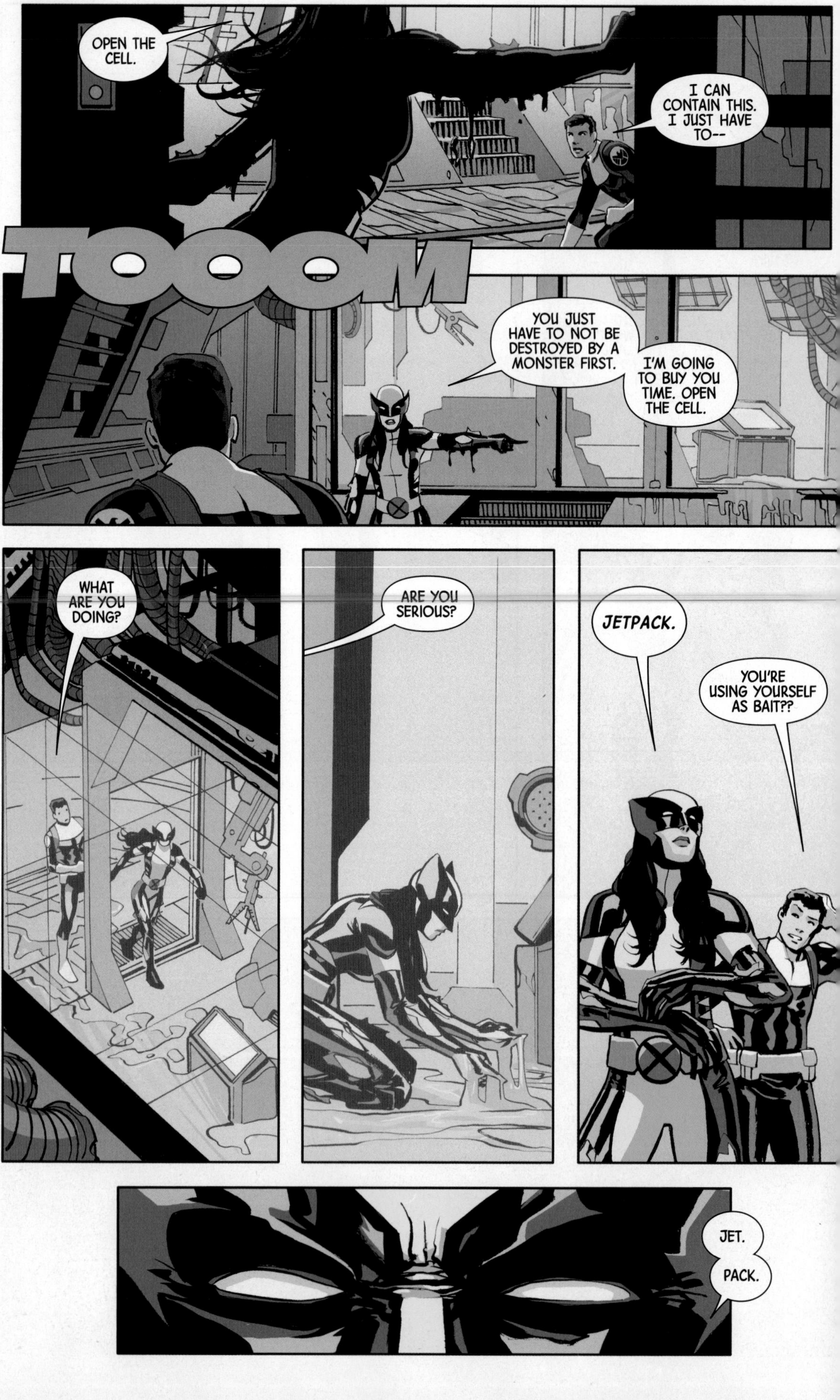
OPEN THE CELL.
I CAN CONTAIN THIS. I JUST HAVE TO--
TOOOM
YOU JUST HAVE TO NOT BE DESTROYED BY A MONSTER FIRST.
I'M GOING TO BUY YOU TIME. OPEN THE CELL.
WHAT ARE YOU DOING?
ARE YOU SERIOUS?
JETPACK.
YOU'RE USING YOURSELF AS BAIT??
JET.
PACK.

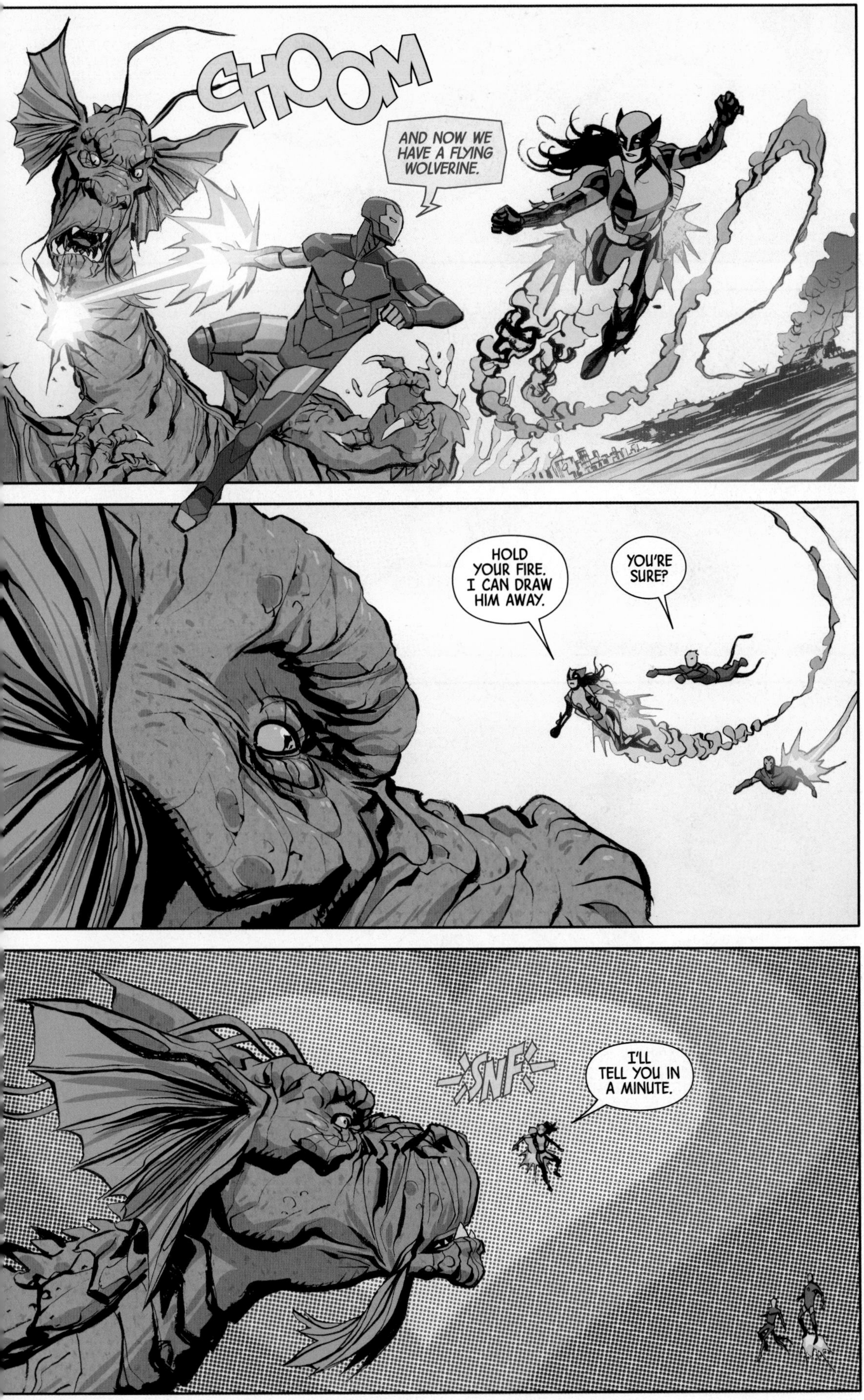
CHOOM
AND NOW WE HAVE A FLYING WOLVERINE.
HOLD YOUR FIRE. I CAN DRAW HIM AWAY.
YOU'RE SURE?
SNF
I'LL TELL YOU IN A MINUTE.

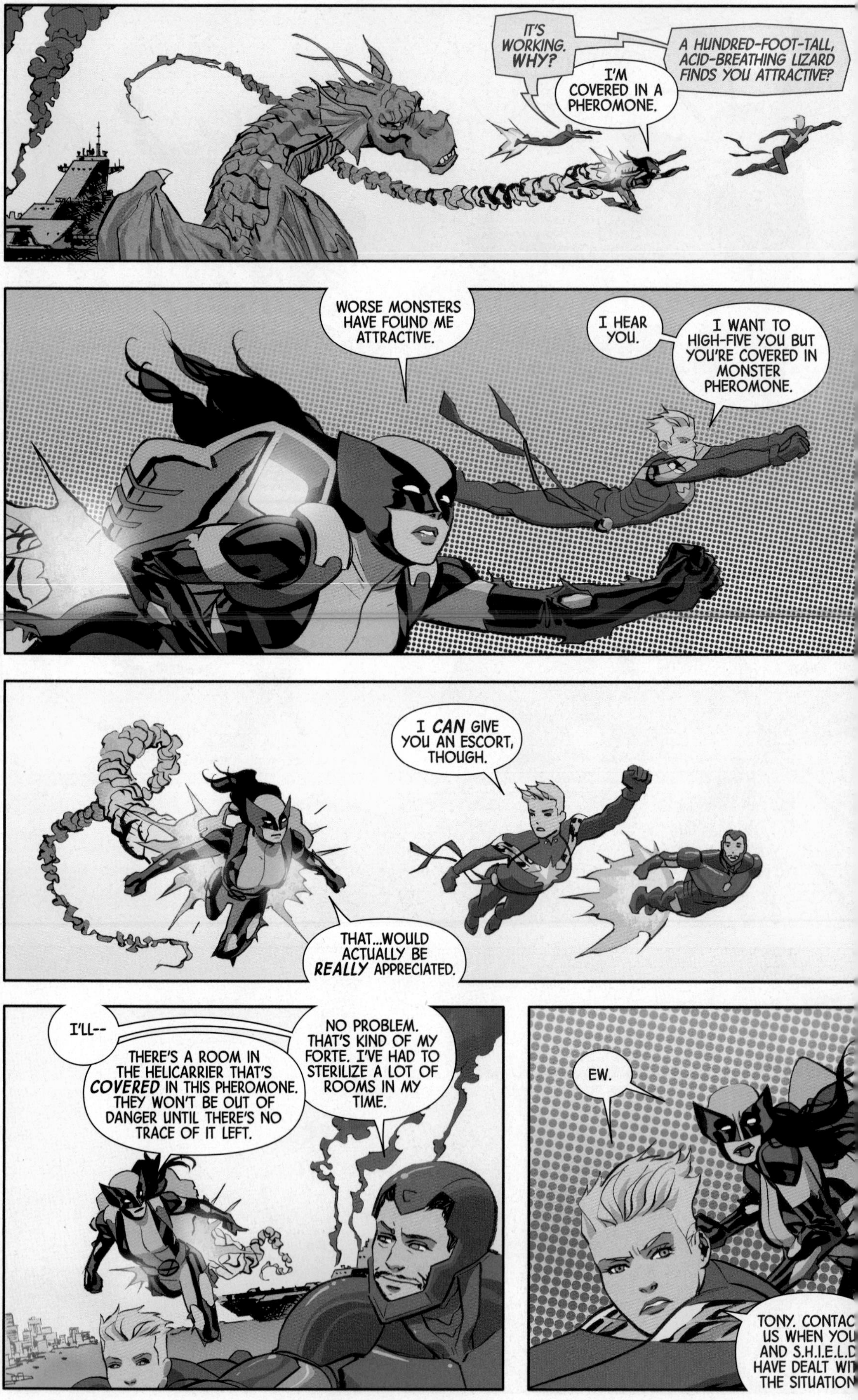

IT'S WORKING. WHY?
A HUNDRED-FOOT-TALL, ACID-BREATHING LIZARD FINDS YOU ATTRACTIVE?
I'M COVERED IN A PHEROMONE.
WORSE MONSTERS HAVE FOUND ME ATTRACTIVE.
I HEAR YOU.
I WANT TO HIGH-FIVE YOU BUT YOU'RE COVERED IN MONSTER PHEROMONE.
I CAN GIVE YOU AN ESCORT, THOUGH.
THAT...WOULD ACTUALLY BE REALLY APPRECIATED.
I'LL--
THERE'S A ROOM IN THE HELICARRIER THAT'S COVERED IN THIS PHEROMONE. THEY WON'T BE OUT OF DANGER UNTIL THERE'S NO TRACE OF IT LEFT.
NO PROBLEM. THAT'S KIND OF MY FORTE. I'VE HAD TO STERILIZE A LOT OF ROOMS IN MY TIME.
EW.
TONY. CONTAC US WHEN YOU AND S.H.I.E.L.D HAVE DEALT WIT THE SITUATION

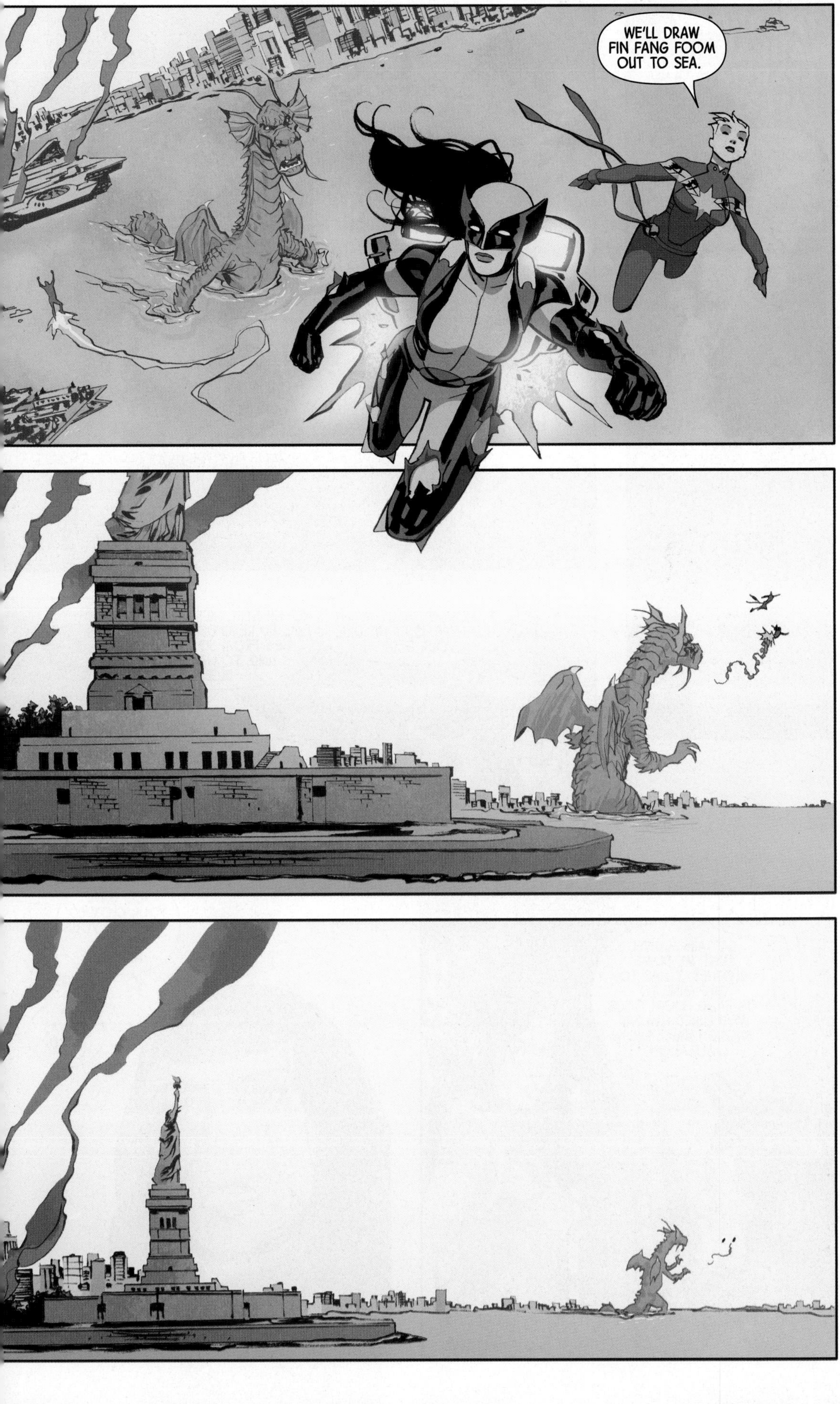
WE'LL DRAW FIN FANG FOOM OUT TO SEA.

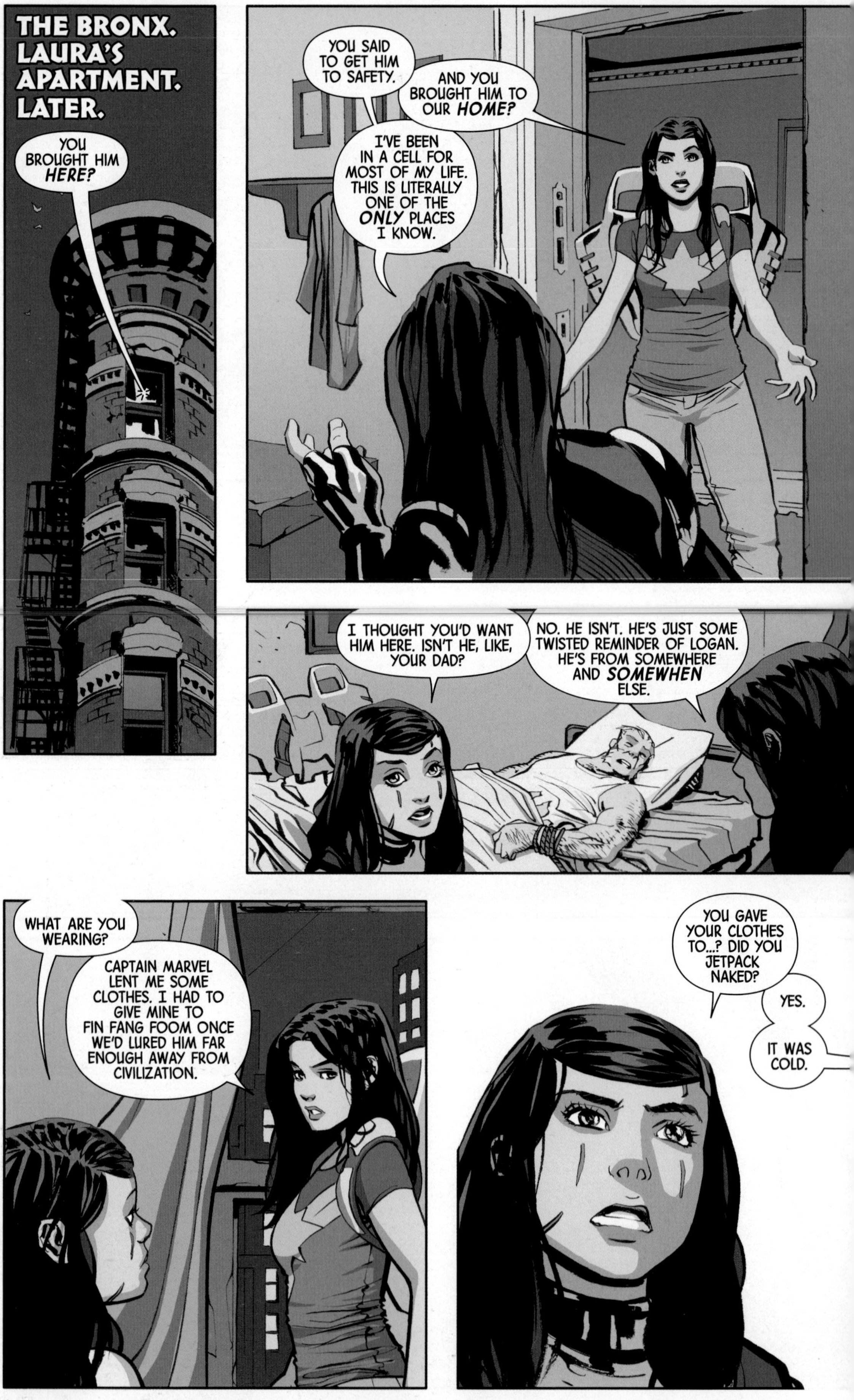
THE BRONX. LAURA'S APARTMENT. LATER.
YOU BROUGHT HIM HERE?
YOU SAID TO GET HIM TO SAFETY.
AND YOU BROUGHT HIM TO OUR HOME?
I'VE BEEN IN A CELL FOR MOST OF MY LIFE. THIS IS LITERALLY ONE OF THE ONLY PLACES I KNOW.
I THOUGHT YOU'D WANT HIM HERE. ISN'T HE, LIKE, YOUR DAD?
NO. HE ISN'T. HE'S JUST SOME TWISTED REMINDER OF LOGAN. HE'S FROM SOMEWHERE AND SOMEWHEN ELSE.
WHAT ARE YOU WEARING?
CAPTAIN MARVEL LENT ME SOME CLOTHES. I HAD TO GIVE MINE TO FIN FANG FOOM ONCE WE'D LURED HIM FAR ENOUGH AWAY FROM CIVILIZATION.
YOU GAVE YOUR CLOTHES TO...? DID YOU JETPACK NAKED?
YES.
IT WAS COLD.

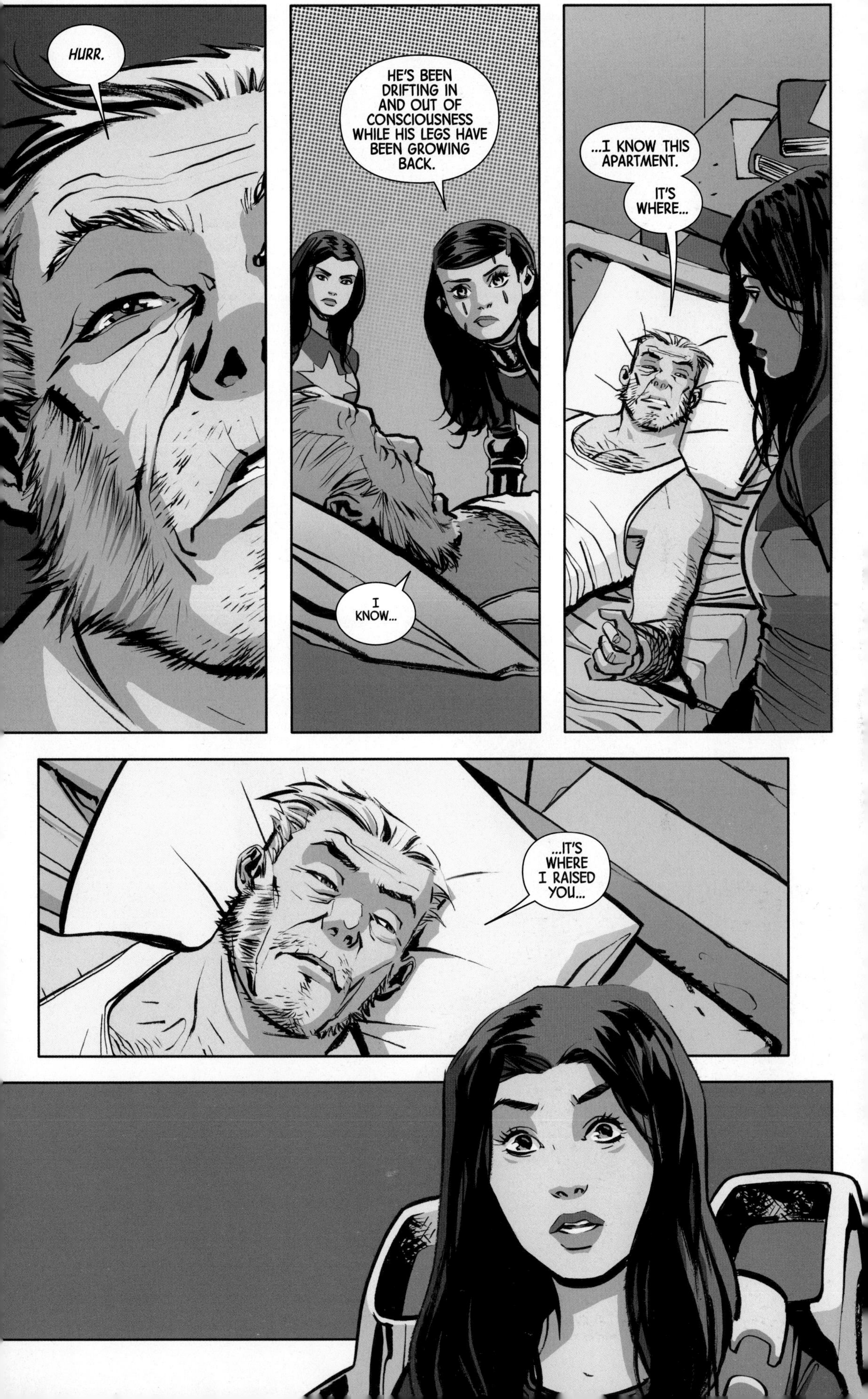
HURR.
HE'S BEEN DRIFTING IN AND OUT OF CONSCIOUSNESS WHILE HIS LEGS HAVE BEEN GROWING BACK.
I KNOW...
...I KNOW THIS APARTMENT.
IT'S WHERE...
...IT'S WHERE I RAISED YOU...

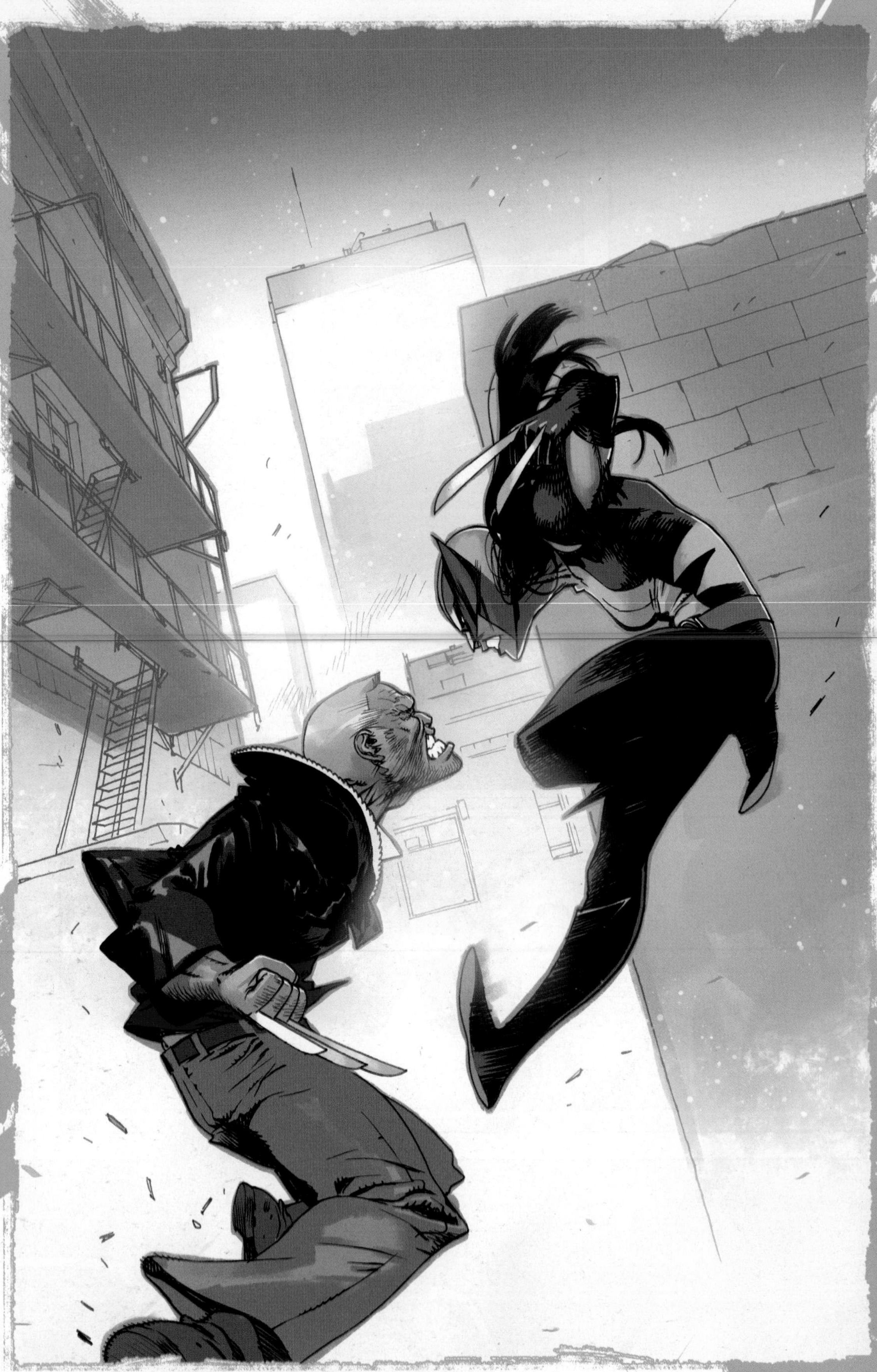

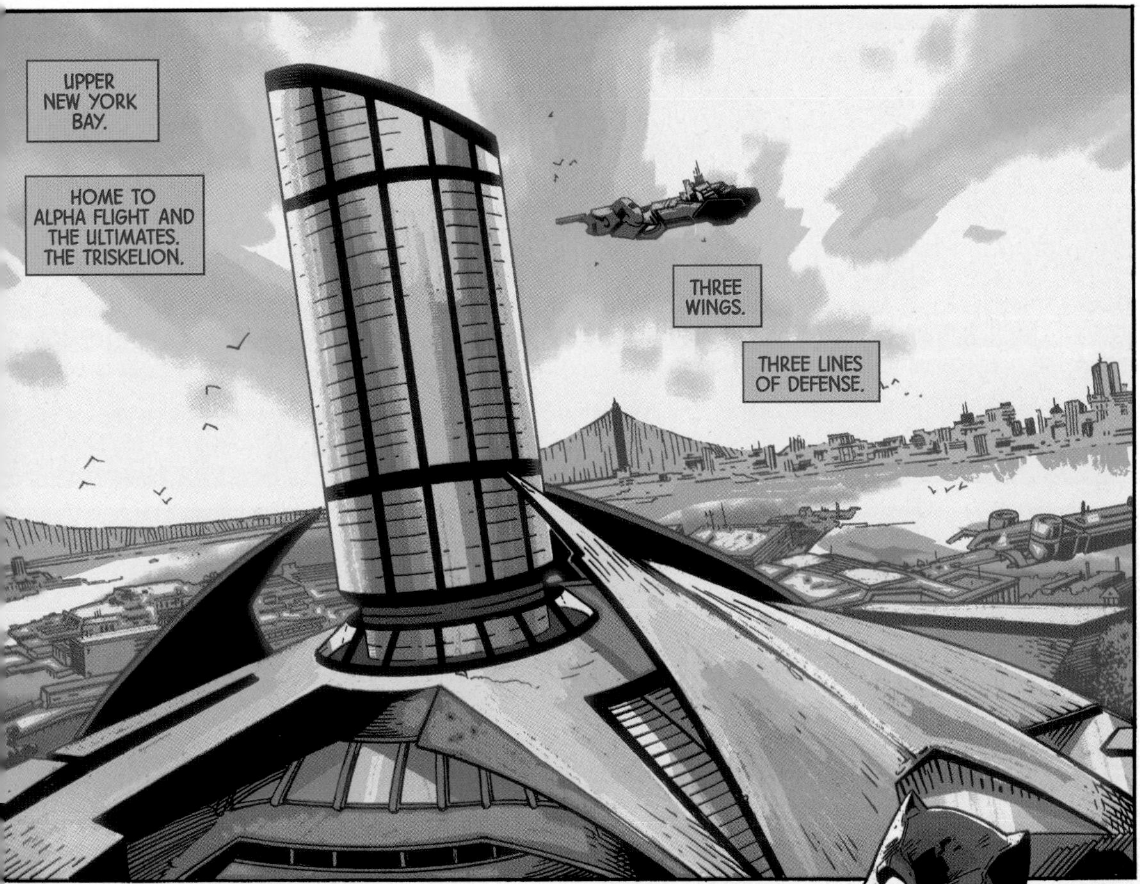
UPPER NEW YORK BAY.
HOME TO ALPHA FLIGHT AND THE ULTIMATES. THE TRISKELION.
THREE WINGS.
THREE LINES OF DEFENSE.
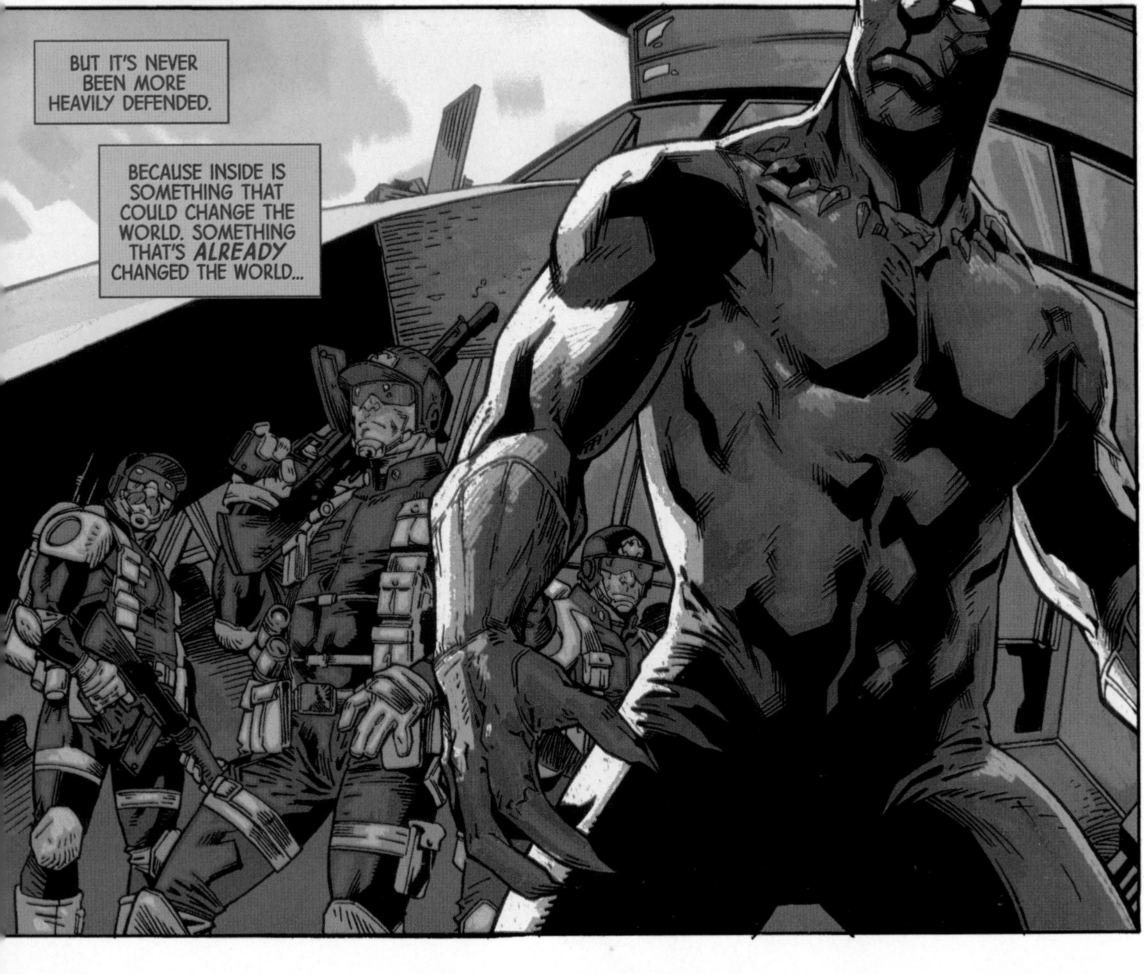
BUT IT'S NEVER BEEN MORE HEAVILY DEFENDED.
BECAUSE INSIDE IS SOMETHING THAT COULD CHANGE THE WORLD. SOMETHING THAT'S *ALREADY* CHANGED THE WORLD...

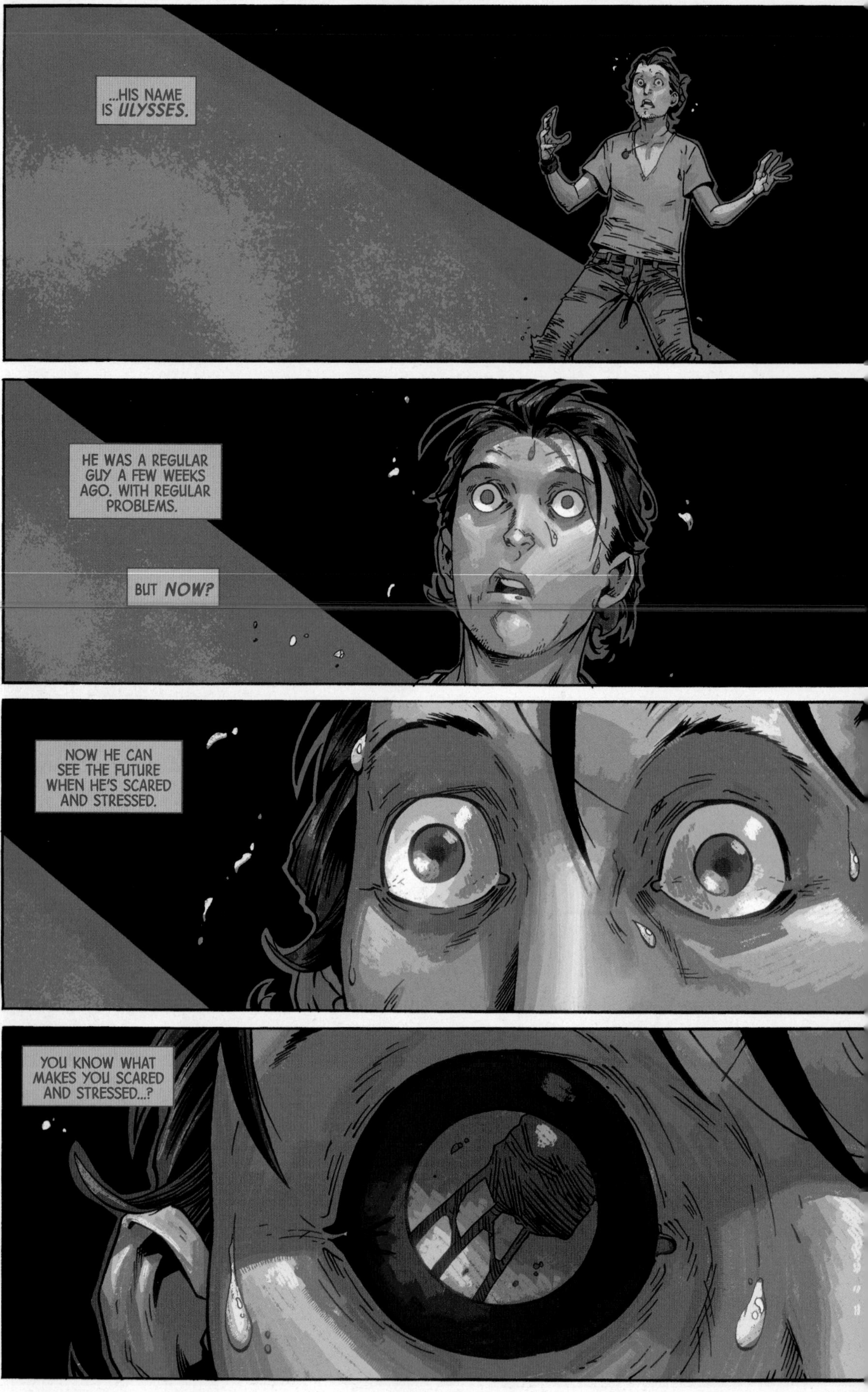
...HIS NAME IS ULYSSES.
HE WAS A REGULAR GUY A FEW WEEKS AGO. WITH REGULAR PROBLEMS.
BUT NOW?
NOW HE CAN SEE THE FUTURE WHEN HE'S SCARED AND STRESSED.
YOU KNOW WHAT MAKES YOU SCARED AND STRESSED...?

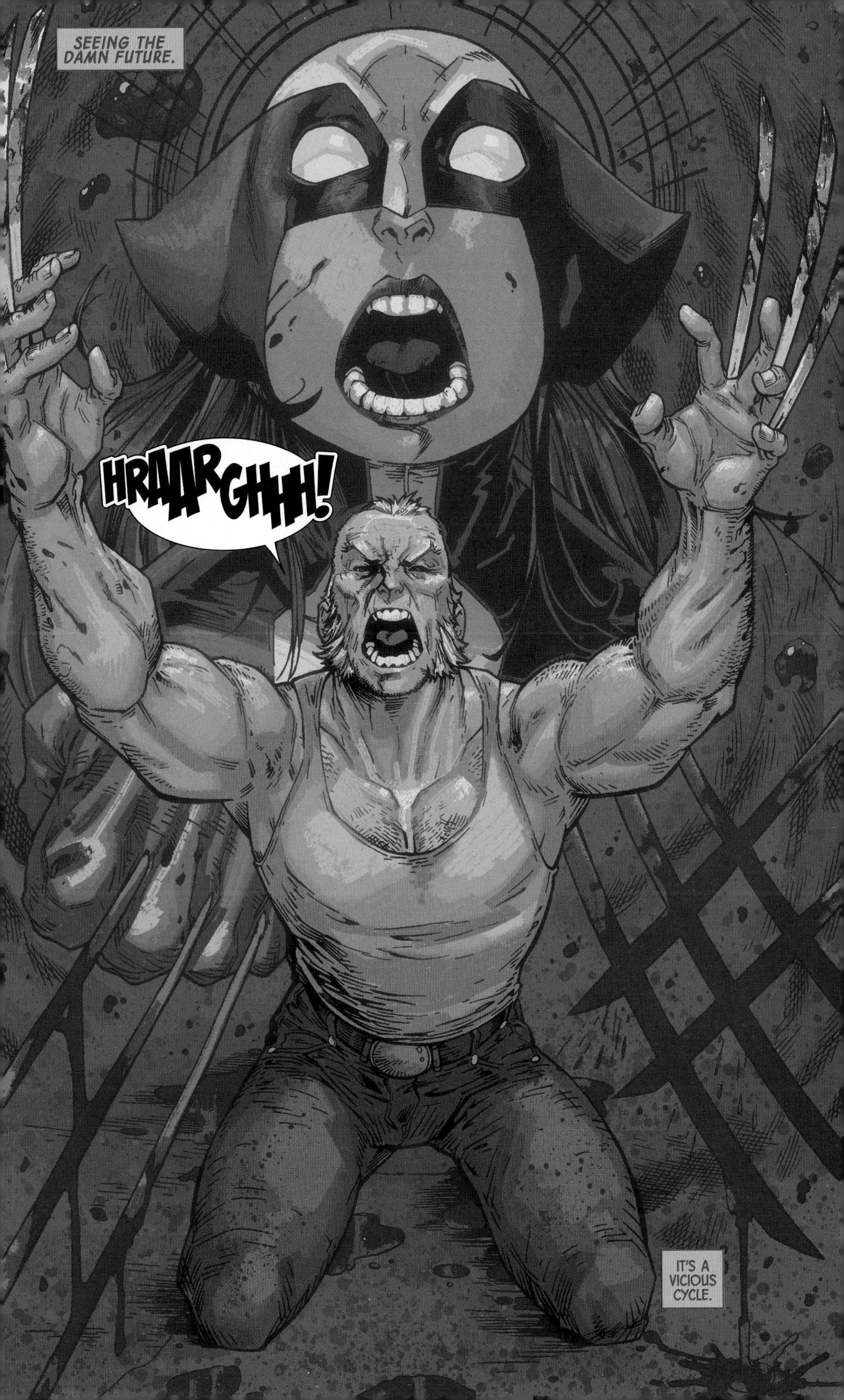
SEEING THE DAMN FUTURE.
HRAAARGHHH!
IT'S A VICIOUS CYCLE.

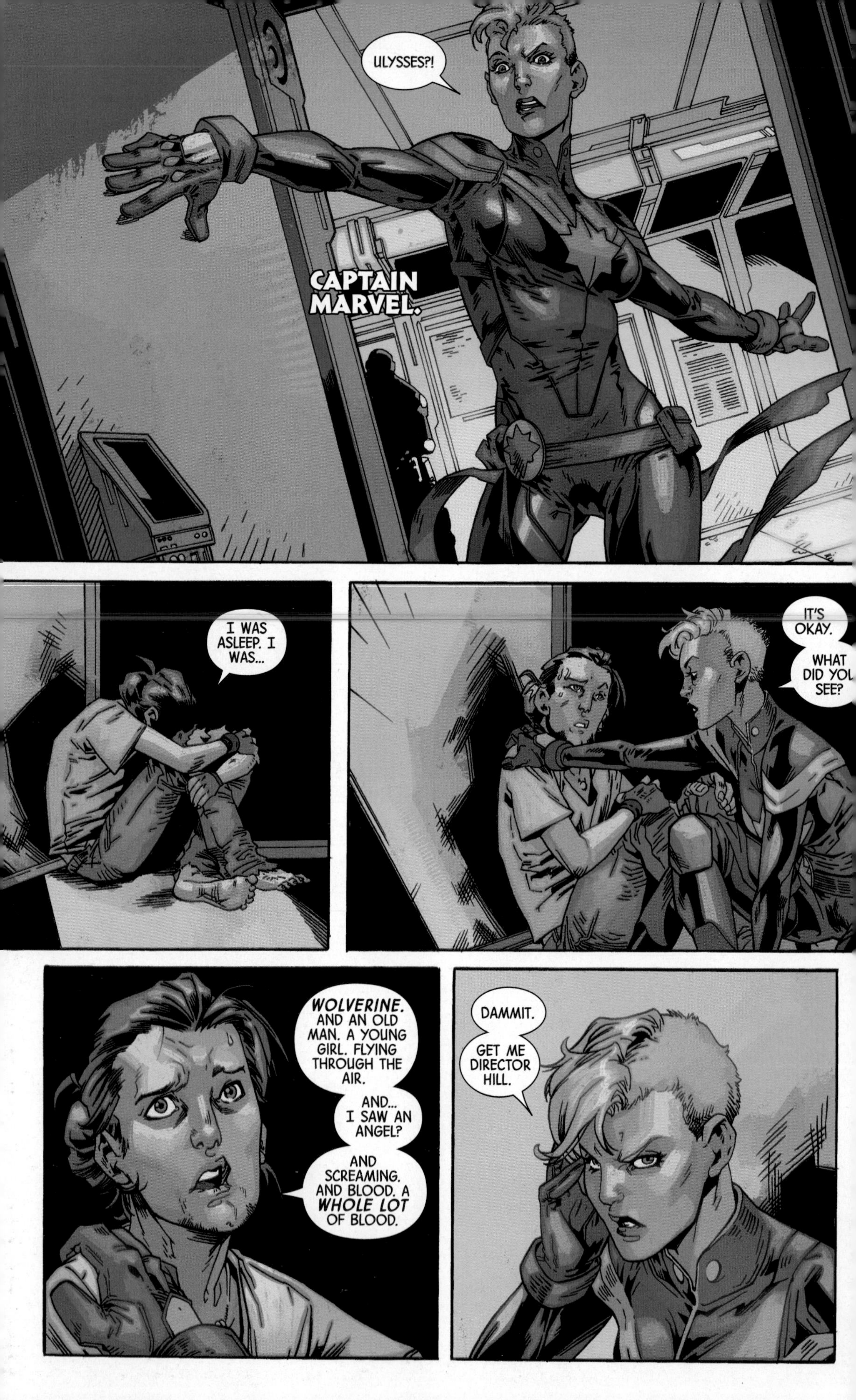
ULYSSES?!
CAPTAIN MARVEL.
I WAS ASLEEP. I WAS...
IT'S OKAY.
WHAT DID YOU SEE?
WOLVERINE. AND AN OLD MAN. A YOUNG GIRL. FLYING THROUGH THE AIR.
AND... I SAW AN ANGEL?
AND SCREAMING. AND BLOOD. A WHOLE LOT OF BLOOD.
DAMMIT.
GET ME DIRECTOR HILL.

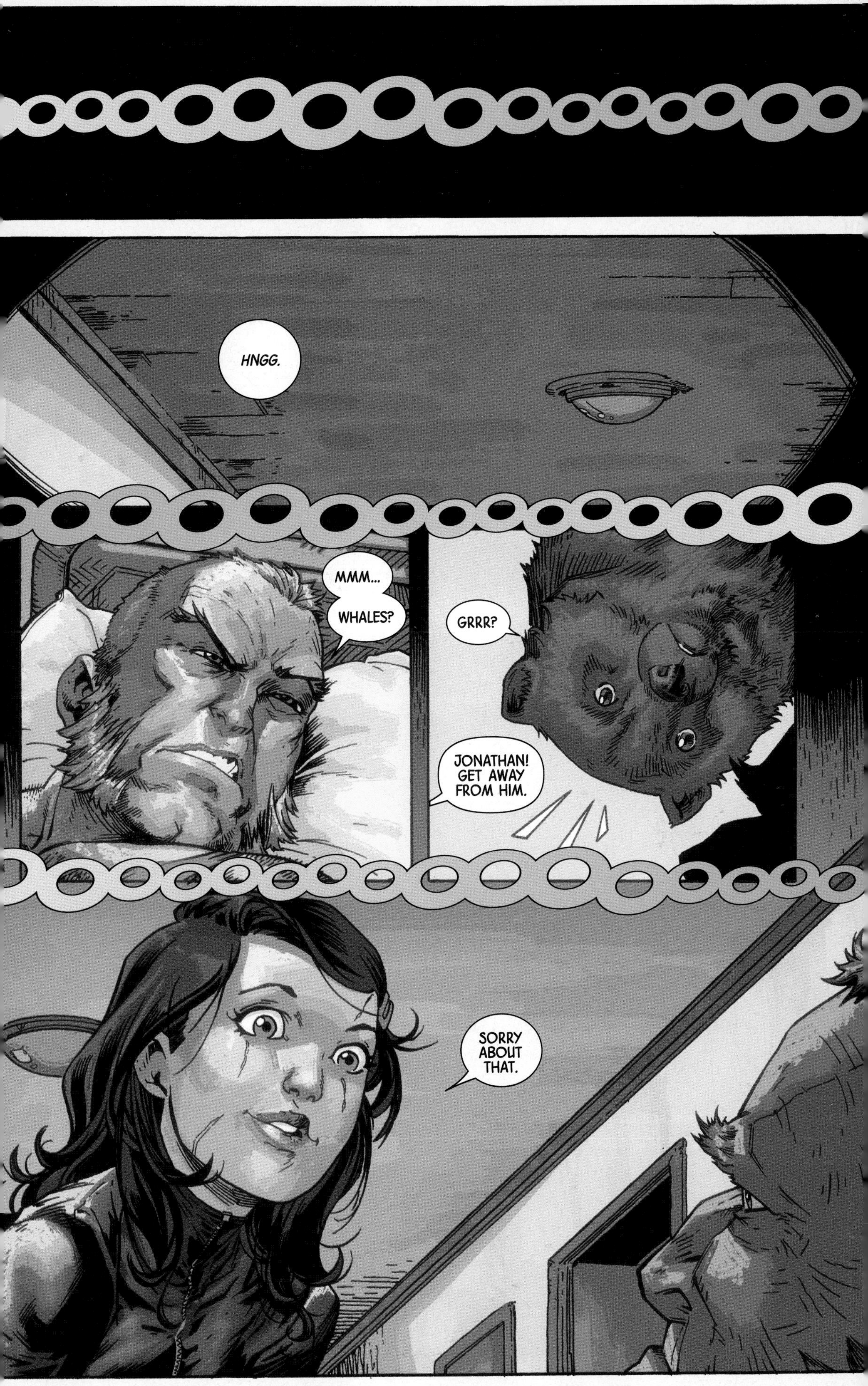
HNGG.
MMM...
WHALES?
GRRR?
JONATHAN! GET AWAY FROM HIM.
SORRY ABOUT THAT.

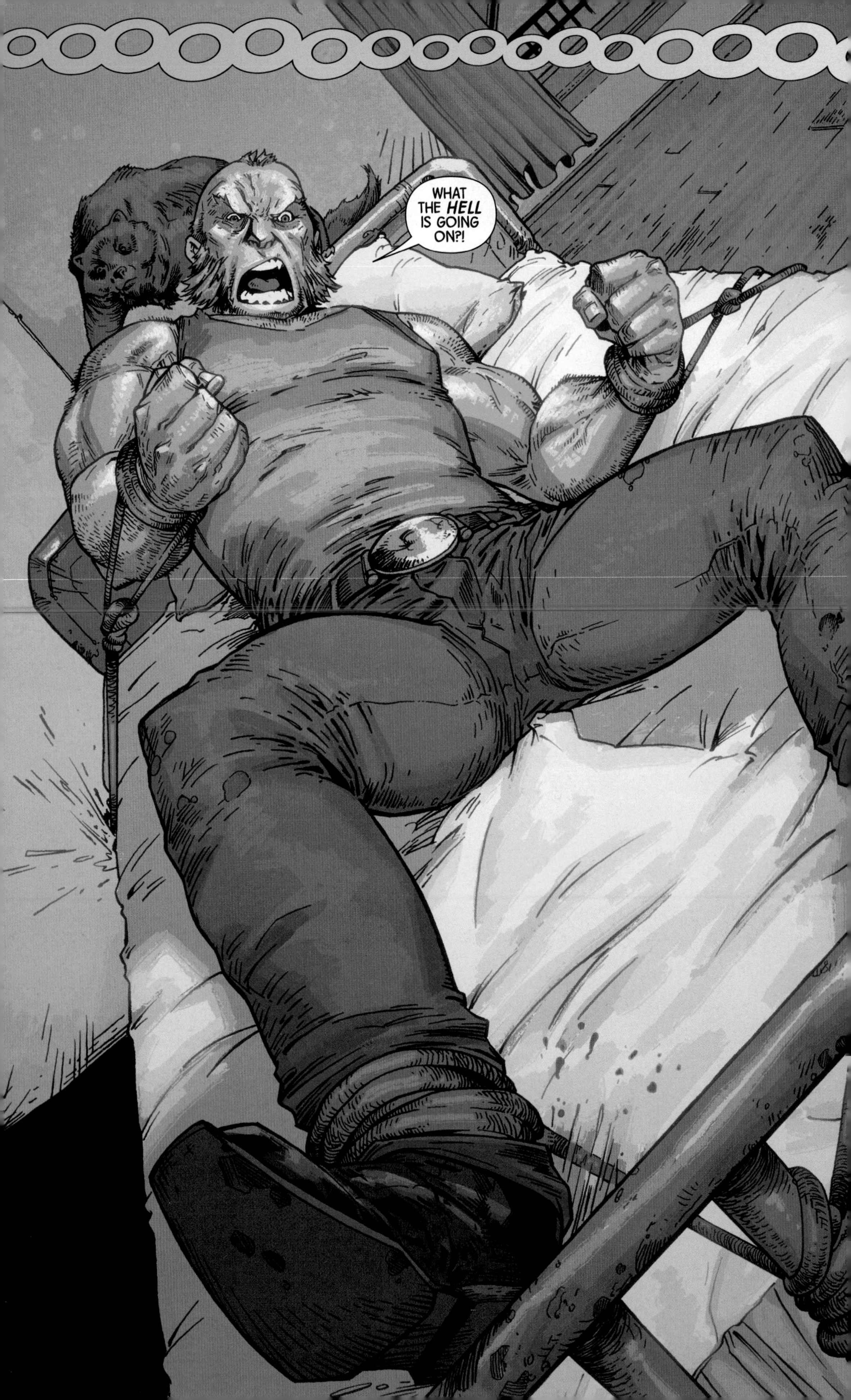
WHAT THE HELL IS GOING ON?!

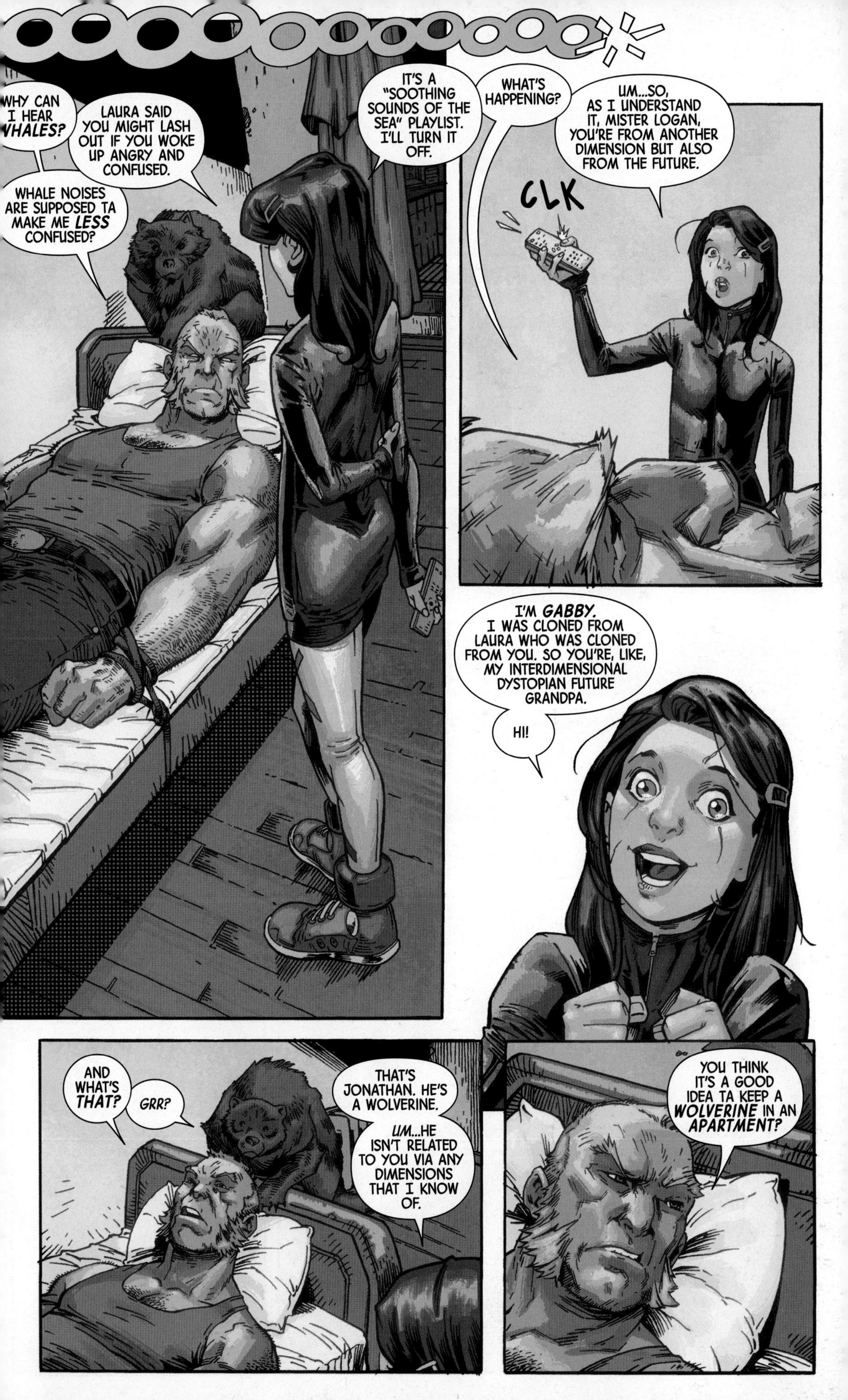
OOOOOOOOOOOOO
WHY CAN I HEAR WHALES?
LAURA SAID YOU MIGHT LASH OUT IF YOU WOKE UP ANGRY AND CONFUSED.
WHALE NOISES ARE SUPPOSED TA MAKE ME LESS CONFUSED?
IT'S A "SOOTHING SOUNDS OF THE SEA" PLAYLIST. I'LL TURN IT OFF.
WHAT'S HAPPENING?
UM...SO, AS I UNDERSTAND IT, MISTER LOGAN, YOU'RE FROM ANOTHER DIMENSION BUT ALSO FROM THE FUTURE.
CLK
I'M GABBY. I WAS CLONED FROM LAURA WHO WAS CLONED FROM YOU. SO YOU'RE, LIKE, MY INTERDIMENSIONAL DYSTOPIAN FUTURE GRANDPA.
HI!
AND WHAT'S THAT?
GRR?
THAT'S JONATHAN. HE'S A WOLVERINE.
UM...HE ISN'T RELATED TO YOU VIA ANY DIMENSIONS THAT I KNOW OF.
YOU THINK IT'S A GOOD IDEA TA KEEP A WOLVERINE IN AN APARTMENT?

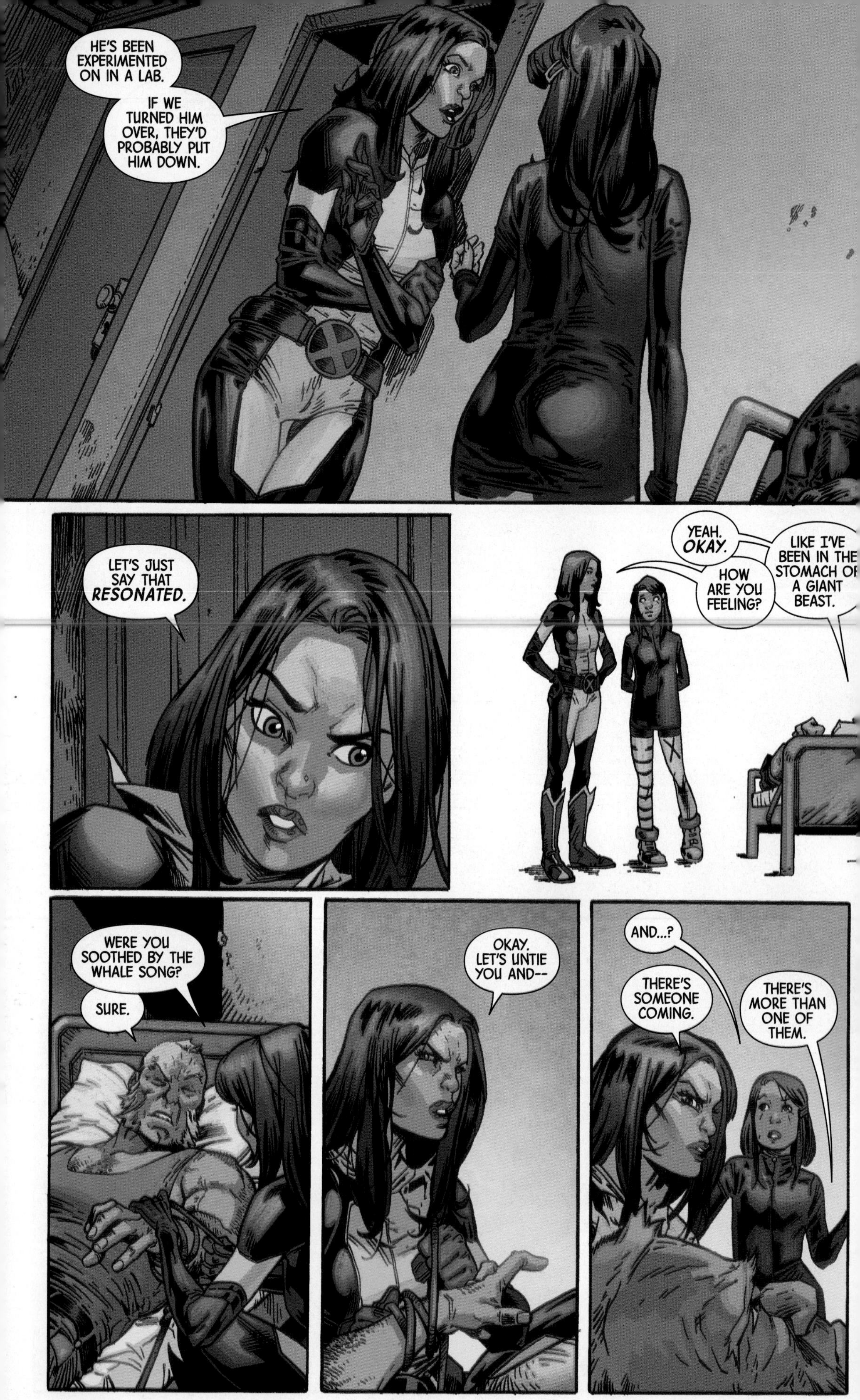
HE'S BEEN EXPERIMENTED ON IN A LAB.
IF WE TURNED HIM OVER, THEY'D PROBABLY PUT HIM DOWN.
LET'S JUST SAY THAT RESONATED.
YEAH. OKAY.
HOW ARE YOU FEELING?
LIKE I'VE BEEN IN THE STOMACH OF A GIANT BEAST.
WERE YOU SOOTHED BY THE WHALE SONG?
SURE.
OKAY. LET'S UNTIE YOU AND--
AND...?
THERE'S SOMEONE COMING.
THERE'S MORE THAN ONE OF THEM.

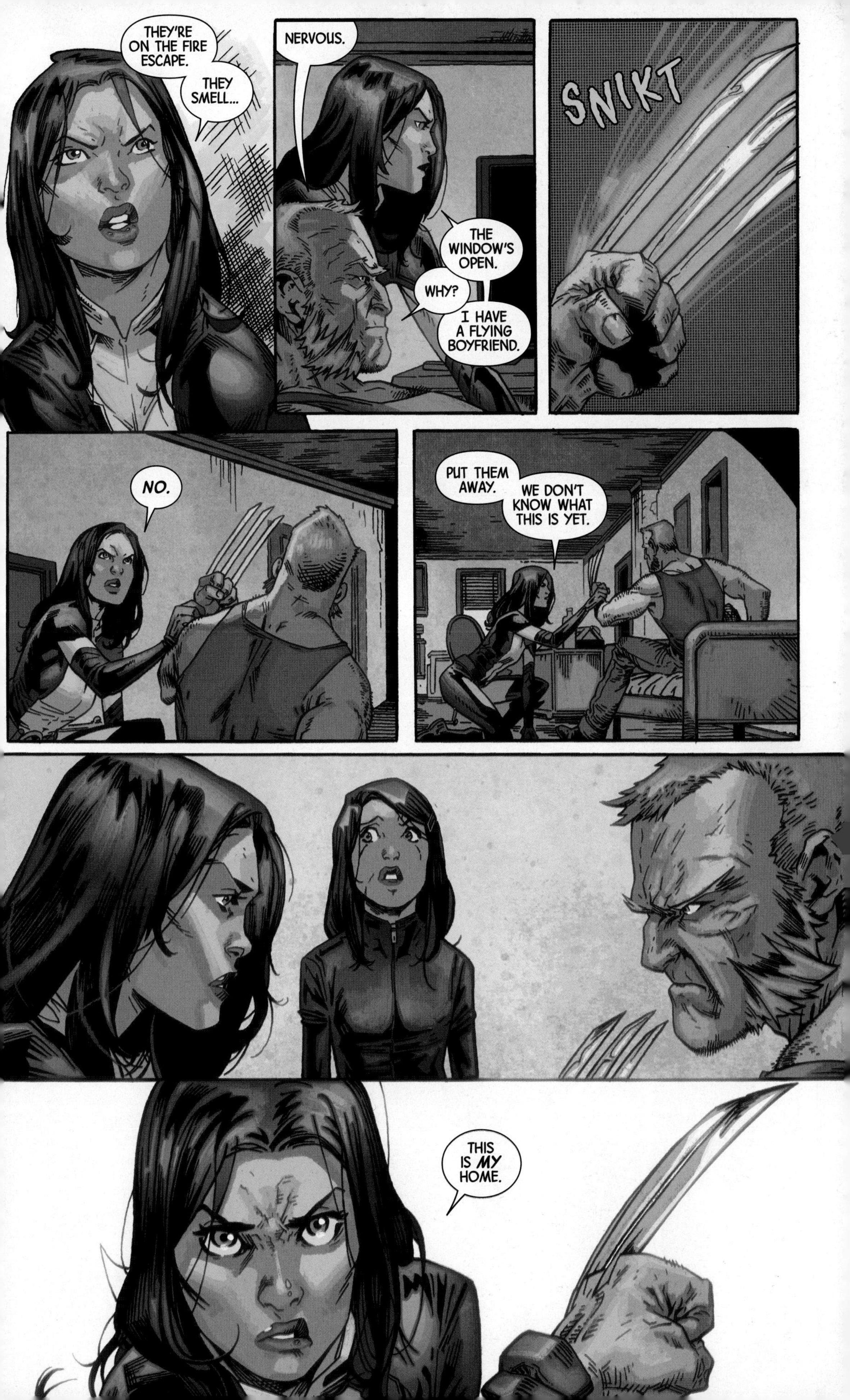
THEY'RE ON THE FIRE ESCAPE.
THEY SMELL...
NERVOUS.
THE WINDOW'S OPEN.
WHY?
I HAVE A FLYING BOYFRIEND.
SNIKT
NO.
PUT THEM AWAY.
WE DON'T KNOW WHAT THIS IS YET.
THIS IS MY HOME.

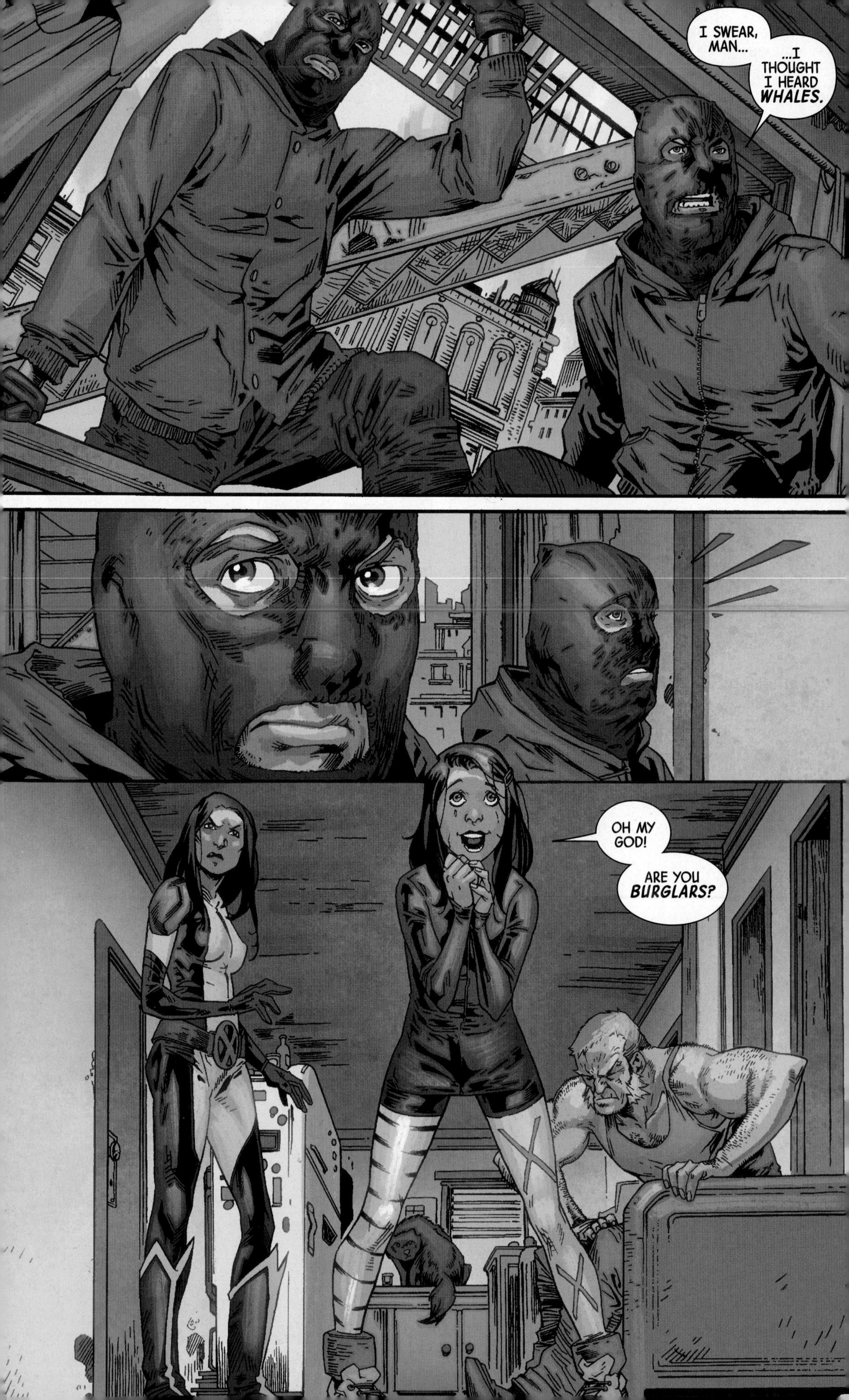
I SWEAR, MAN...
...I THOUGHT I HEARD WHALES.
OH MY GOD!
ARE YOU BURGLARS?

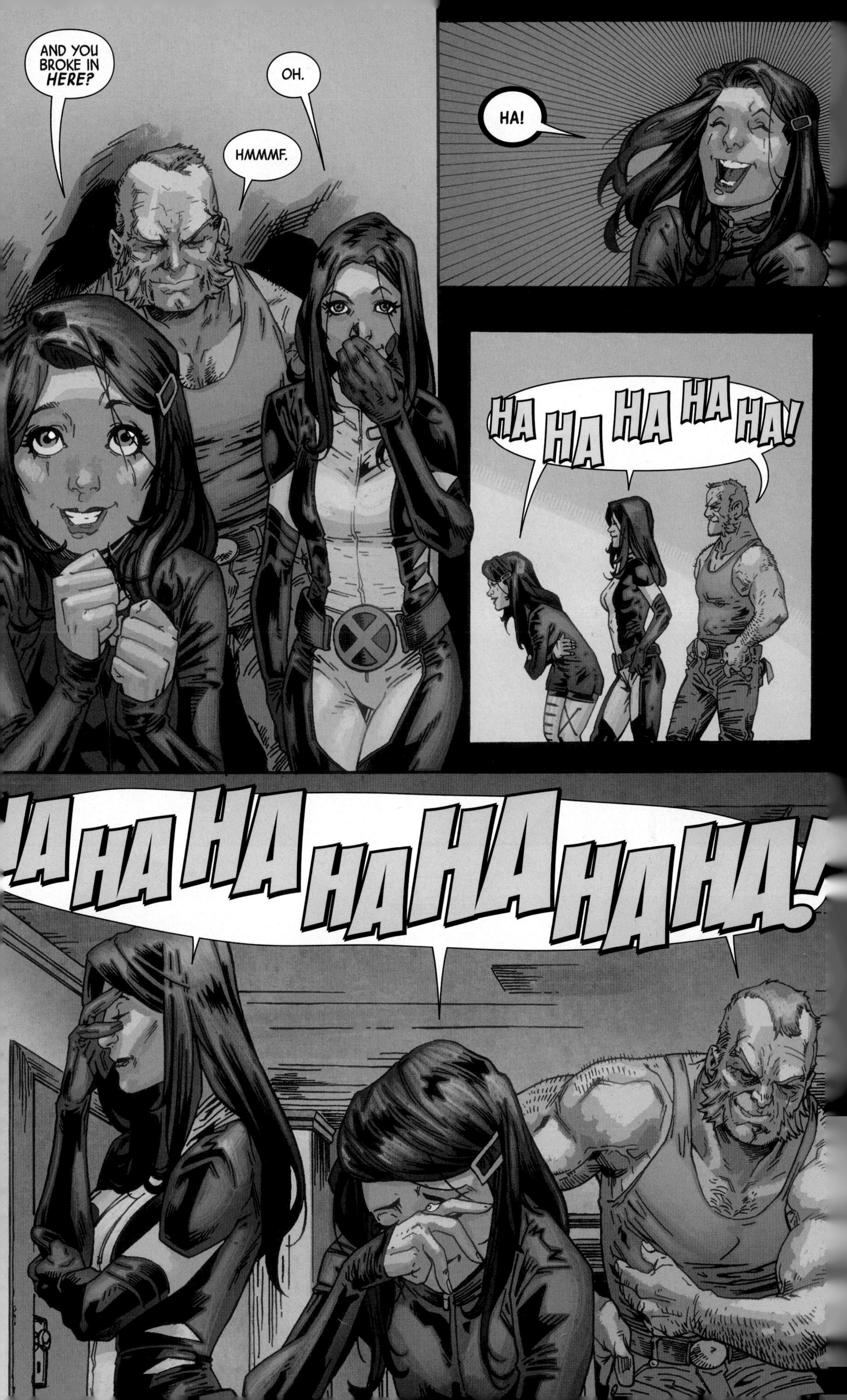
AND YOU BROKE IN *HERE?*
HMMMF.
OH.
HA!
HA HA HA HA HA!
HA HA HA HA HA HA HA HA!

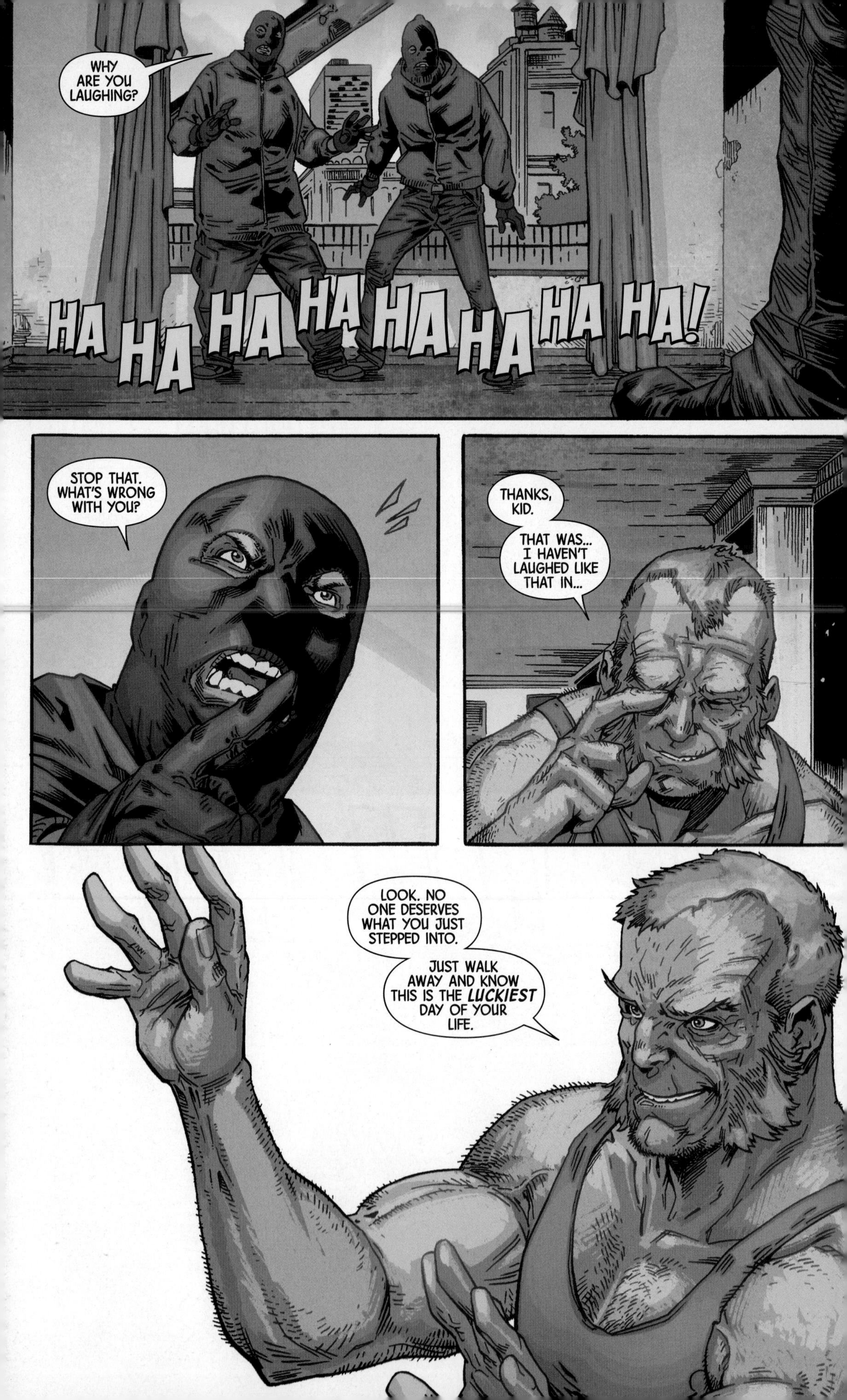
WHY ARE YOU LAUGHING?
HA HA HA HA HA HA HA HA HA!
STOP THAT. WHAT'S WRONG WITH YOU?
THANKS, KID.
THAT WAS... I HAVEN'T LAUGHED LIKE THAT IN...
LOOK. NO ONE DESERVES WHAT YOU JUST STEPPED INTO.
JUST WALK AWAY AND KNOW THIS IS THE *LUCKIEST* DAY OF YOUR LIFE.

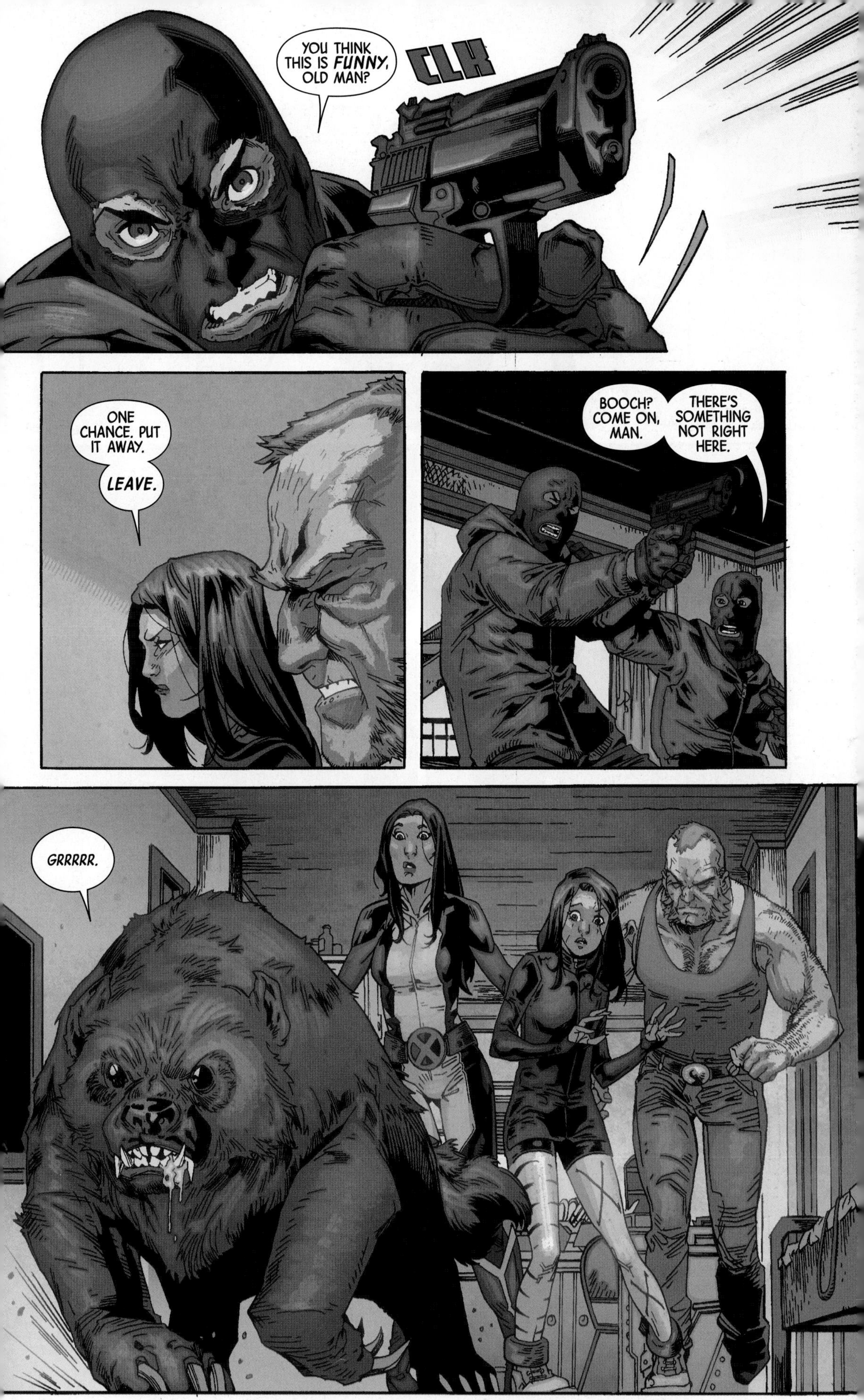
YOU THINK THIS IS FUNNY, OLD MAN?
CLK
ONE CHANCE. PUT IT AWAY.
LEAVE.
BOOCH? COME ON, MAN.
THERE'S SOMETHING NOT RIGHT HERE.
GRRRRR.

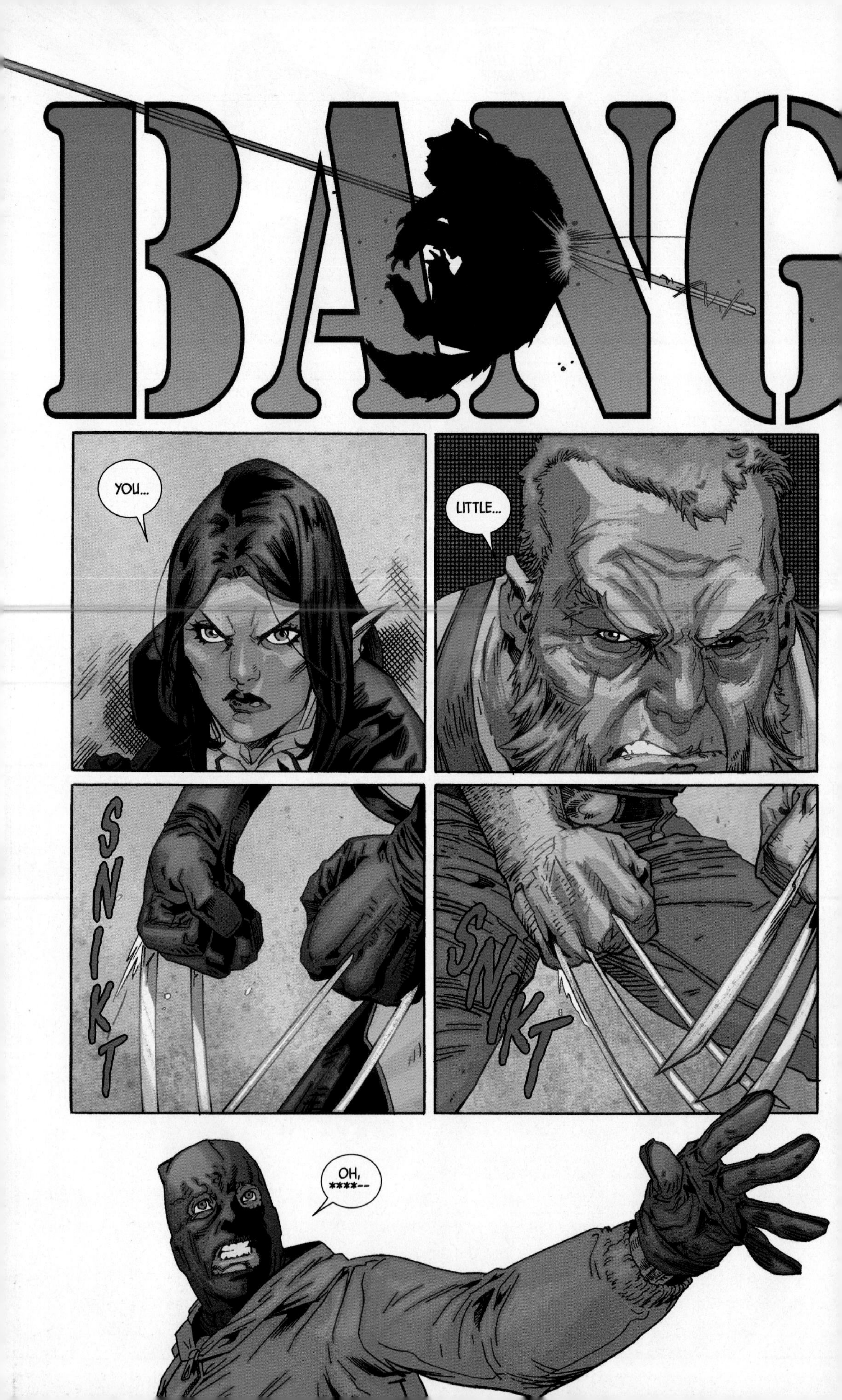
BANG
YOU...
LITTLE...
SNIKT
SNIKT
OH,
****--

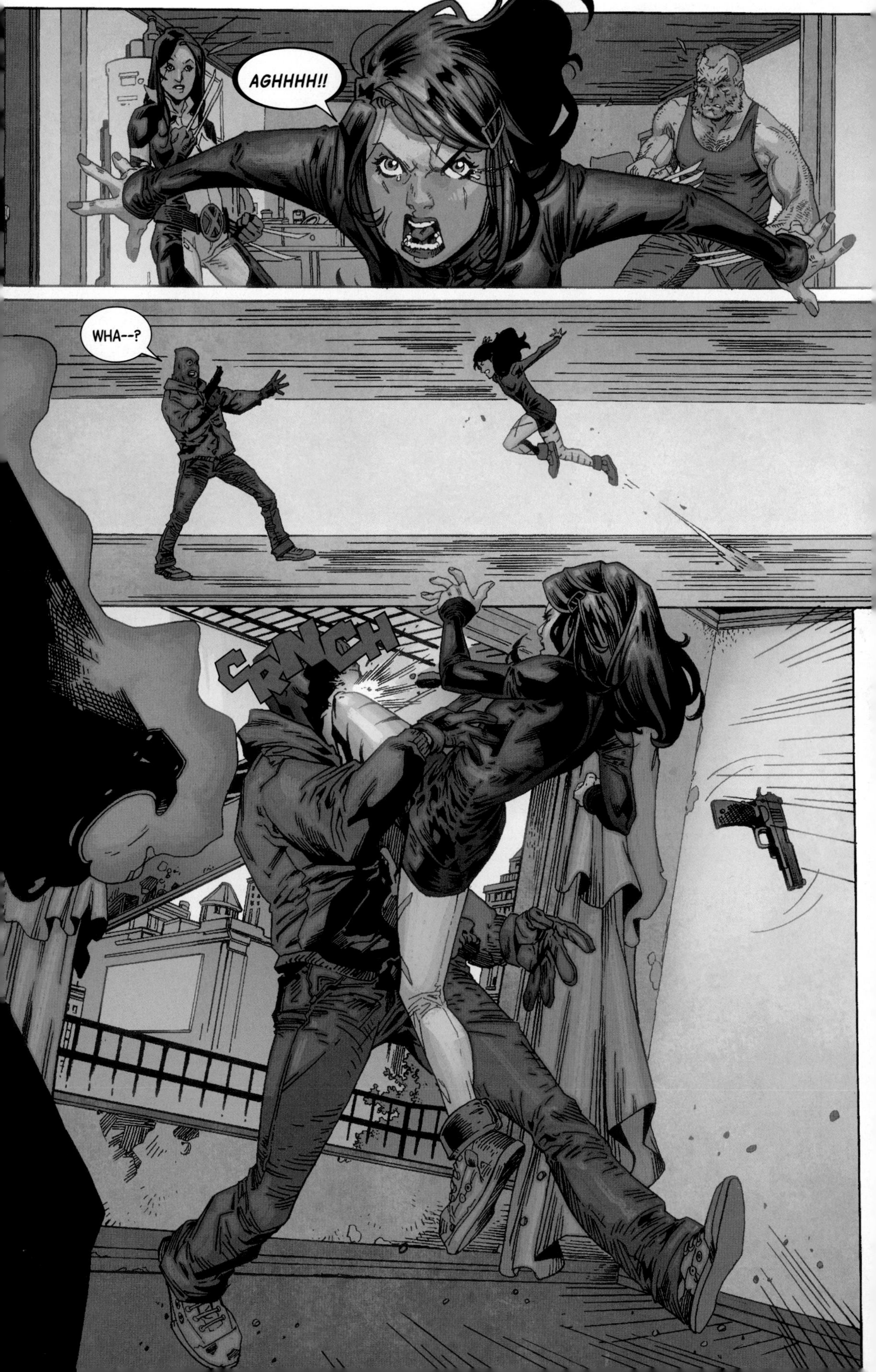
AGHHHH!!
WHA--?
CRNCH

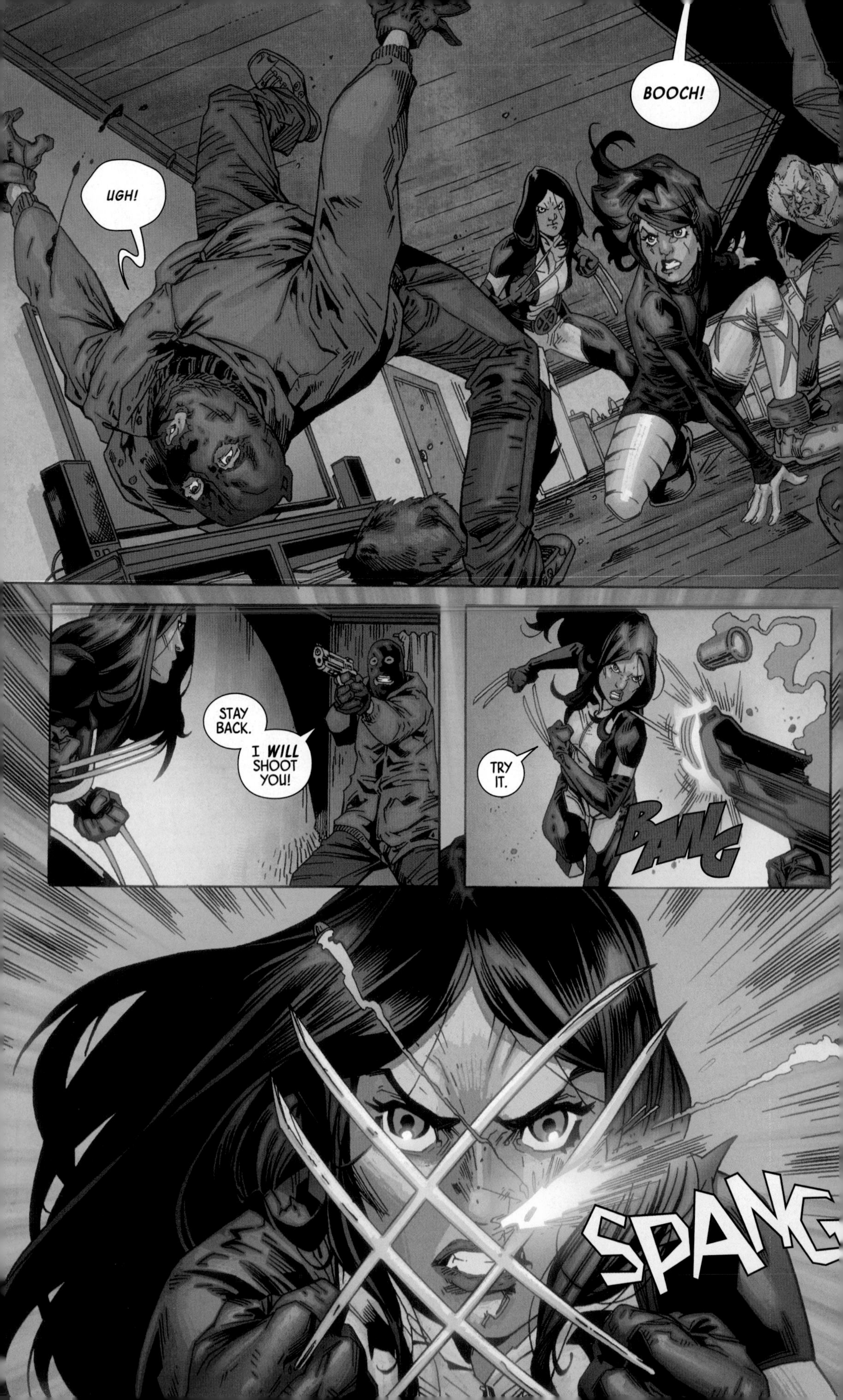
BOOCH!
UGH!
STAY BACK.
I WILL SHOOT YOU!
TRY IT.
BANG
SPANG

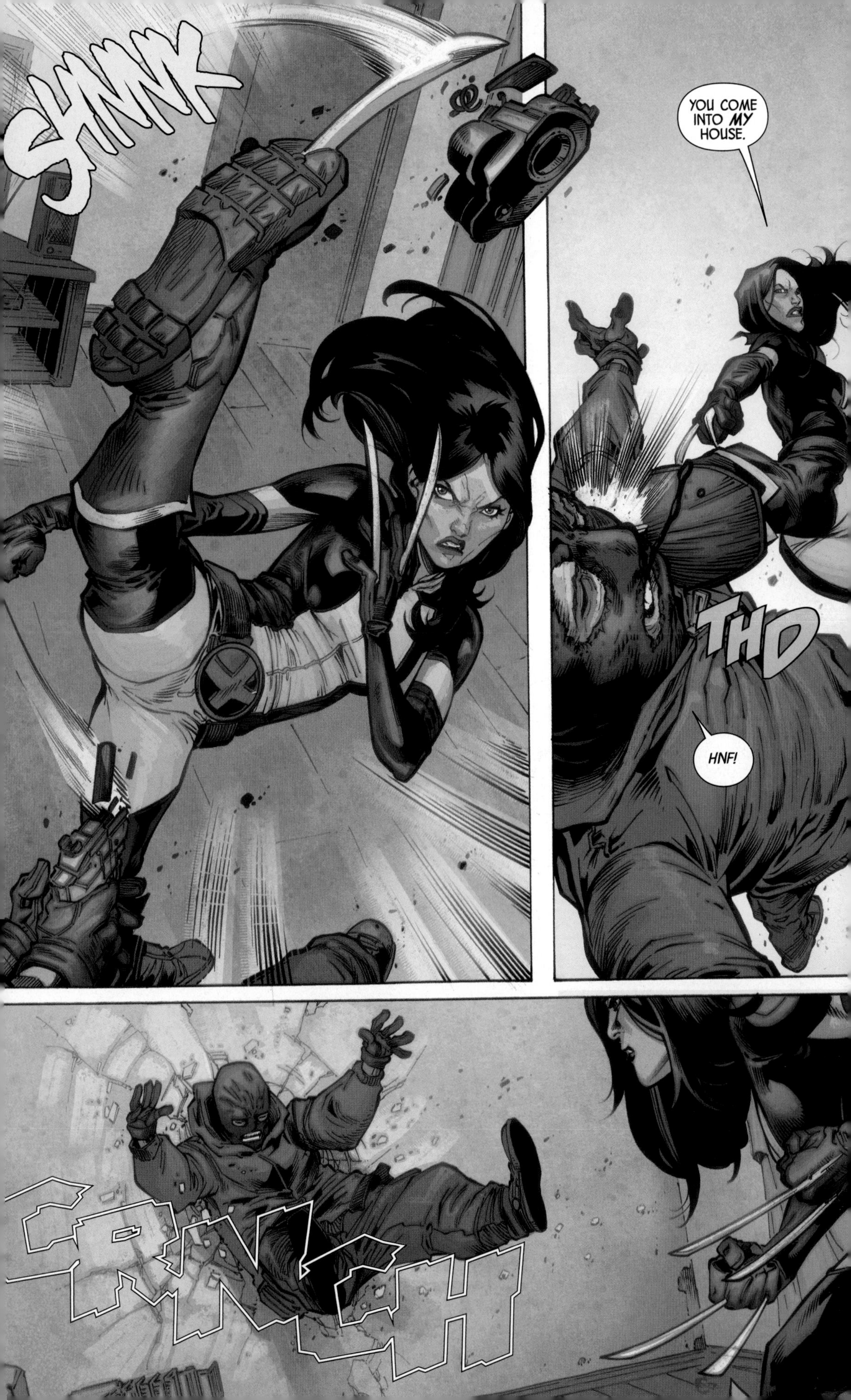
SHNNK
YOU COME INTO MY HOUSE.
THD
HNF!
CRUNCH

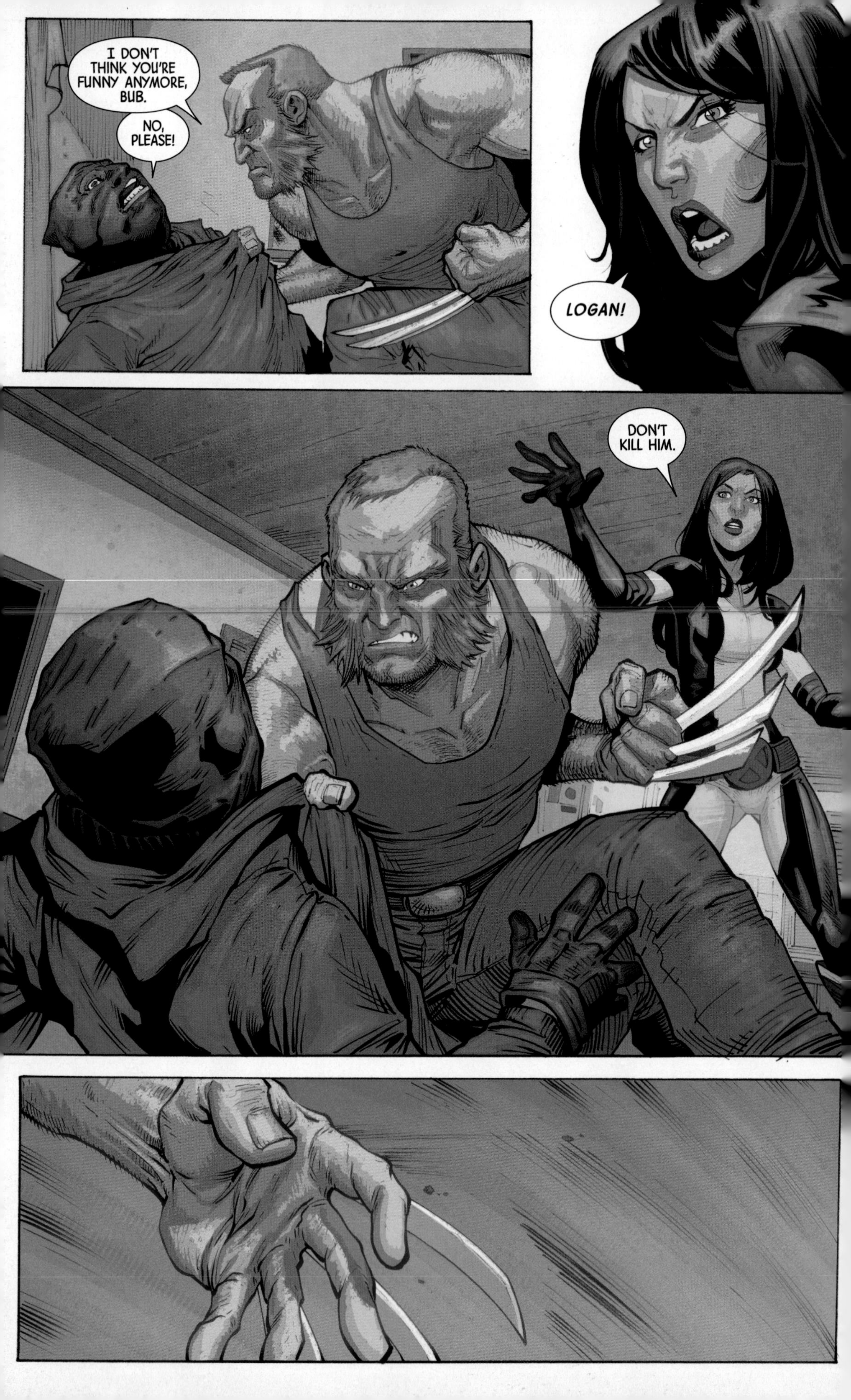
I DON'T THINK YOU'RE FUNNY ANYMORE, BUB.
NO, PLEASE!
LOGAN!
DON'T KILL HIM.

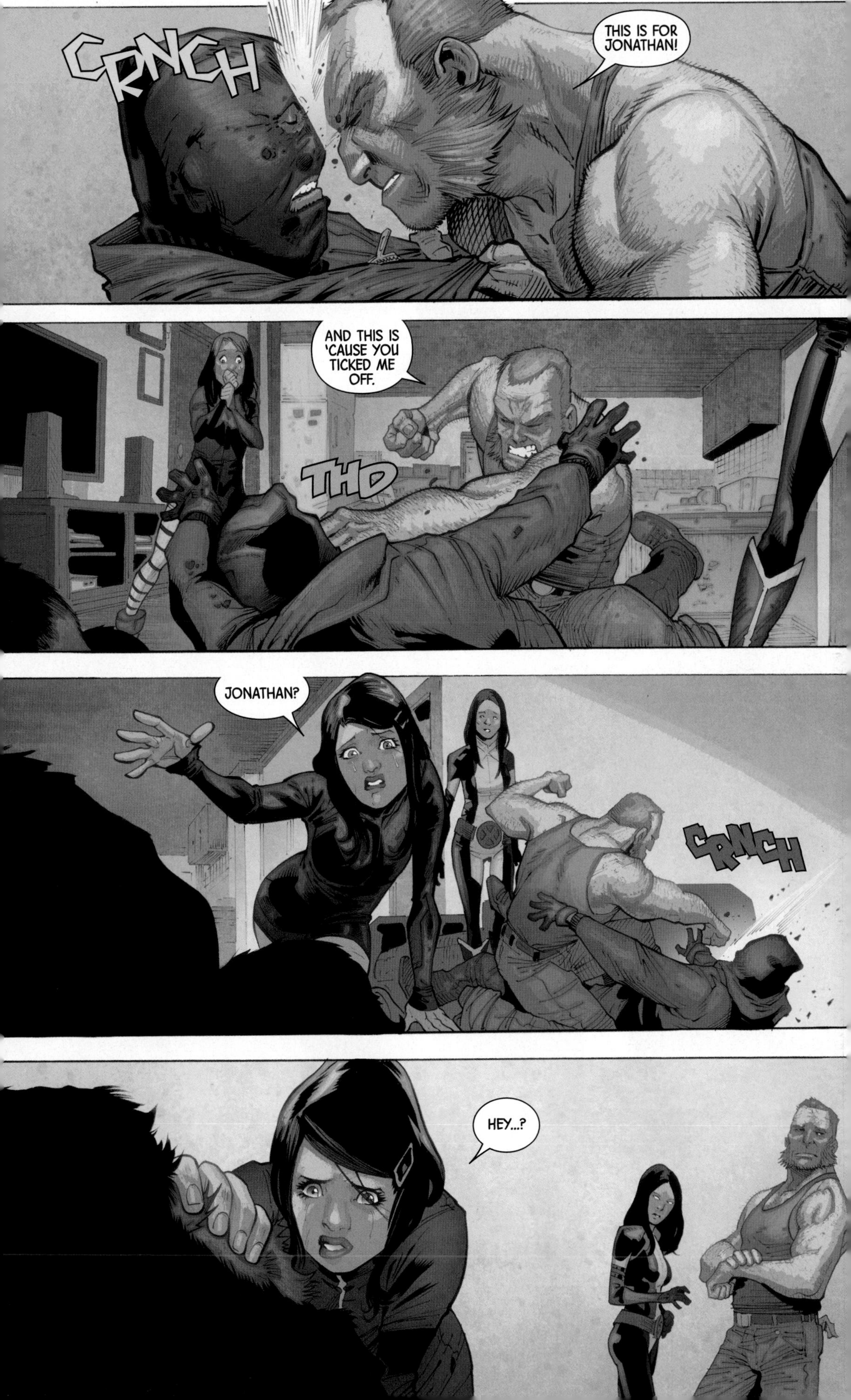
CRNCH
THIS IS FOR JONATHAN!
AND THIS IS 'CAUSE YOU TICKED ME OFF.
THD
JONATHAN?
CRNCH
HEY...?

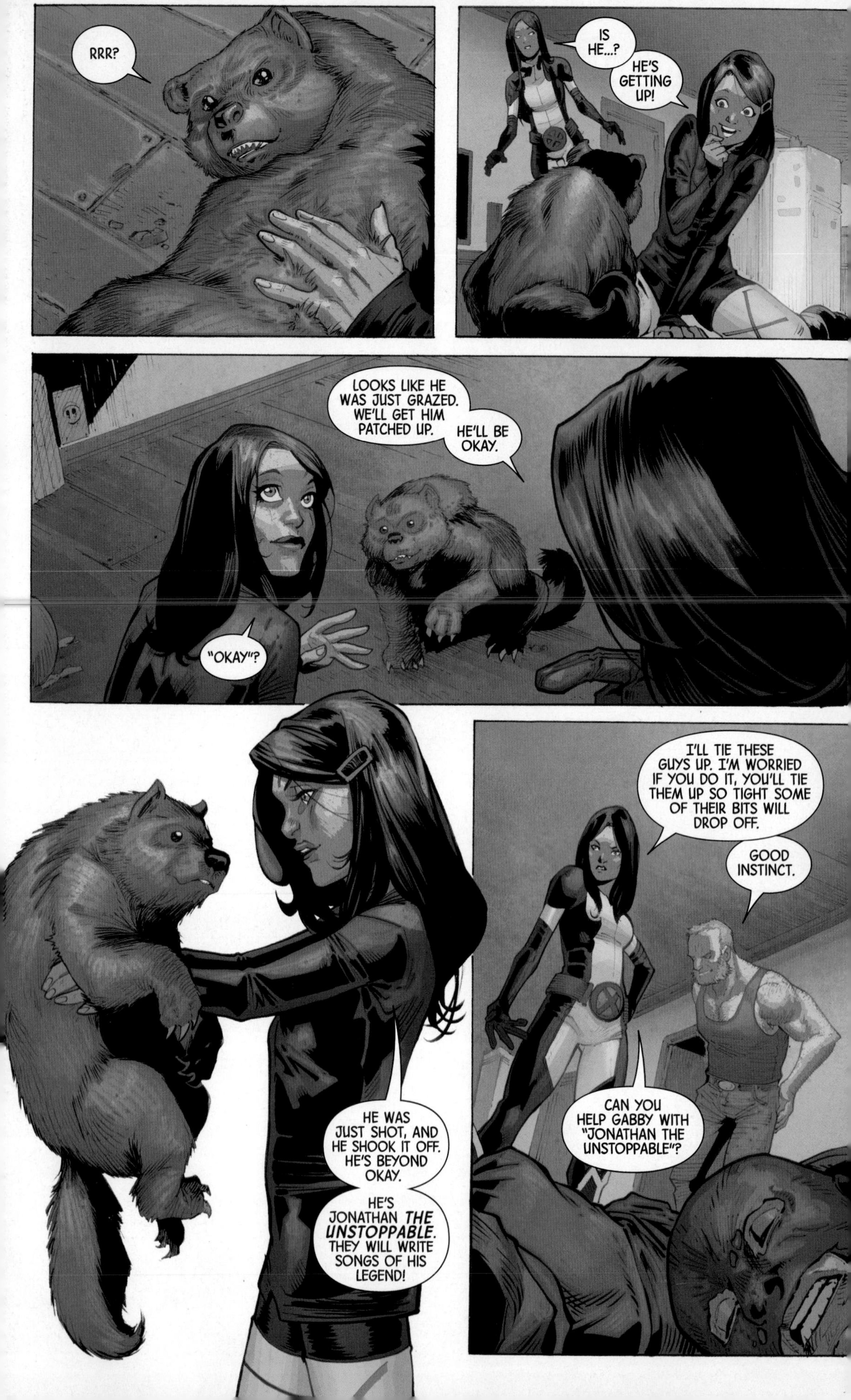
RRR?
IS HE...?
HE'S GETTING UP!
LOOKS LIKE HE WAS JUST GRAZED. WE'LL GET HIM PATCHED UP.
HE'LL BE OKAY.
"OKAY"?
HE WAS JUST SHOT, AND HE SHOOK IT OFF. HE'S BEYOND OKAY.
HE'S JONATHAN *THE UNSTOPPABLE.* THEY WILL WRITE SONGS OF HIS LEGEND!
I'LL TIE THESE GUYS UP. I'M WORRIED IF YOU DO IT, YOU'LL TIE THEM UP SO TIGHT SOME OF THEIR BITS WILL DROP OFF.
GOOD INSTINCT.
CAN YOU HELP GABBY WITH "JONATHAN THE UNSTOPPABLE"?

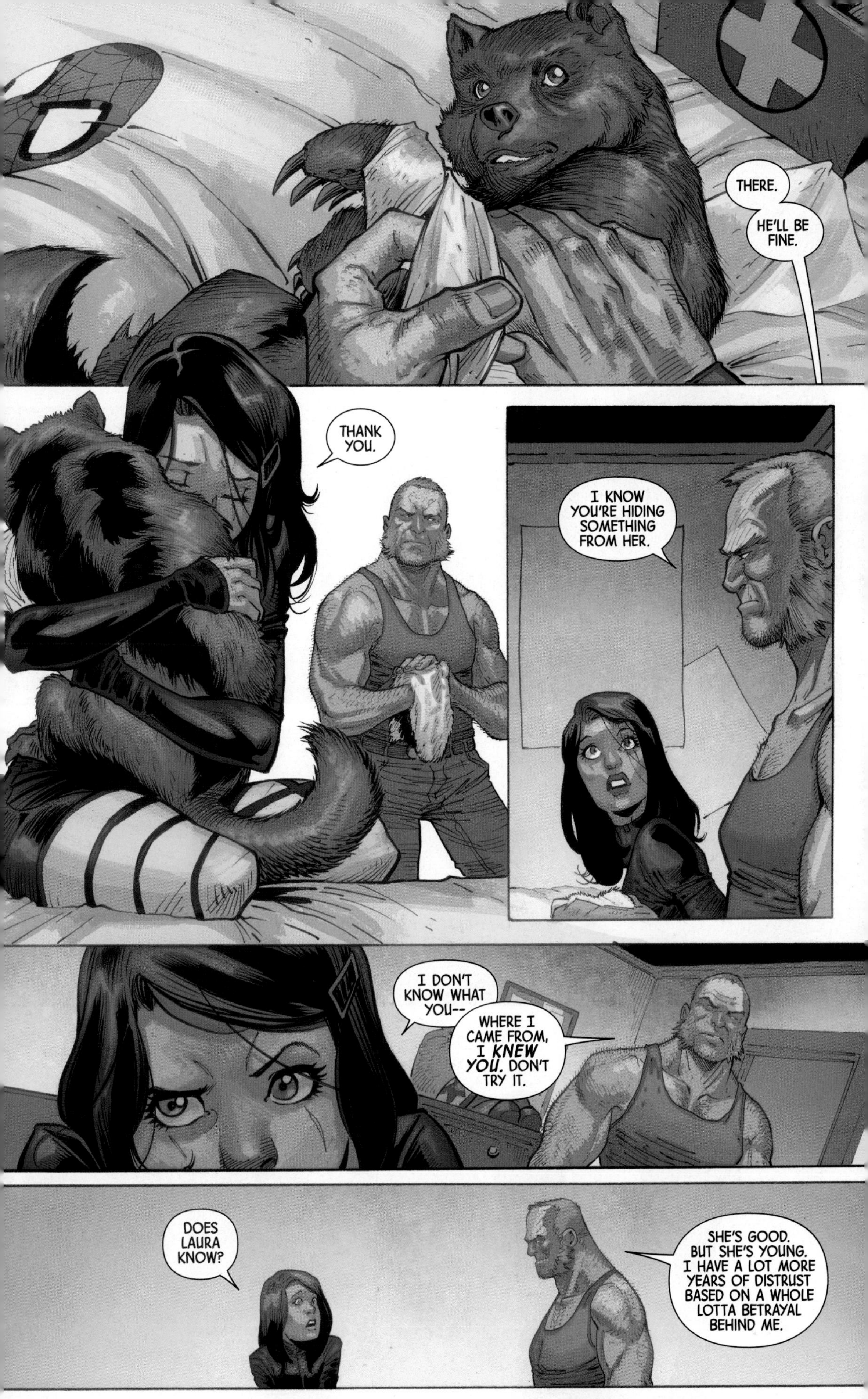

THERE.
HE'LL BE FINE.
THANK YOU.
I KNOW YOU'RE HIDING SOMETHING FROM HER.
I DON'T KNOW WHAT YOU--
WHERE I CAME FROM, I *KNEW YOU.* DON'T TRY IT.
DOES LAURA KNOW?
SHE'S GOOD. BUT SHE'S YOUNG. I HAVE A LOT MORE YEARS OF DISTRUST BASED ON A WHOLE LOTTA BETRAYAL BEHIND ME.

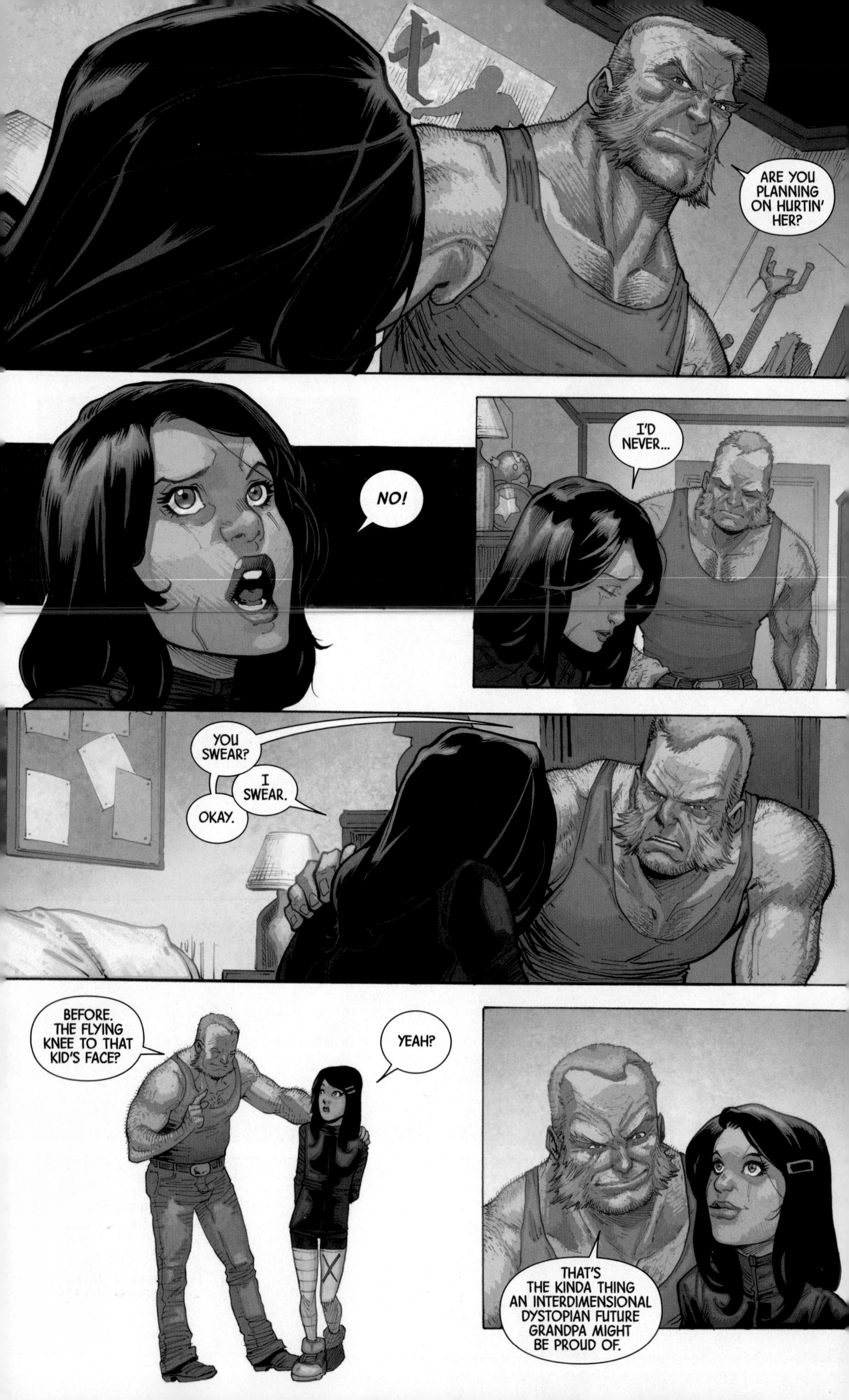
ARE YOU PLANNING ON HURTIN' HER?
NO!
I'D NEVER...
YOU SWEAR?
I SWEAR.
OKAY.
BEFORE. THE FLYING KNEE TO THAT KID'S FACE?
YEAH?
THAT'S THE KINDA THING AN INTERDIMENSIONAL DYSTOPIAN FUTURE GRANDPA MIGHT BE PROUD OF.

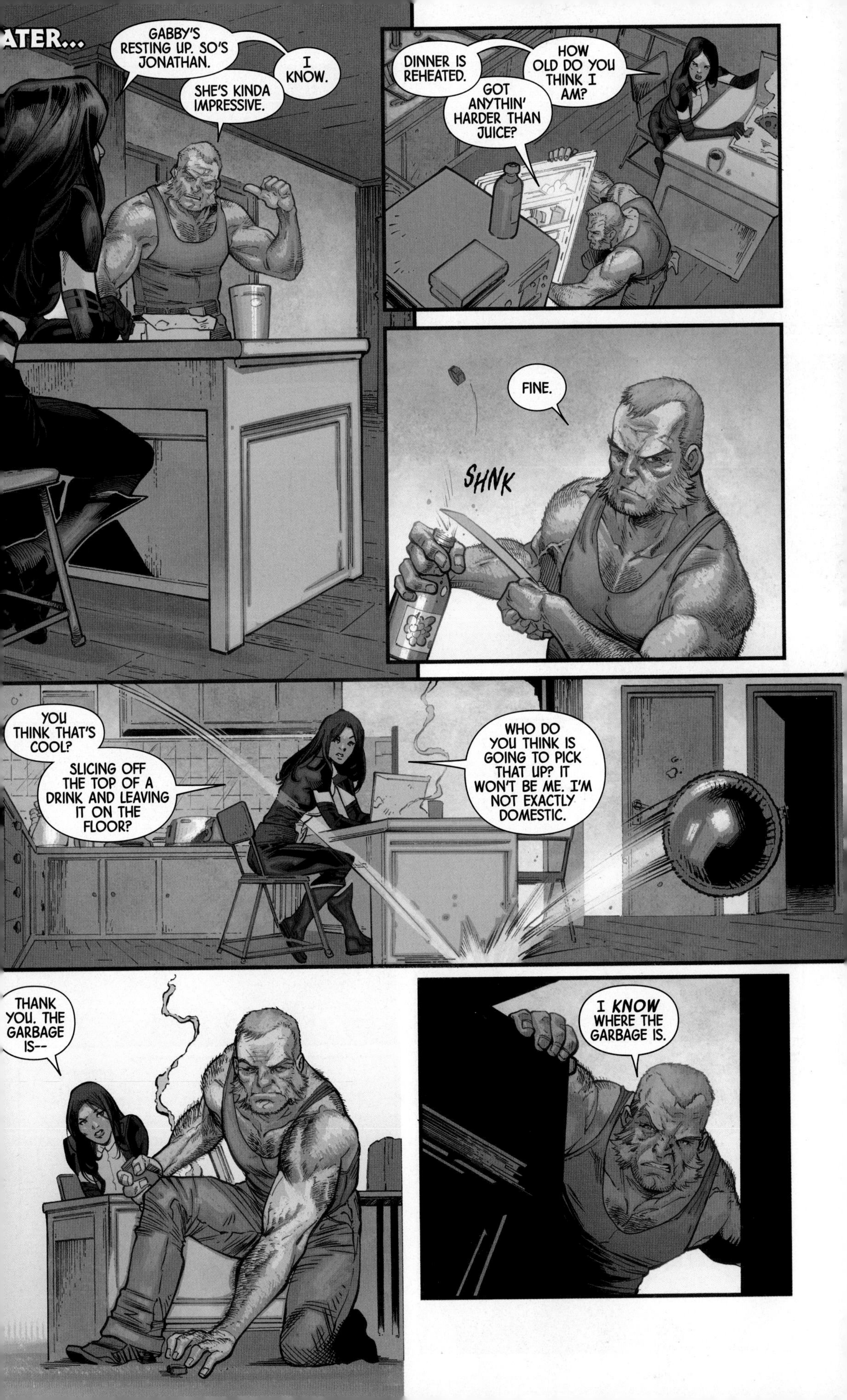

...ATER...
GABBY'S RESTING UP. SO'S JONATHAN.
I KNOW.
SHE'S KINDA IMPRESSIVE.
DINNER IS REHEATED.
HOW OLD DO YOU THINK I AM?
GOT ANYTHIN' HARDER THAN JUICE?
FINE.
SHNK
YOU THINK THAT'S COOL?
SLICING OFF THE TOP OF A DRINK AND LEAVING IT ON THE FLOOR?
WHO DO YOU THINK IS GOING TO PICK THAT UP? IT WON'T BE ME. I'M NOT EXACTLY DOMESTIC.
THANK YOU. THE GARBAGE IS--
I KNOW WHERE THE GARBAGE IS.

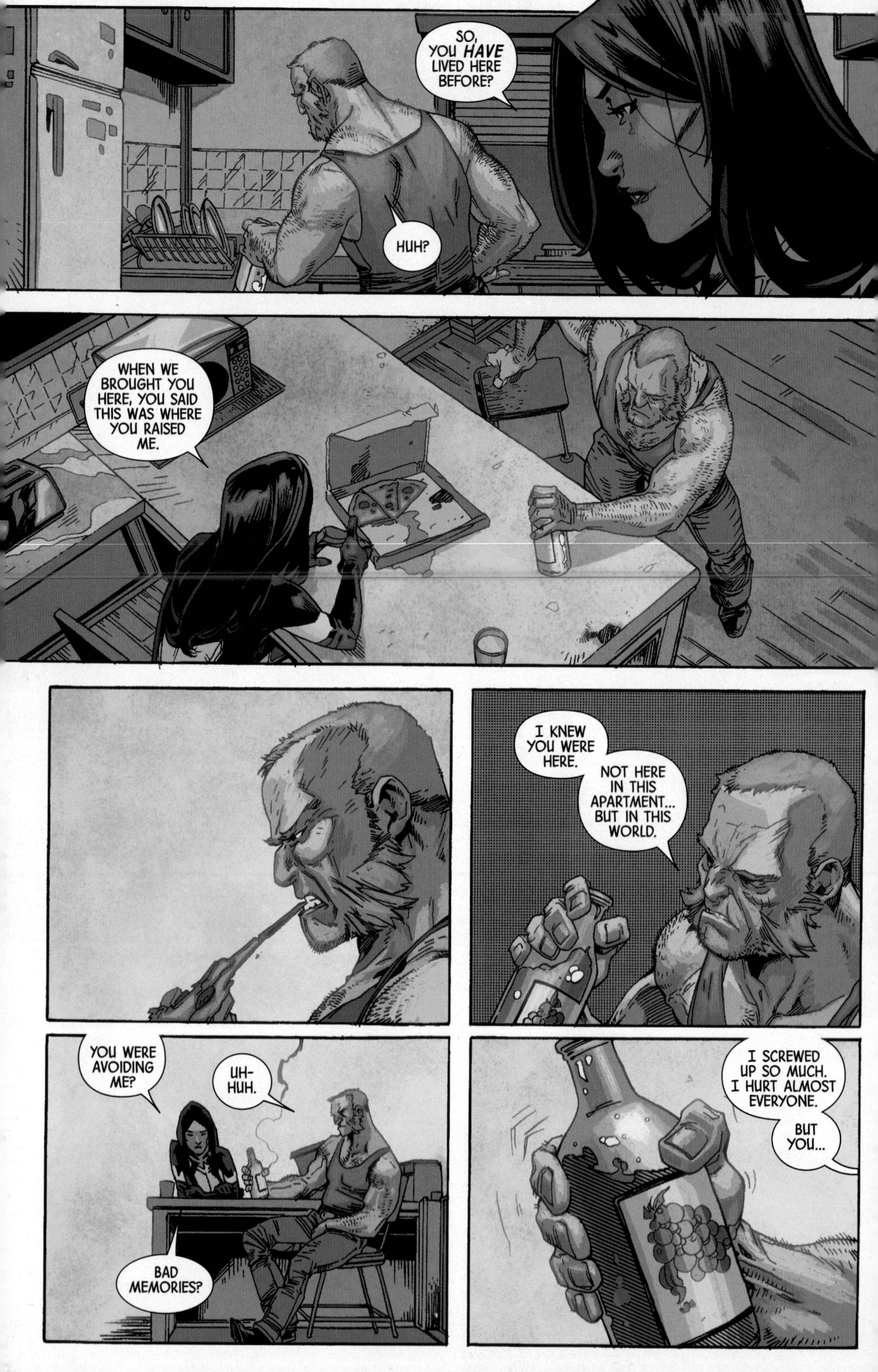
SO, YOU HAVE LIVED HERE BEFORE?
HUH?
WHEN WE BROUGHT YOU HERE, YOU SAID THIS WAS WHERE YOU RAISED ME.
I KNEW YOU WERE HERE.
NOT HERE IN THIS APARTMENT... BUT IN THIS WORLD.
YOU WERE AVOIDING ME?
UH-HUH.
BAD MEMORIES?
I SCREWED UP SO MUCH. I HURT ALMOST EVERYONE.
BUT YOU...

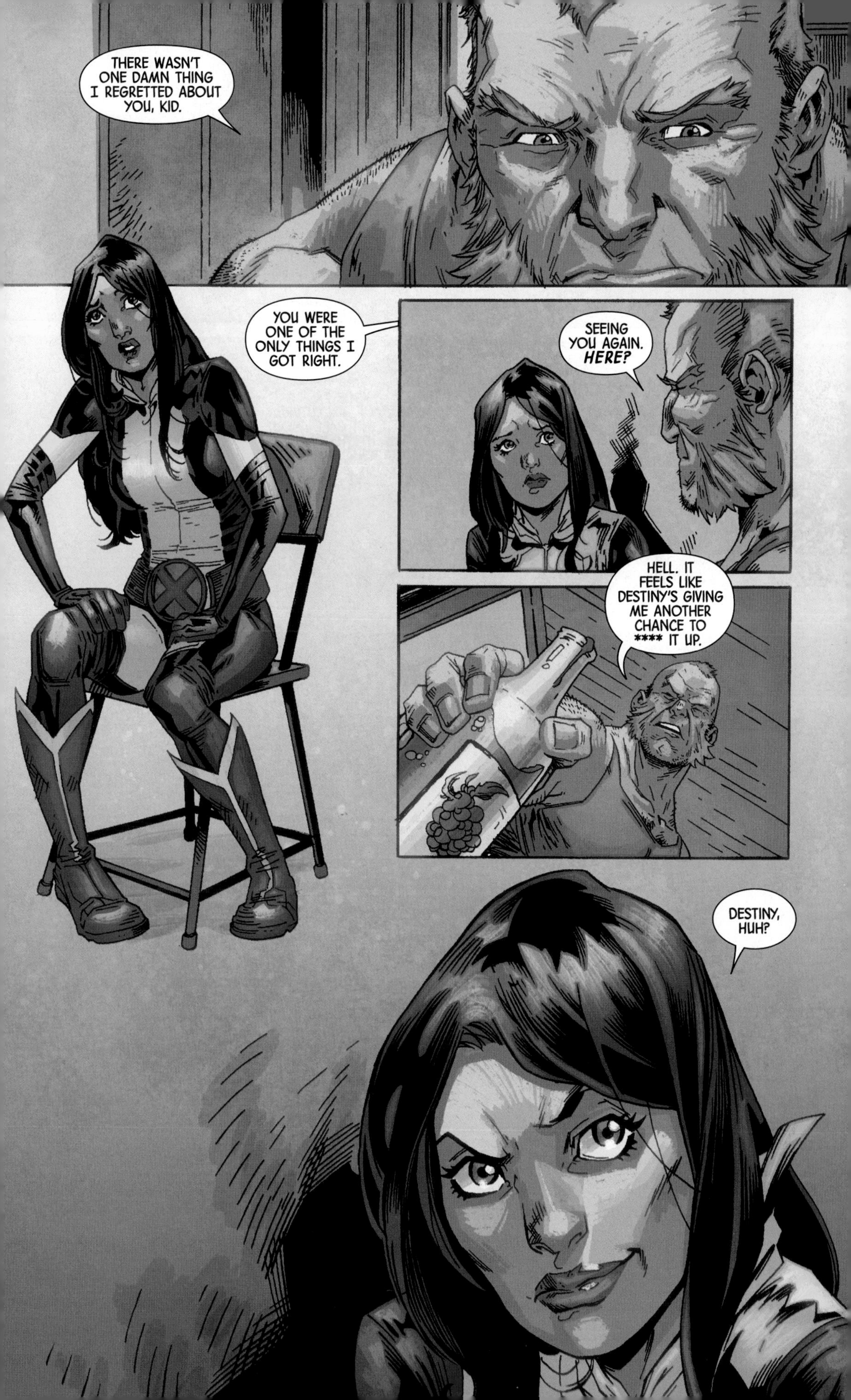
THERE WASN'T ONE DAMN THING I REGRETTED ABOUT YOU, KID.
YOU WERE ONE OF THE ONLY THINGS I GOT RIGHT.
SEEING YOU AGAIN. *HERE?*
HELL. IT FEELS LIKE DESTINY'S GIVING ME ANOTHER CHANCE TO **** IT UP.
DESTINY, HUH?

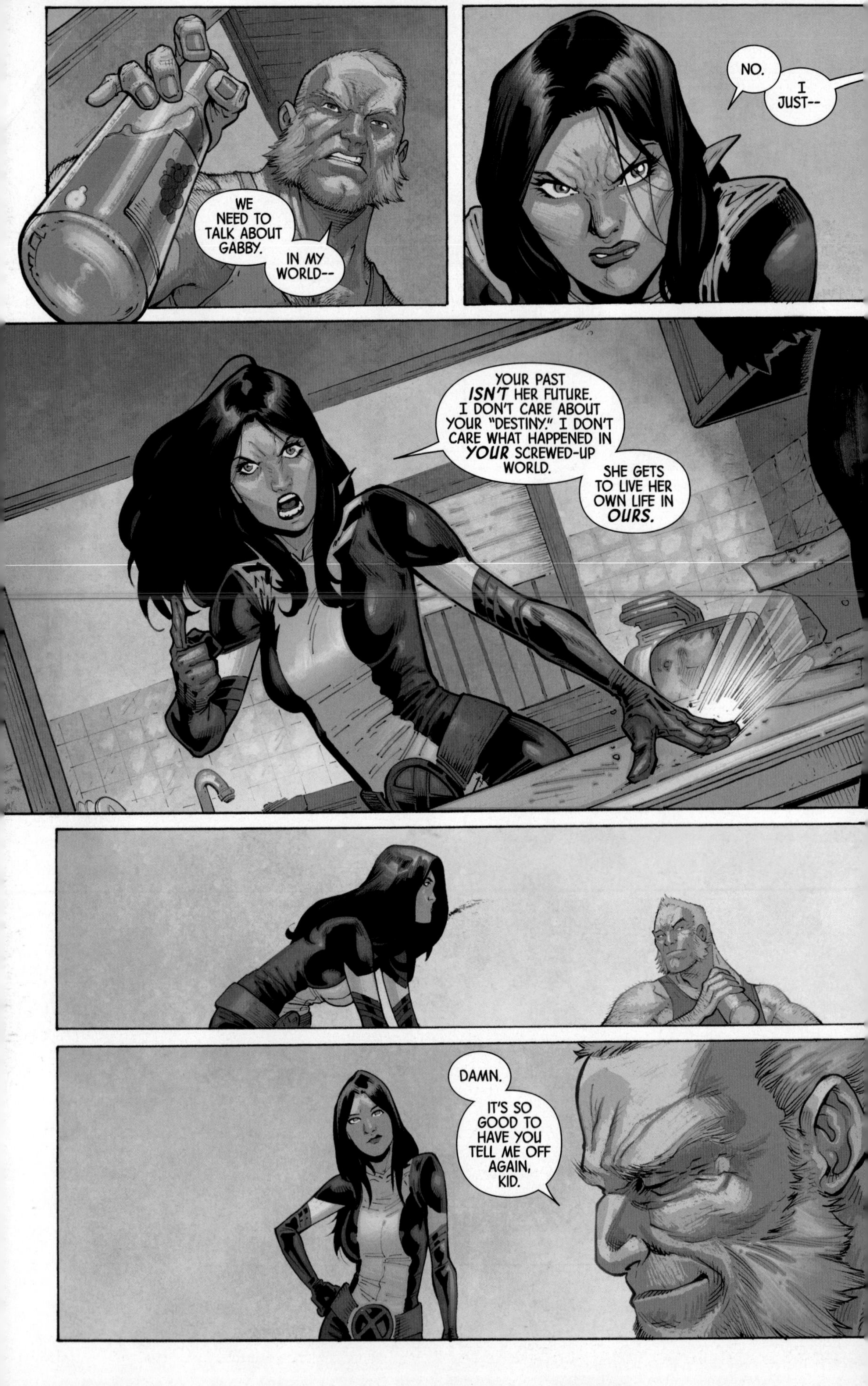
WE NEED TO TALK ABOUT GABBY.
IN MY WORLD--
NO.
I JUST--
YOUR PAST ISN'T HER FUTURE. I DON'T CARE ABOUT YOUR "DESTINY." I DON'T CARE WHAT HAPPENED IN YOUR SCREWED-UP WORLD.
SHE GETS TO LIVE HER OWN LIFE IN OURS.
DAMN.
IT'S SO GOOD TO HAVE YOU TELL ME OFF AGAIN, KID.

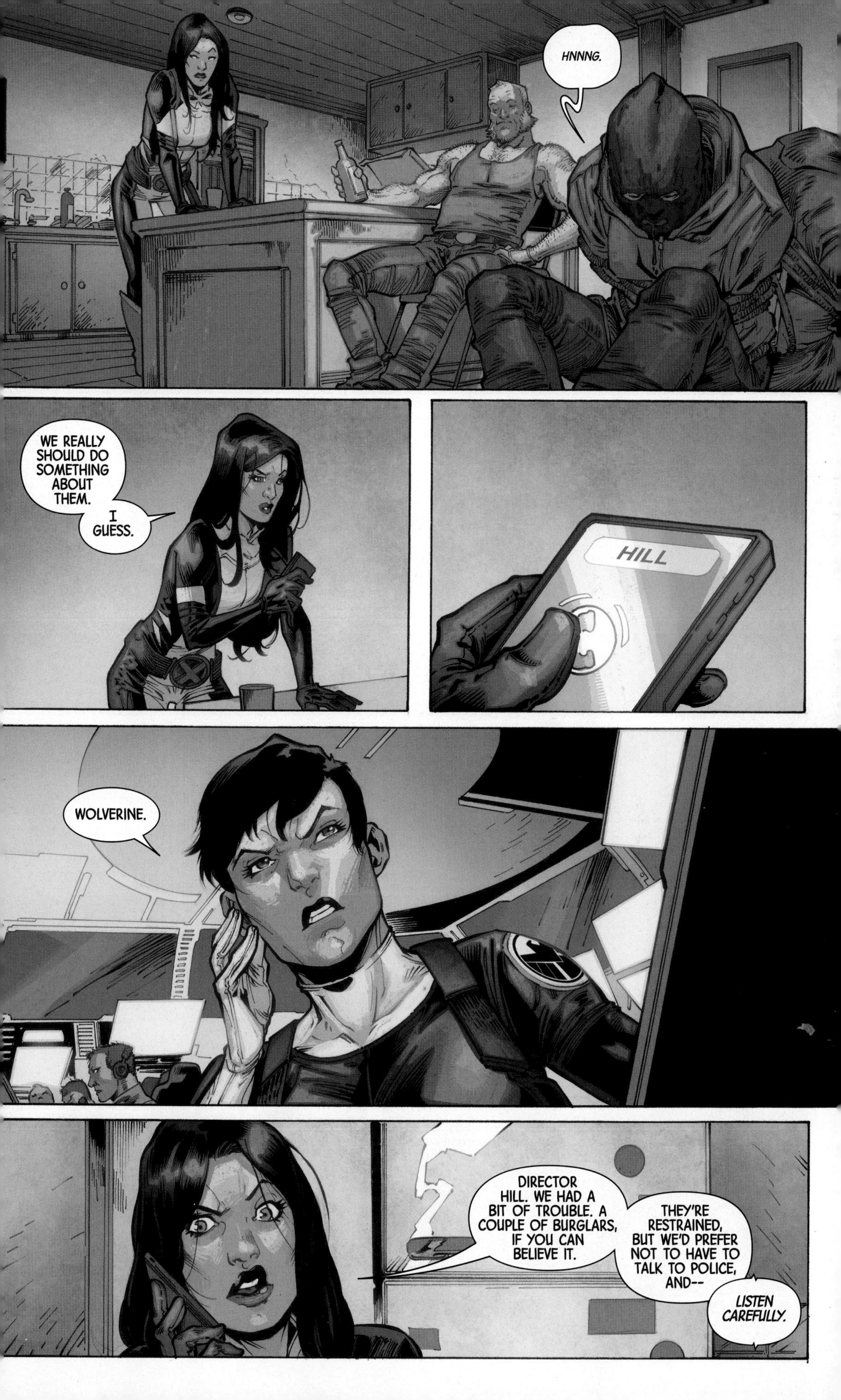
HNNNG.
WE REALLY SHOULD DO SOMETHING ABOUT THEM.
I GUESS.
HILL
WOLVERINE.
DIRECTOR HILL. WE HAD A BIT OF TROUBLE. A COUPLE OF BURGLARS, IF YOU CAN BELIEVE IT.
THEY'RE RESTRAINED, BUT WE'D PREFER NOT TO HAVE TO TALK TO POLICE, AND--
LISTEN CAREFULLY.

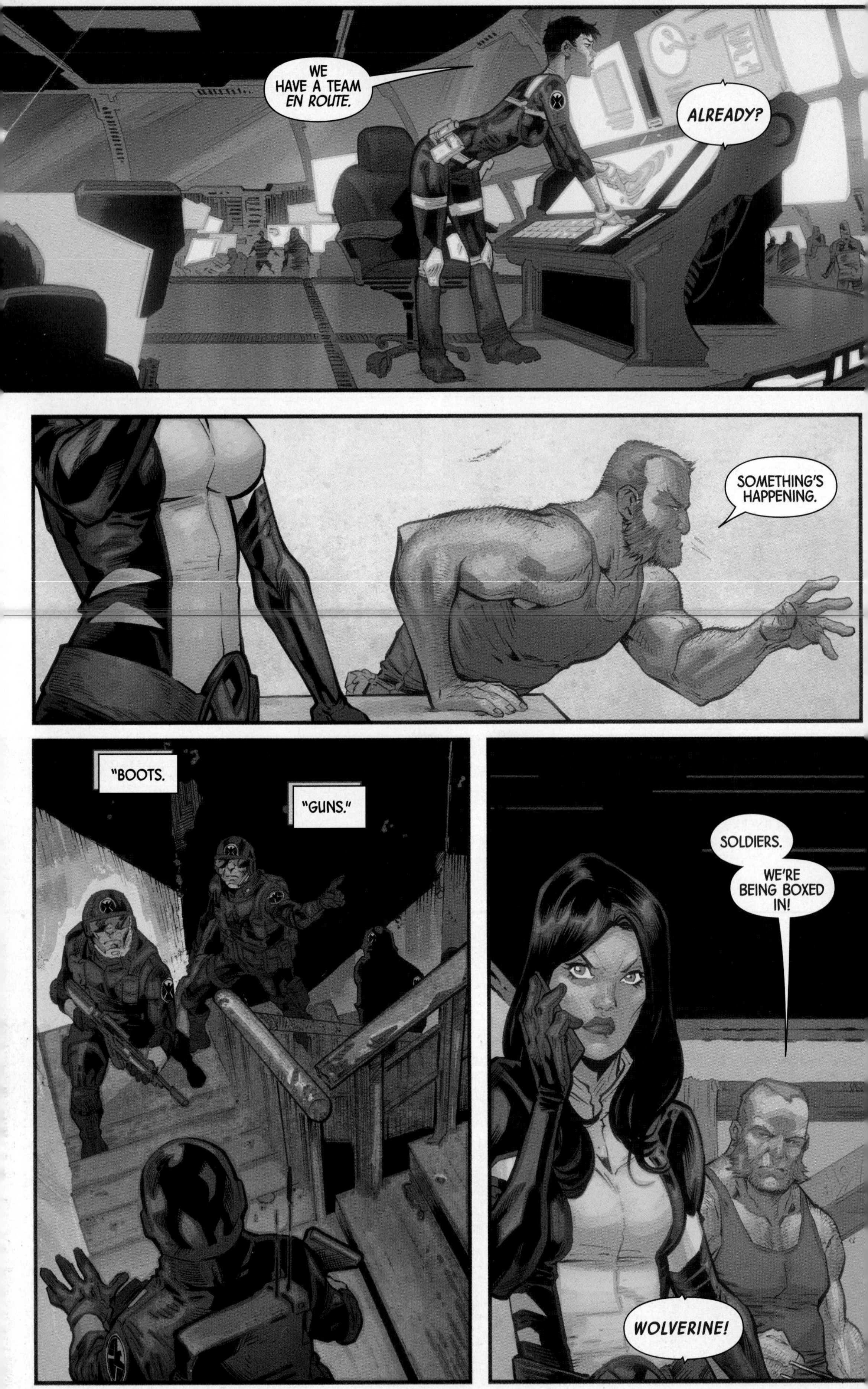

WE HAVE A TEAM EN ROUTE.
ALREADY?
SOMETHING'S HAPPENING.
"BOOTS.
"GUNS."
SOLDIERS.
WE'RE BEING BOXED IN!
WOLVERINE!

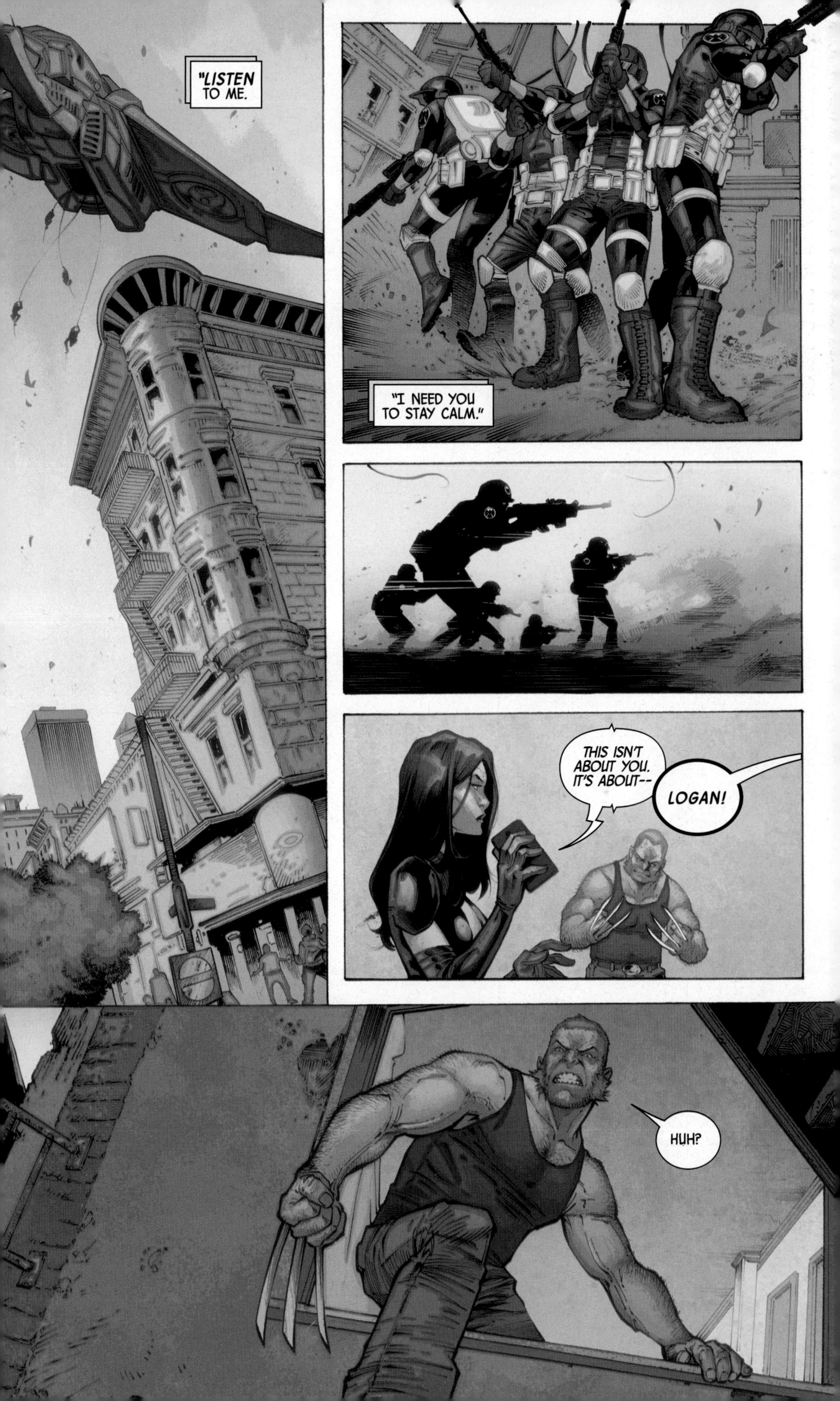
"LISTEN TO ME.
"I NEED YOU TO STAY CALM."
THIS ISN'T ABOUT YOU. IT'S ABOUT--
LOGAN!
HUH?

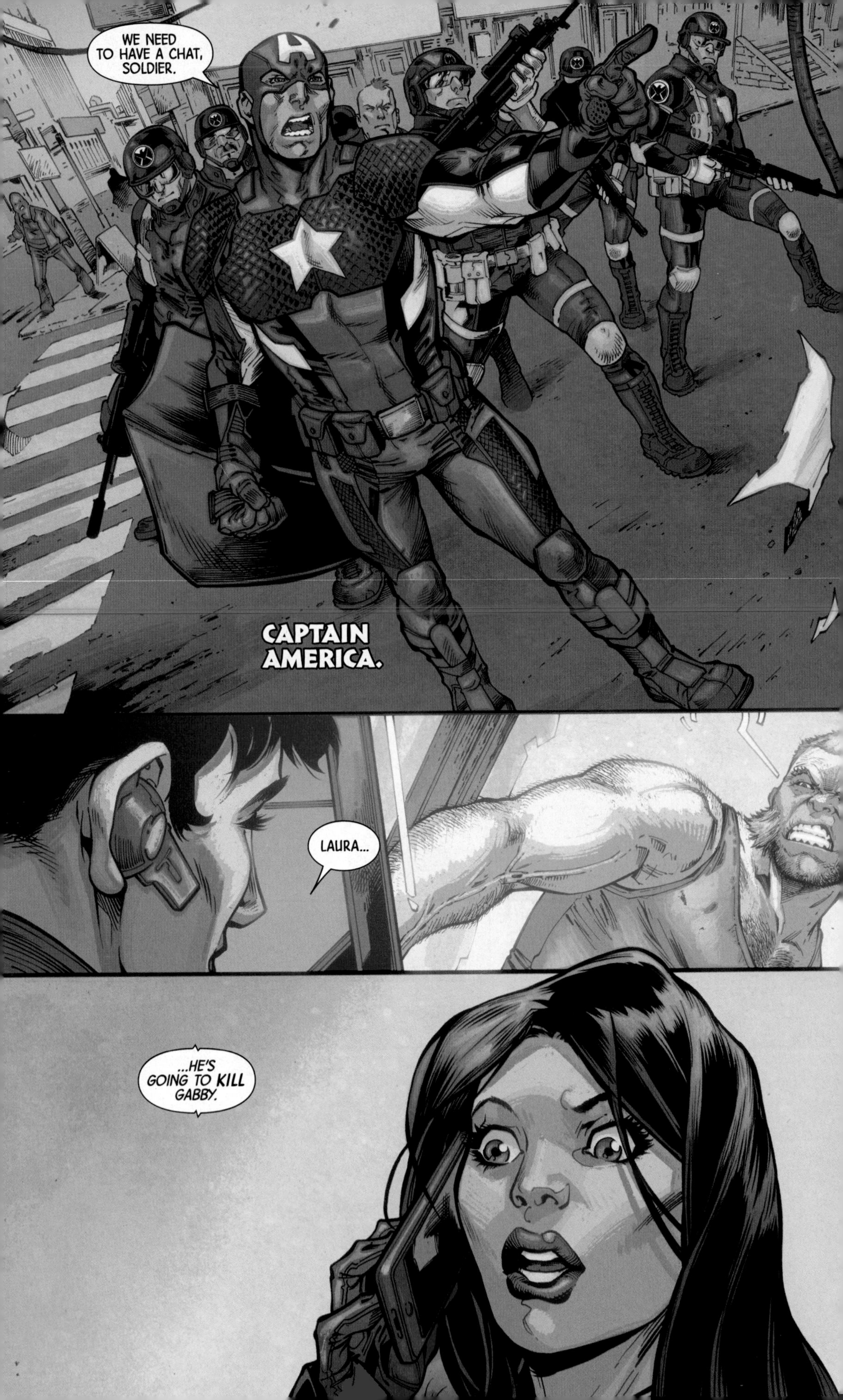
WE NEED TO HAVE A CHAT, SOLDIER.
CAPTAIN AMERICA.
LAURA...
...HE'S GOING TO KILL GABBY.

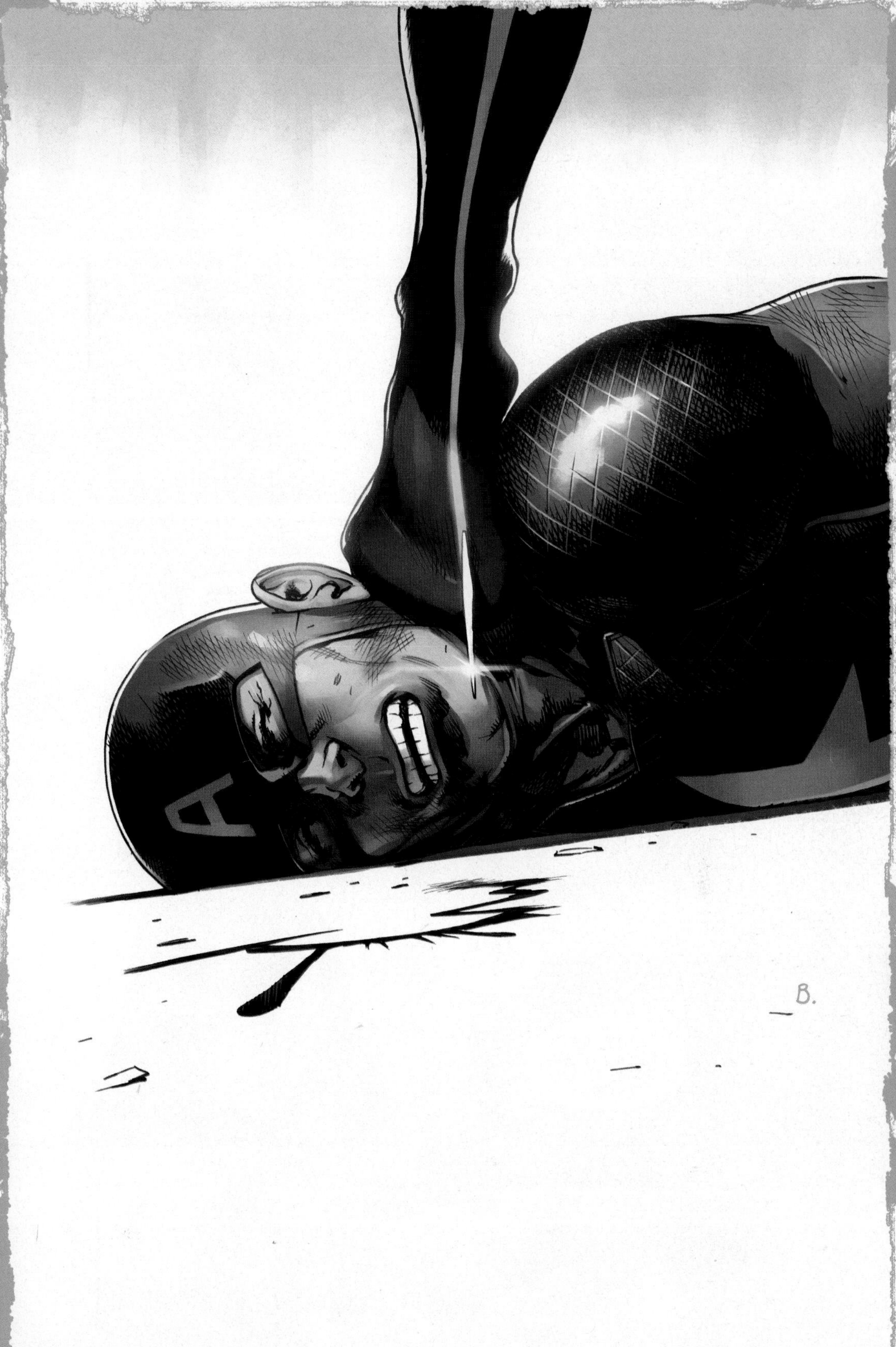
B.

11

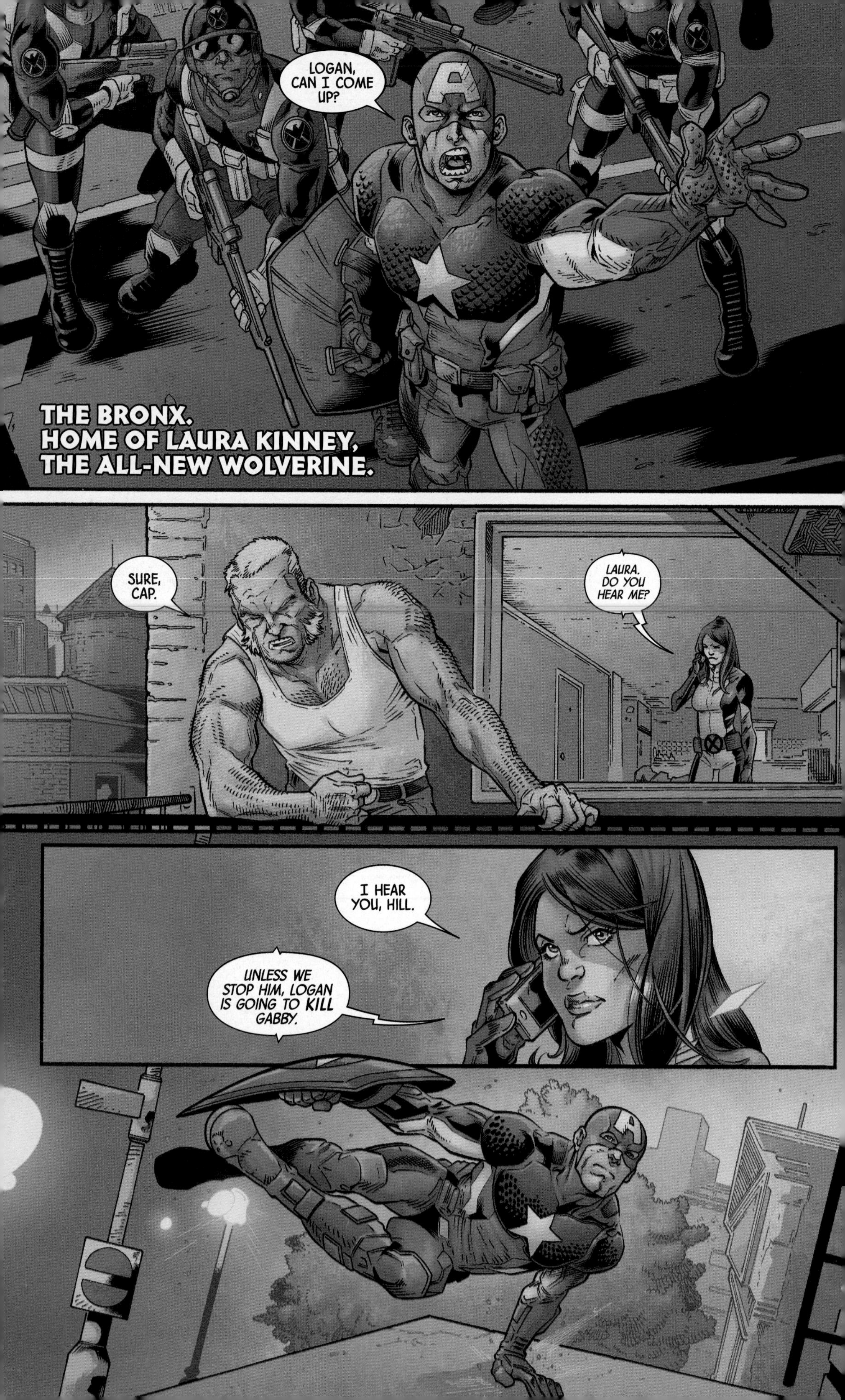

LOGAN, CAN I COME UP?
THE BRONX. HOME OF LAURA KINNEY, THE ALL-NEW WOLVERINE.
SURE, CAP.
LAURA. DO YOU HEAR ME?
I HEAR YOU, HILL.
UNLESS WE STOP HIM, LOGAN IS GOING TO KILL GABBY.

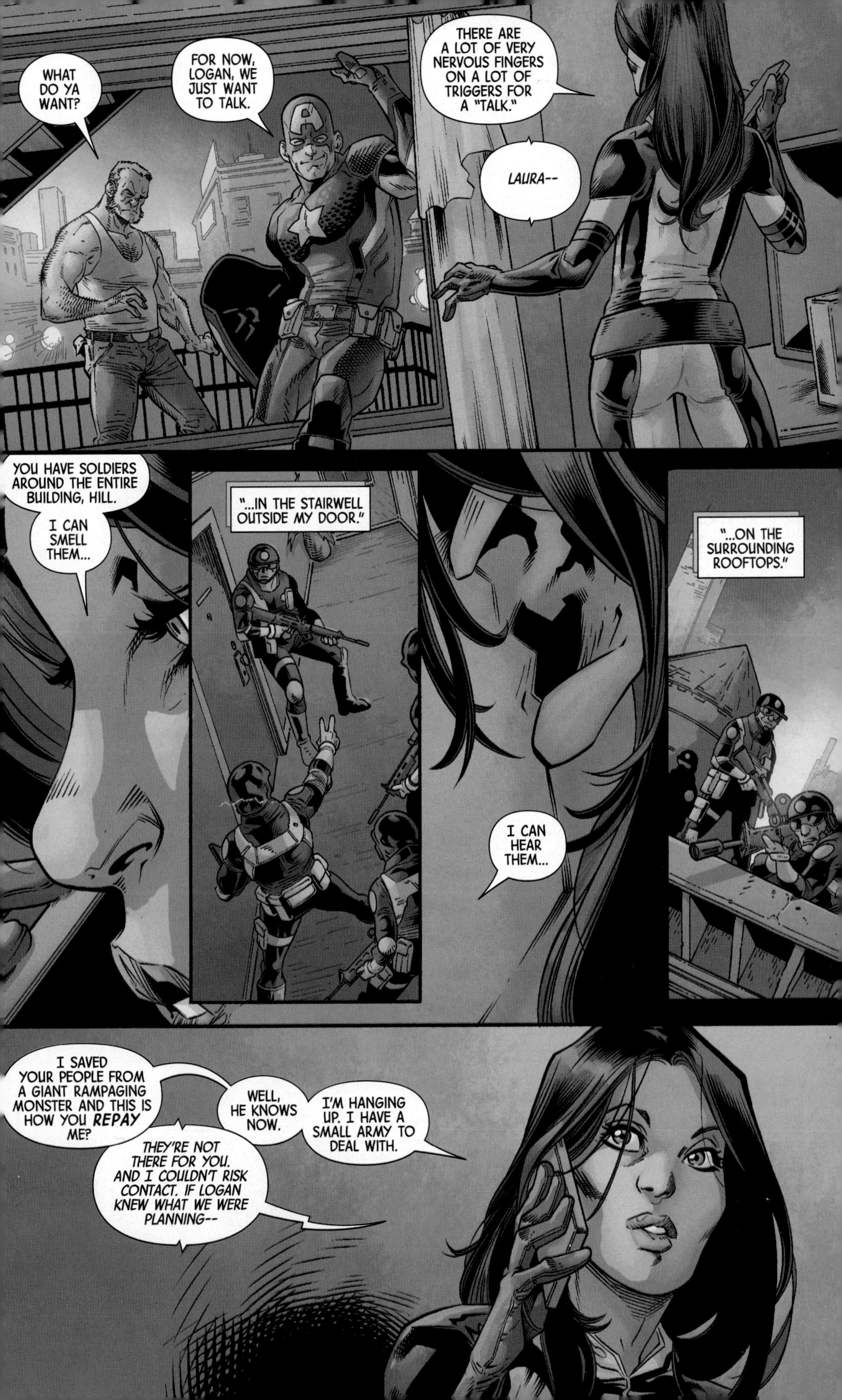
WHAT DO YA WANT?
FOR NOW, LOGAN, WE JUST WANT TO TALK.
THERE ARE A LOT OF VERY NERVOUS FINGERS ON A LOT OF TRIGGERS FOR A "TALK."
LAURA--
YOU HAVE SOLDIERS AROUND THE ENTIRE BUILDING, HILL.
I CAN SMELL THEM...
"...IN THE STAIRWELL OUTSIDE MY DOOR."
I CAN HEAR THEM...
"...ON THE SURROUNDING ROOFTOPS."
I SAVED YOUR PEOPLE FROM A GIANT RAMPAGING MONSTER AND THIS IS HOW YOU ***REPAY*** ME?
THEY'RE NOT THERE FOR YOU. AND I COULDN'T RISK CONTACT. IF LOGAN KNEW WHAT WE WERE PLANNING--
WELL, HE KNOWS NOW.
I'M HANGING UP. I HAVE A SMALL ARMY TO DEAL WITH.

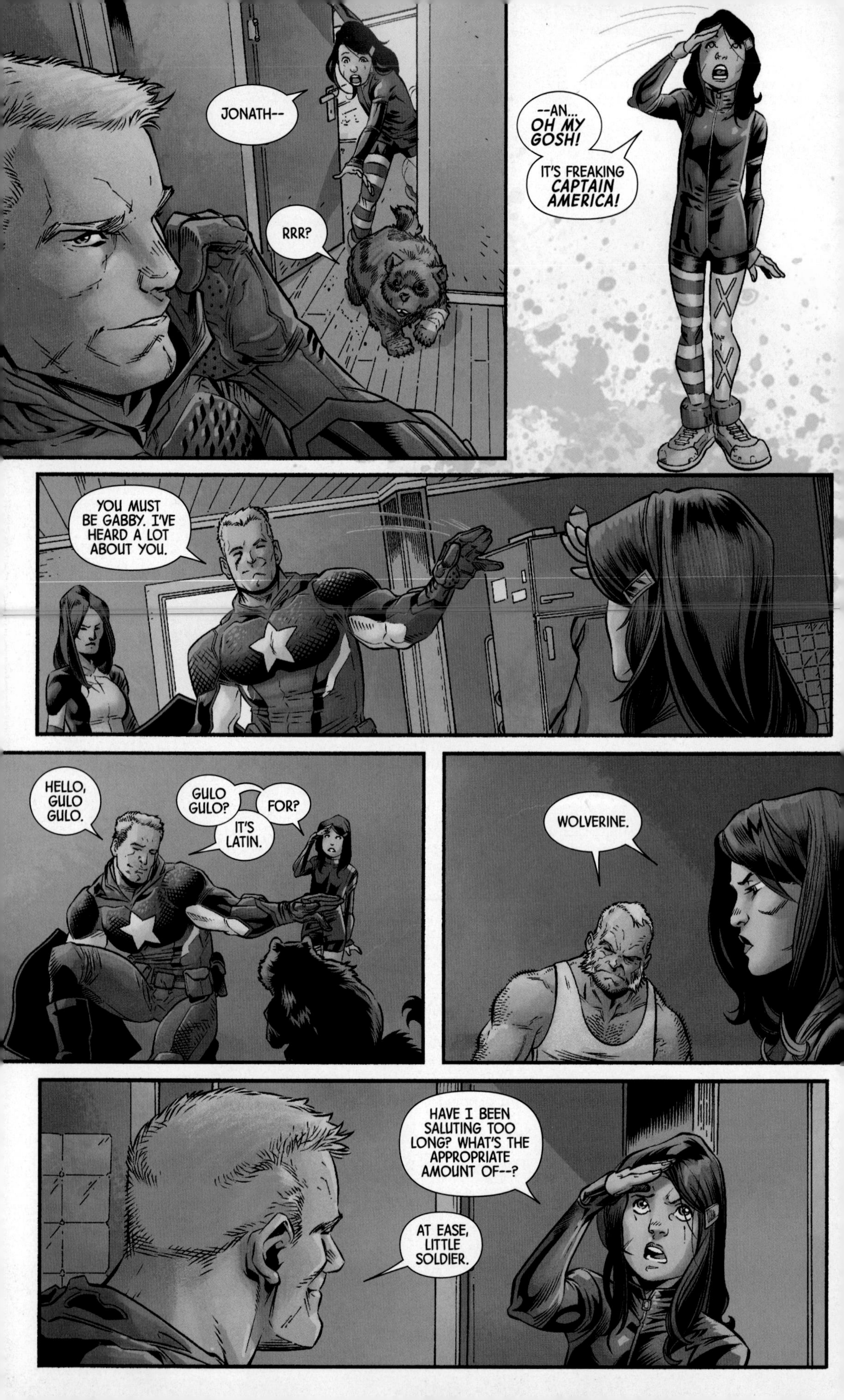
JONATH--
RRR?
--AN... OH MY GOSH!
IT'S FREAKING CAPTAIN AMERICA!
YOU MUST BE GABBY. I'VE HEARD A LOT ABOUT YOU.
HELLO, GULO GULO.
GULO GULO?
FOR?
IT'S LATIN.
WOLVERINE.
HAVE I BEEN SALUTING TOO LONG? WHAT'S THE APPROPRIATE AMOUNT OF--?
AT EASE, LITTLE SOLDIER.

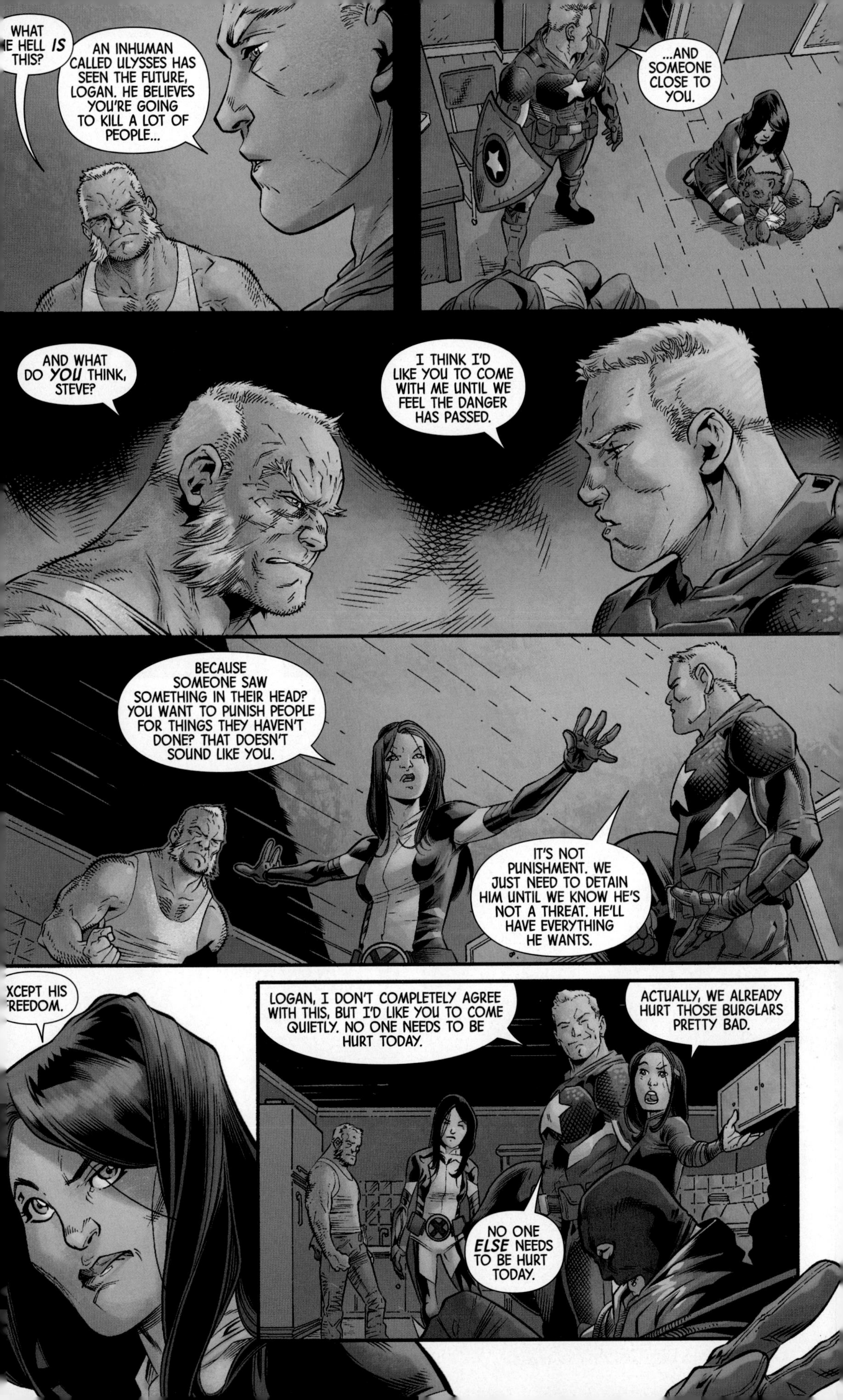
WHAT
E HELL IS THIS?
AN INHUMAN CALLED ULYSSES HAS SEEN THE FUTURE, LOGAN. HE BELIEVES YOU'RE GOING TO KILL A LOT OF PEOPLE...
...AND SOMEONE CLOSE TO YOU.
AND WHAT DO YOU THINK, STEVE?
I THINK I'D LIKE YOU TO COME WITH ME UNTIL WE FEEL THE DANGER HAS PASSED.
BECAUSE SOMEONE SAW SOMETHING IN THEIR HEAD? YOU WANT TO PUNISH PEOPLE FOR THINGS THEY HAVEN'T DONE? THAT DOESN'T SOUND LIKE YOU.
IT'S NOT PUNISHMENT. WE JUST NEED TO DETAIN HIM UNTIL WE KNOW HE'S NOT A THREAT. HE'LL HAVE EVERYTHING HE WANTS.
XCEPT HIS
REEDOM.
LOGAN, I DON'T COMPLETELY AGREE WITH THIS, BUT I'D LIKE YOU TO COME QUIETLY. NO ONE NEEDS TO BE HURT TODAY.
ACTUALLY, WE ALREADY HURT THOSE BURGLARS PRETTY BAD.
NO ONE ELSE NEEDS TO BE HURT TODAY.

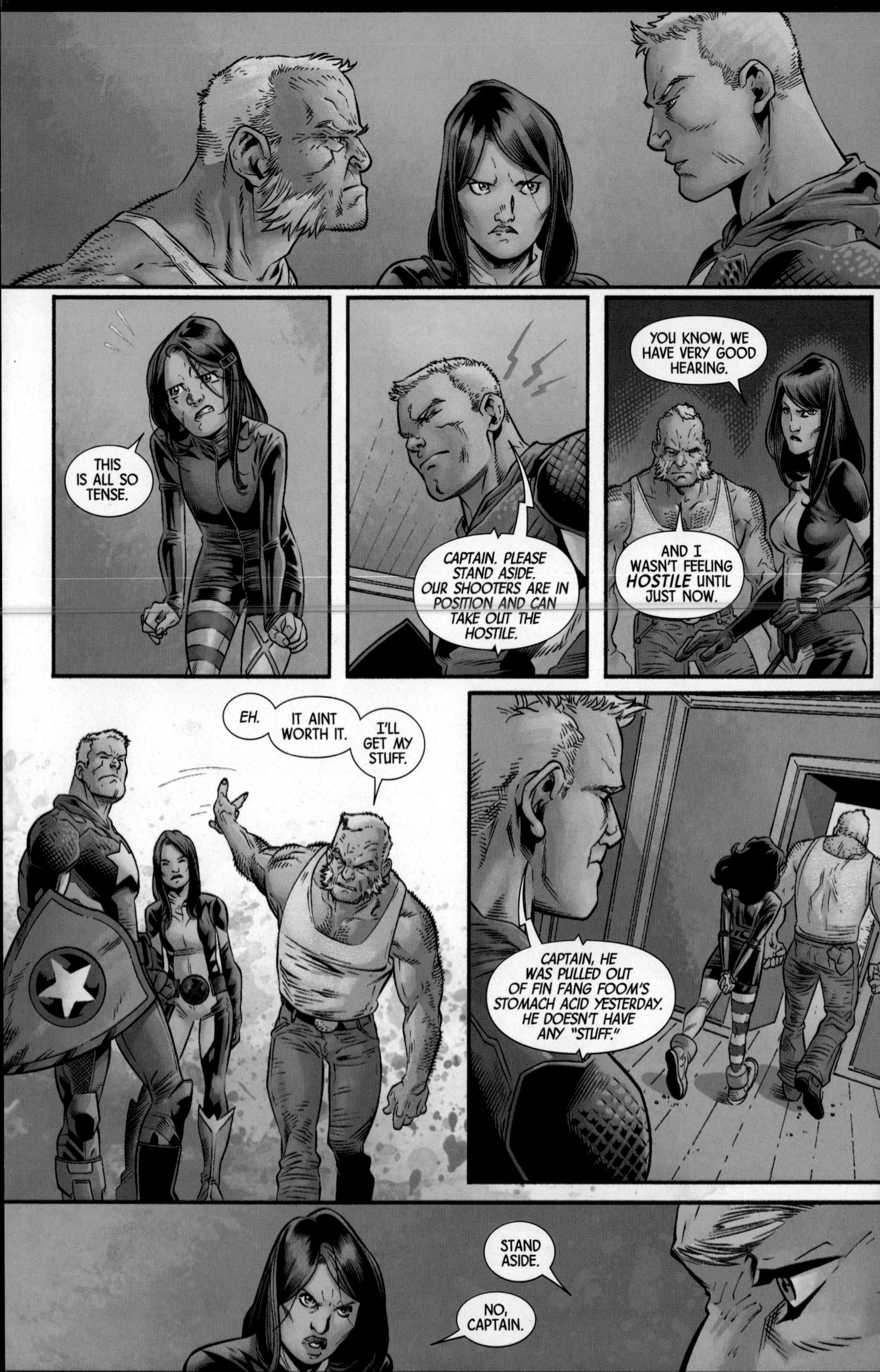
THIS IS ALL SO TENSE.
CAPTAIN. PLEASE STAND ASIDE. OUR SHOOTERS ARE IN POSITION AND CAN TAKE OUT THE HOSTILE.
YOU KNOW, WE HAVE VERY GOOD HEARING.
AND I WASN'T FEELING HOSTILE UNTIL JUST NOW.
EH.
IT AINT WORTH IT.
I'LL GET MY STUFF.
CAPTAIN, HE WAS PULLED OUT OF FIN FANG FOOM'S STOMACH ACID YESTERDAY. HE DOESN'T HAVE ANY "STUFF."
STAND ASIDE.
NO, CAPTAIN.

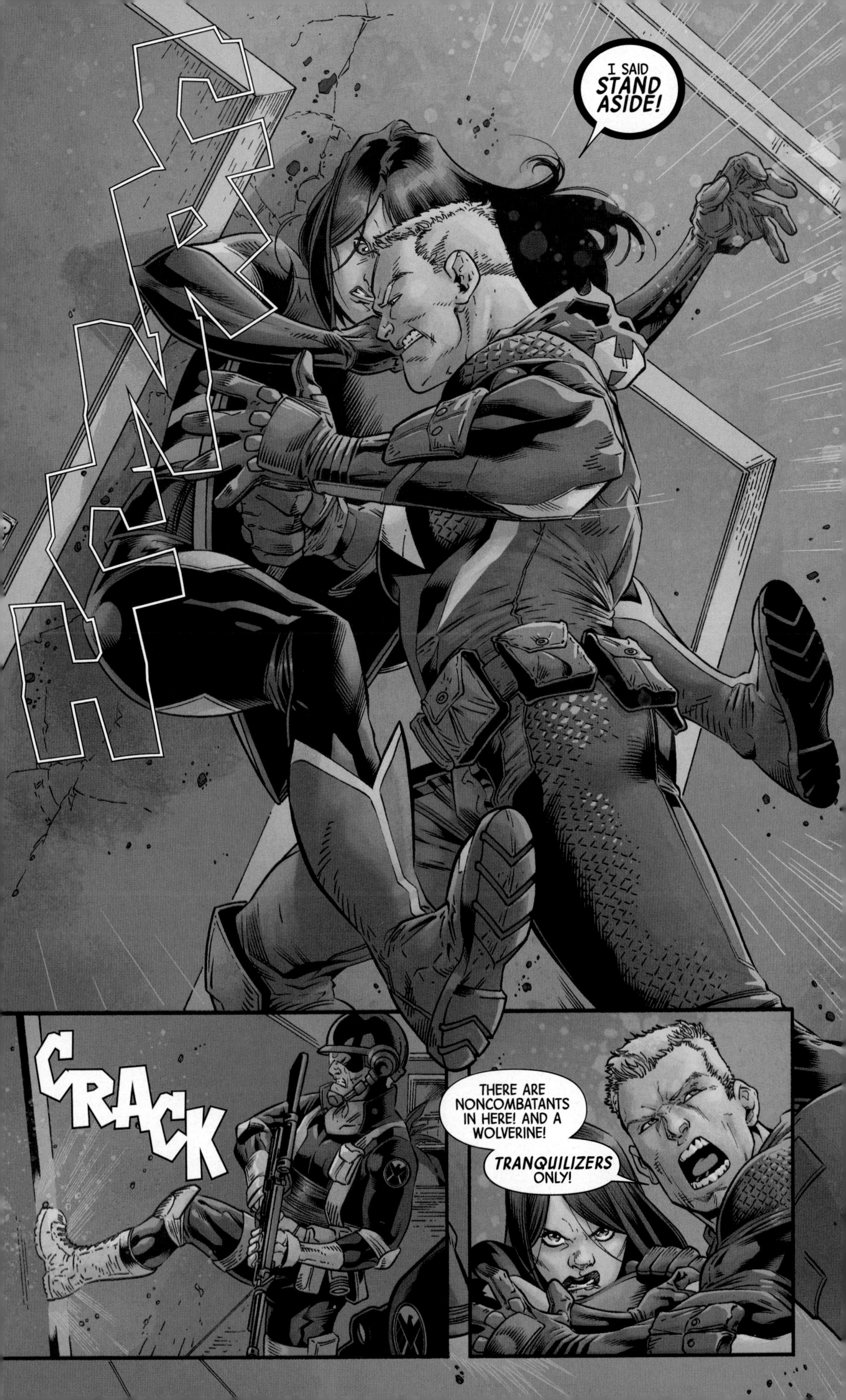
I SAID STAND ASIDE!
CRACK
THERE ARE NONCOMBATANTS IN HERE! AND A WOLVERINE!
TRANQUILIZERS ONLY!

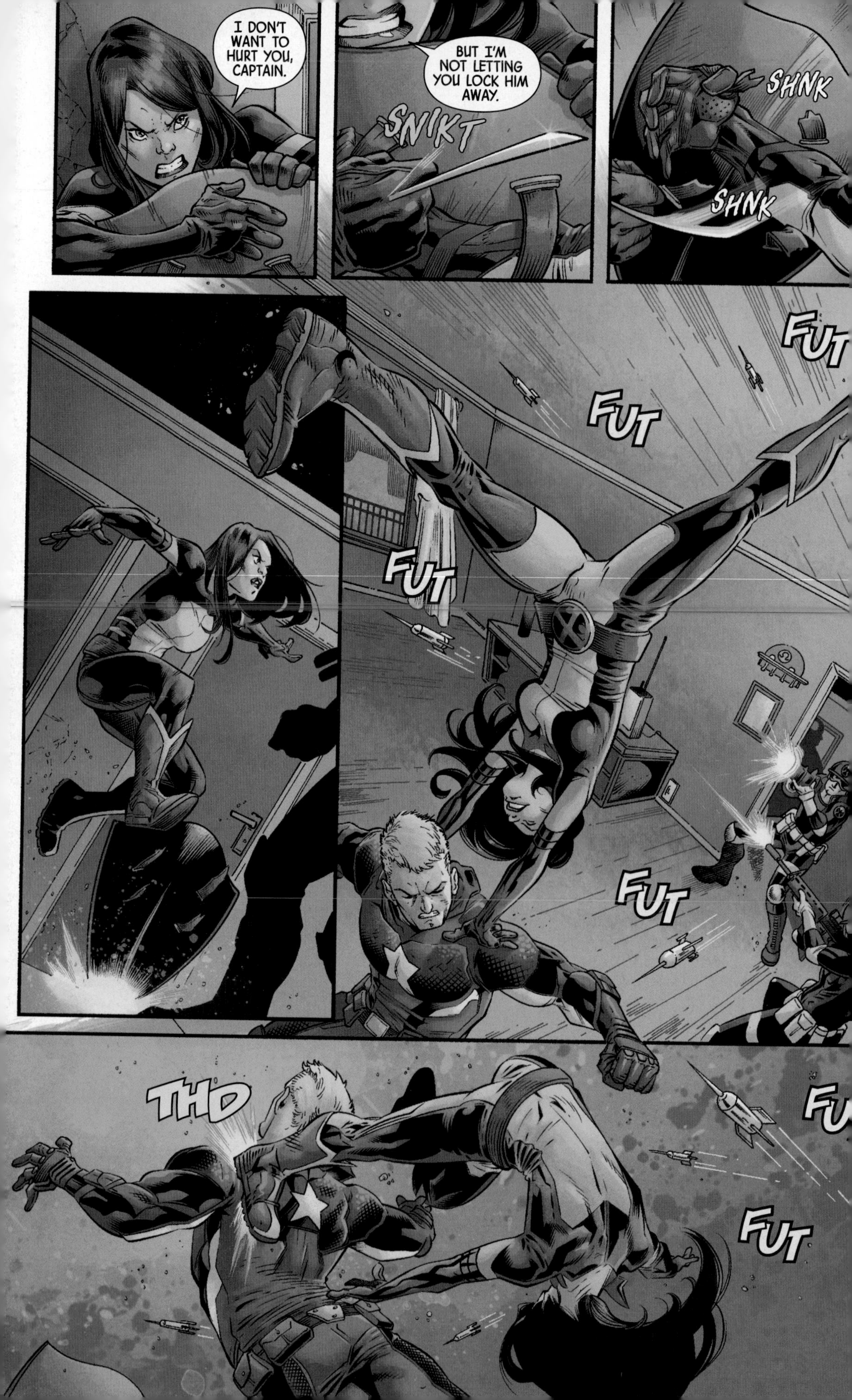

I DON'T WANT TO HURT YOU, CAPTAIN.
BUT I'M NOT LETTING YOU LOCK HIM AWAY.
SNIKT
SHNK
SHNK
FUT
FUT
FUT
FUT
THD
FUT

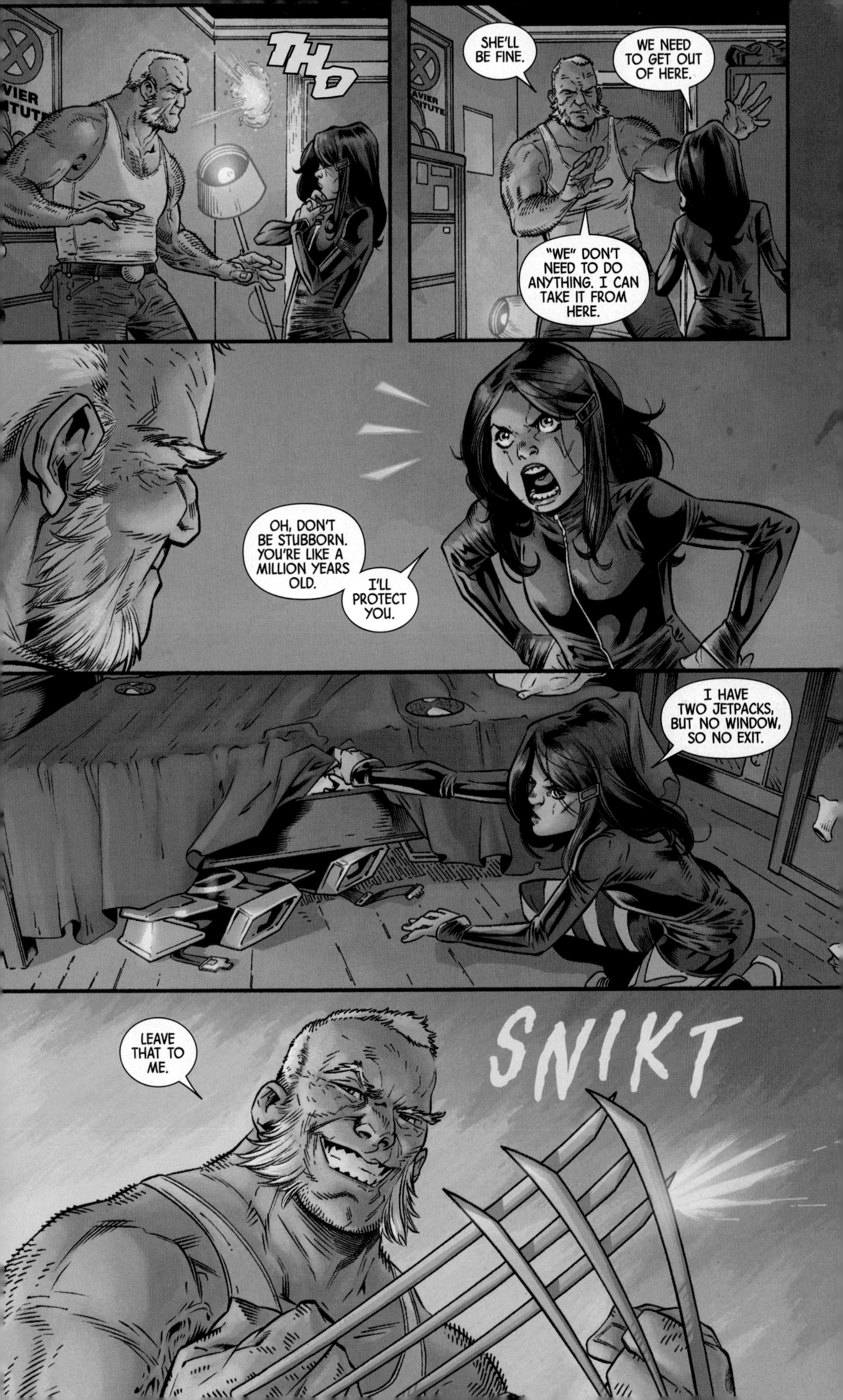
THD
SHE'LL BE FINE.
WE NEED TO GET OUT OF HERE.
"WE" DON'T NEED TO DO ANYTHING. I CAN TAKE IT FROM HERE.
OH, DON'T BE STUBBORN. YOU'RE LIKE A MILLION YEARS OLD.
I'LL PROTECT YOU.
I HAVE TWO JETPACKS, BUT NO WINDOW, SO NO EXIT.
LEAVE THAT TO ME.
SNIKT

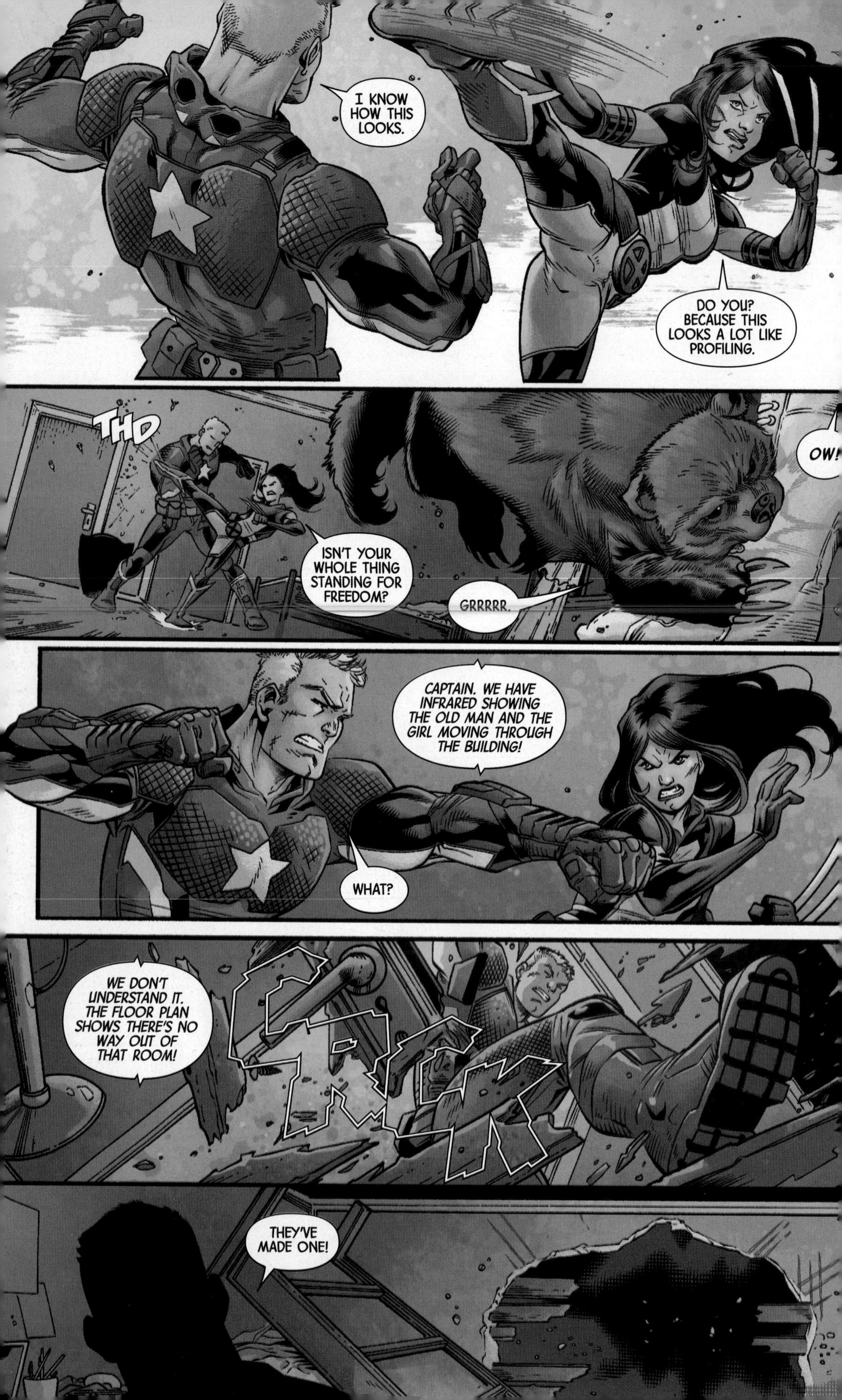
I KNOW HOW THIS LOOKS.
DO YOU? BECAUSE THIS LOOKS A LOT LIKE PROFILING.
THD
ISN'T YOUR WHOLE THING STANDING FOR FREEDOM?
GRRRRR.
OW!
CAPTAIN. WE HAVE INFRARED SHOWING THE OLD MAN AND THE GIRL MOVING THROUGH THE BUILDING!
WHAT?
WE DON'T UNDERSTAND IT. THE FLOOR PLAN SHOWS THERE'S NO WAY OUT OF THAT ROOM!
THEY'VE MADE ONE!

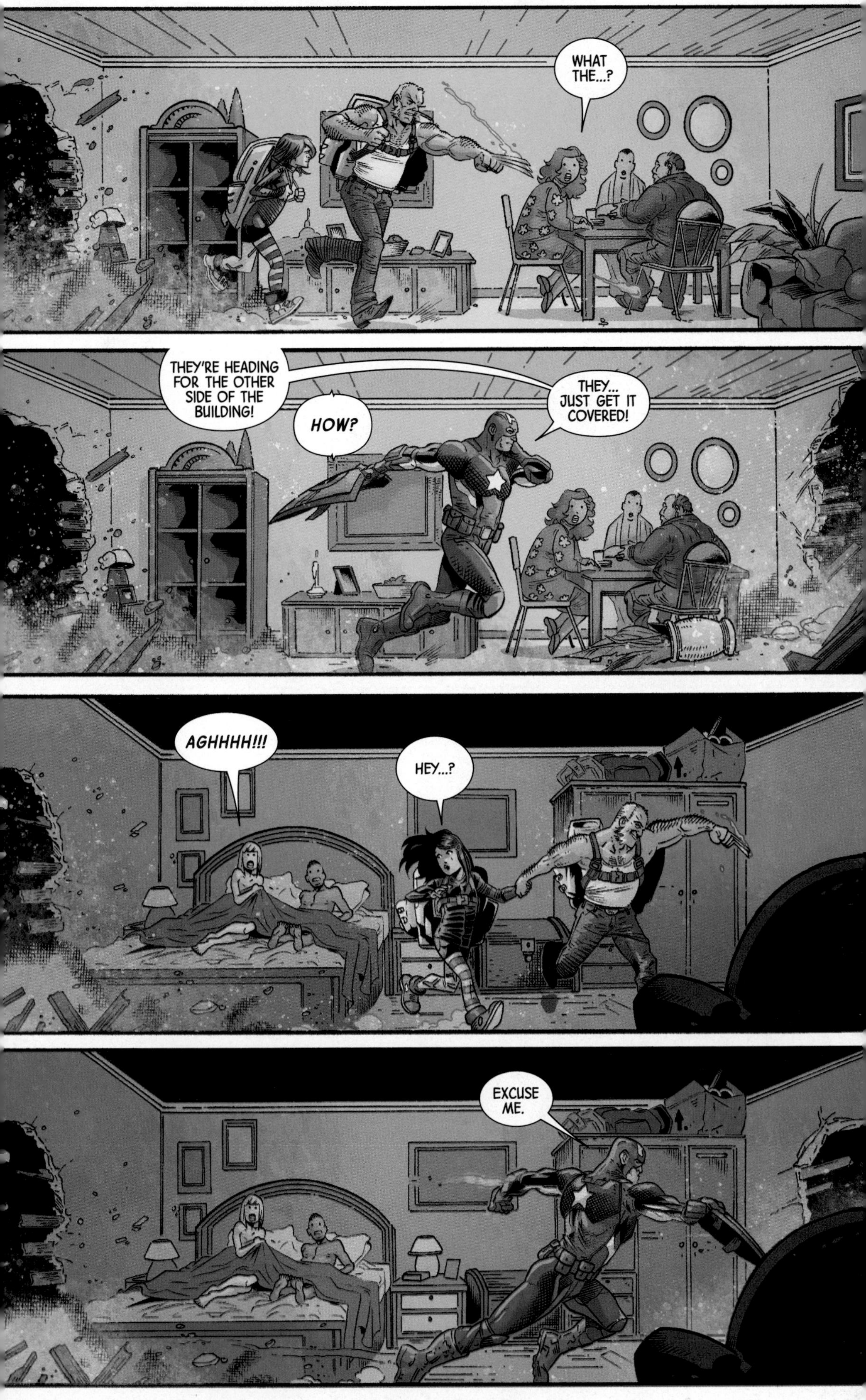
WHAT THE...?
THEY'RE HEADING FOR THE OTHER SIDE OF THE BUILDING!
HOW?
THEY... JUST GET IT COVERED!
AGHHHH!!!
HEY...?
EXCUSE ME.

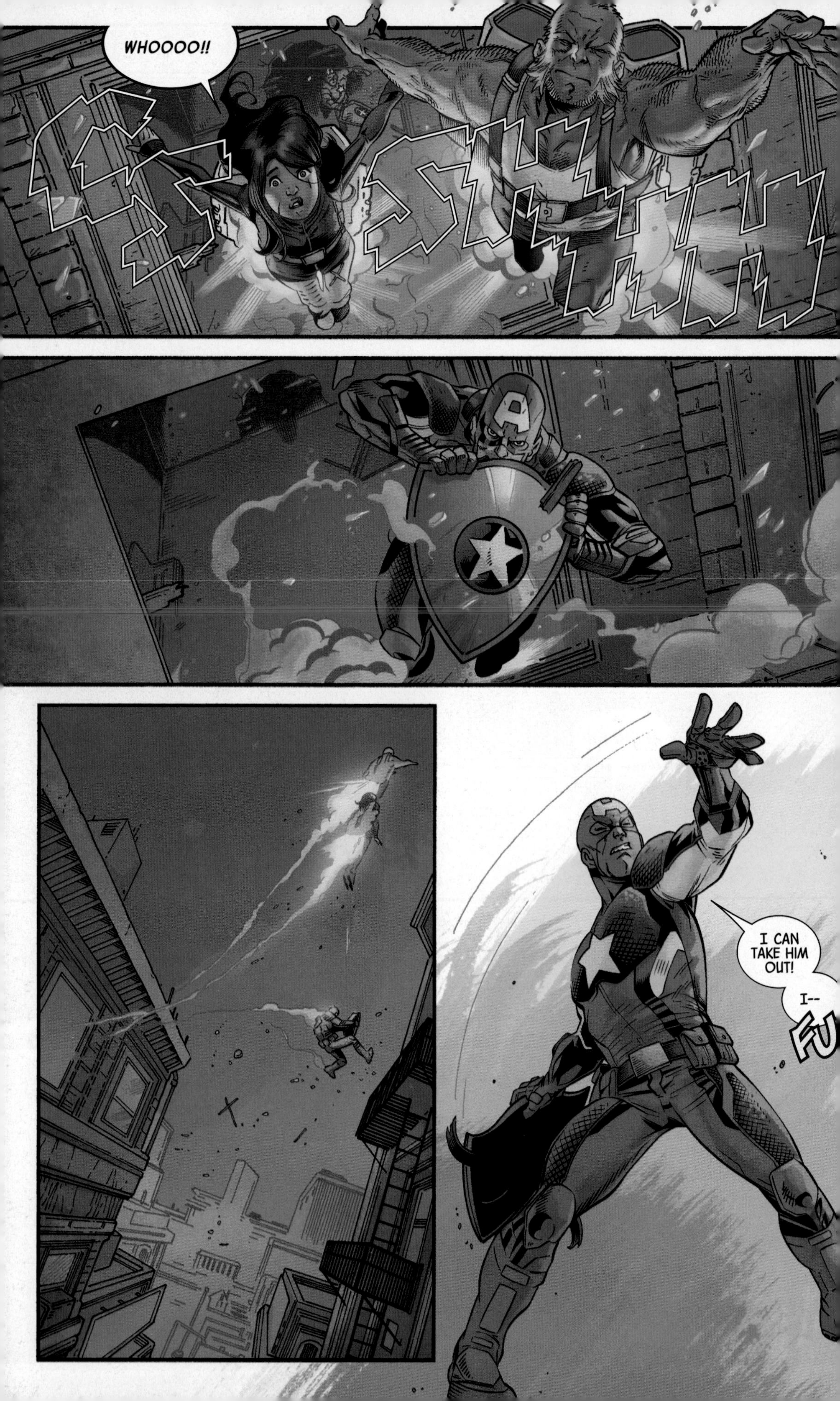
WHOOOO!!
I CAN TAKE HIM OUT!
I--
FU

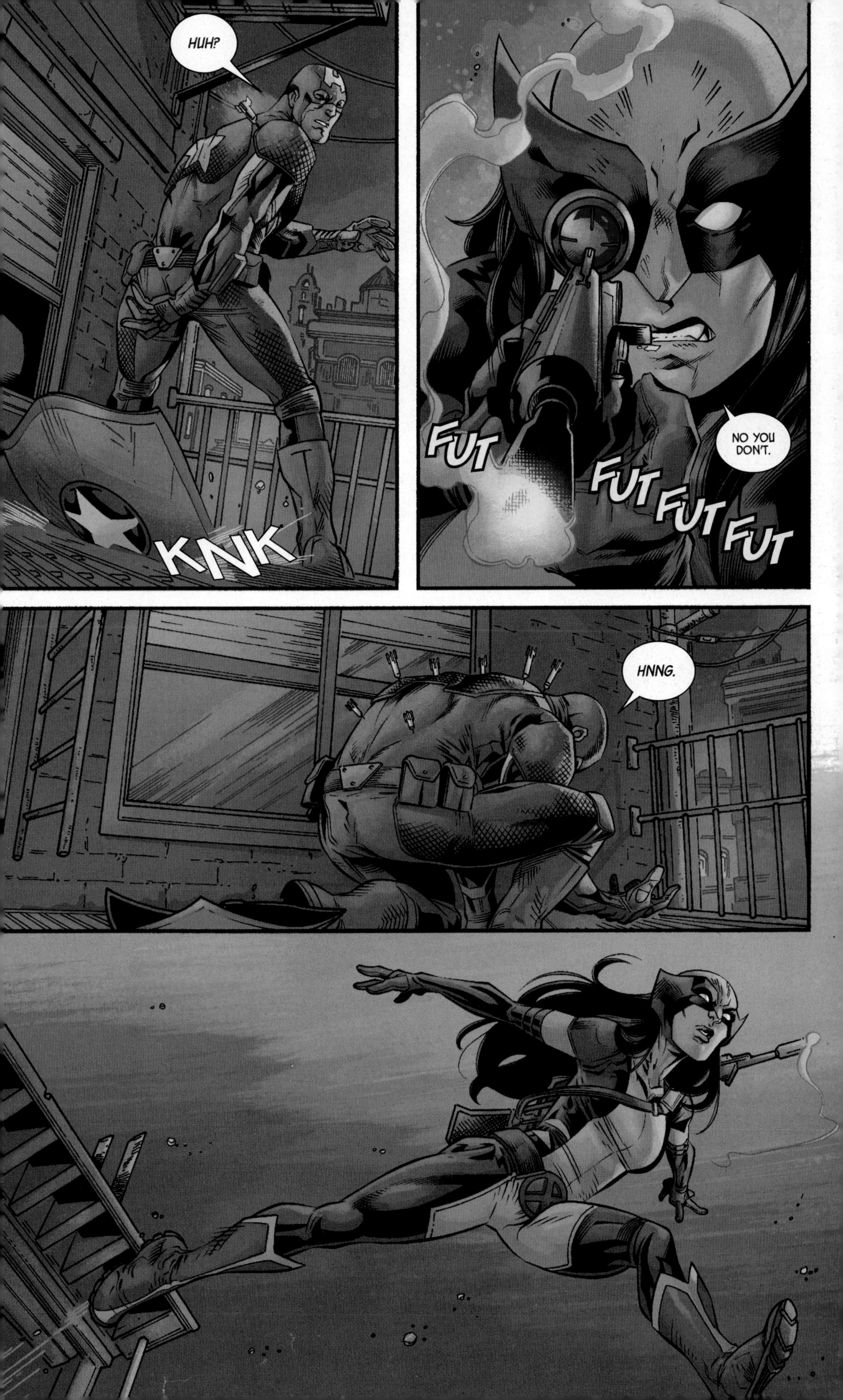
HUH?
KNK
FUT
NO YOU DON'T.
FUT FUT FUT
HNNG.

STAY DOWN.

HE SAID... THEY FLY THROUGH... THE AIR.

WHAT?

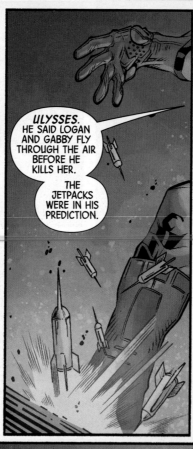

ULYSSES. HE SAID LOGAN AND GABBY FLY THROUGH THE AIR BEFORE HE KILLS HER.

THE JETPACKS WERE IN HIS PREDICTION.

I UNDERSTAND WHY YOU'RE FIGHTING FOR HIM.

IF I DIDN'T KNOW WHAT I KNOW, IF I HADN'T SEEN WHAT I'D SEEN, I'D BE FIGHTING *ALONGSIDE* YOU.

BUT HE'S *NOT* THE MAN YOU WISH HE WAS.

HE'S NOT THE LOGAN *I* WISH HE WAS.

I KNOW WHAT HE'S CAPABLE OF. HE KILLED HIS FRIENDS IN THE WORLD HE CAME FROM. THE X-MEN *DIED* AT HIS HAND.

HE'S CONFUSED AND UNSTABLE. HE'S STEPPED OUT OF A NIGHTMARE.

HE MAY NOT KNOW WHAT HE'S DOING, BUT THERE'S A VERY GOOD CHANCE HE'S GOING TO KILL GABBY AND MANY, *MANY* MORE UNLESS WE STOP HIM.

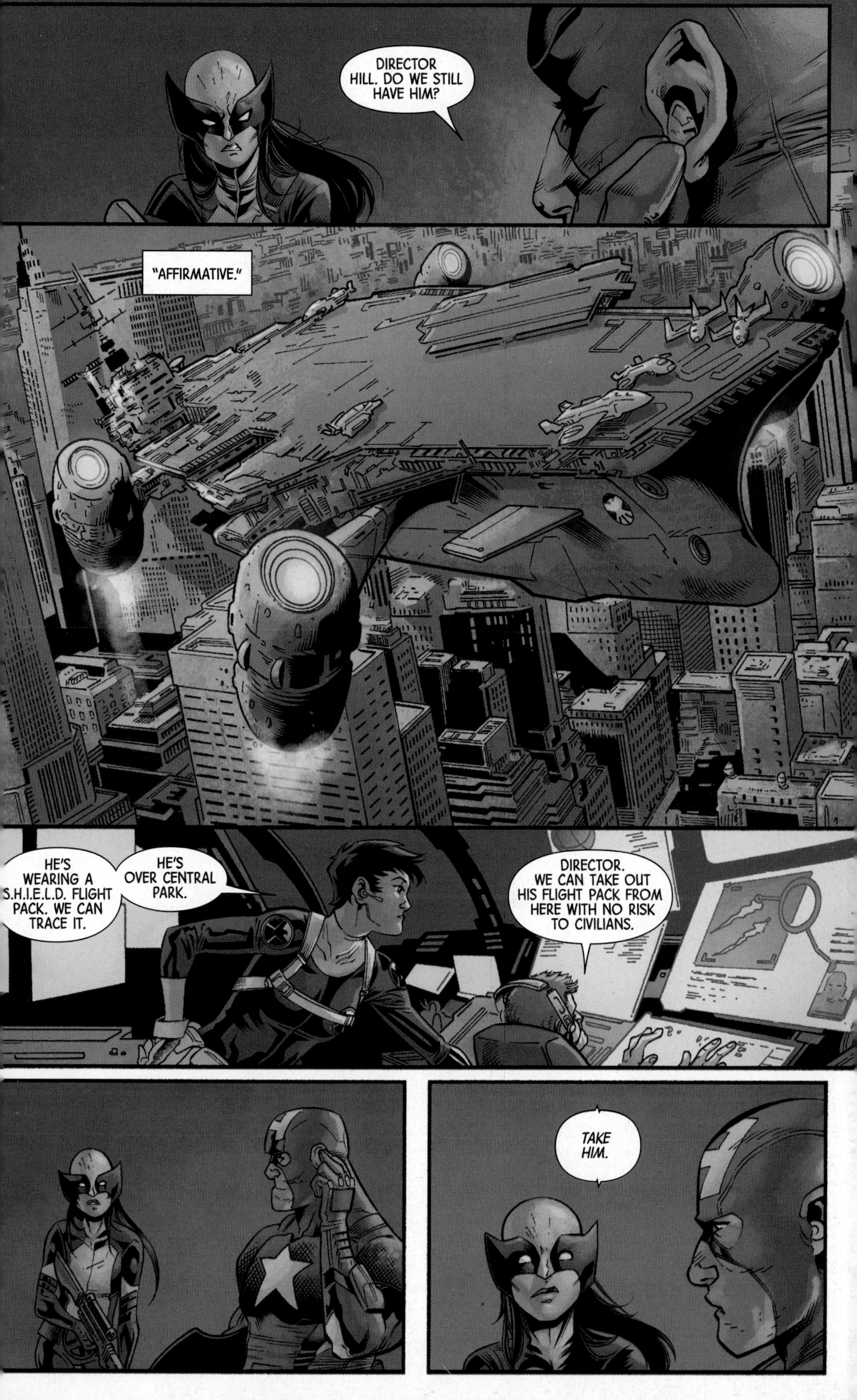
DIRECTOR HILL. DO WE STILL HAVE HIM?
"AFFIRMATIVE."
HE'S WEARING A S.H.I.E.L.D. FLIGHT PACK. WE CAN TRACE IT.
HE'S OVER CENTRAL PARK.
DIRECTOR. WE CAN TAKE OUT HIS FLIGHT PACK FROM HERE WITH NO RISK TO CIVILIANS.
TAKE HIM.

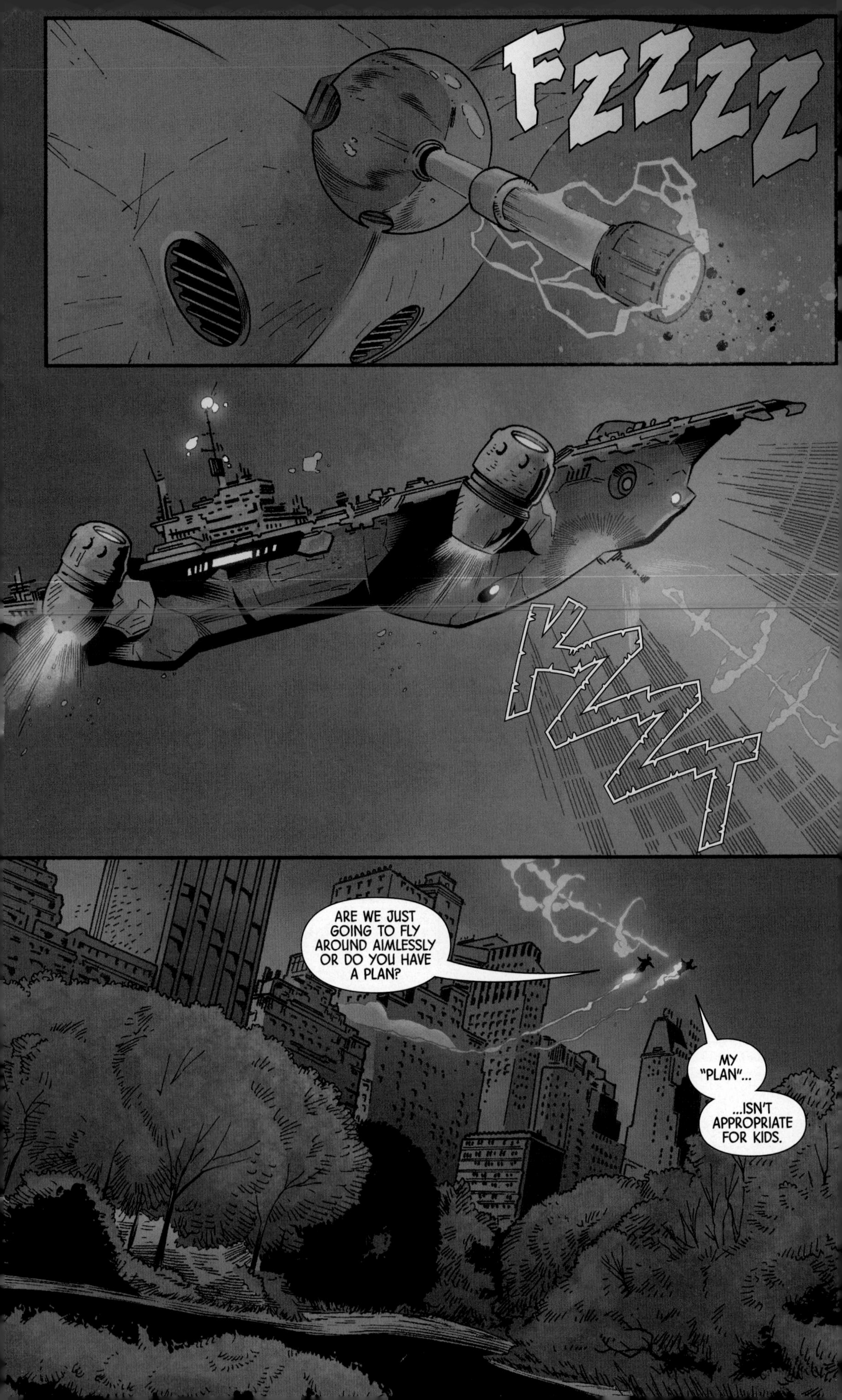
FZZZZZ
KZZZT
ARE WE JUST GOING TO FLY AROUND AIMLESSLY OR DO YOU HAVE A PLAN?
MY "PLAN"...
...ISN'T APPROPRIATE FOR KIDS.

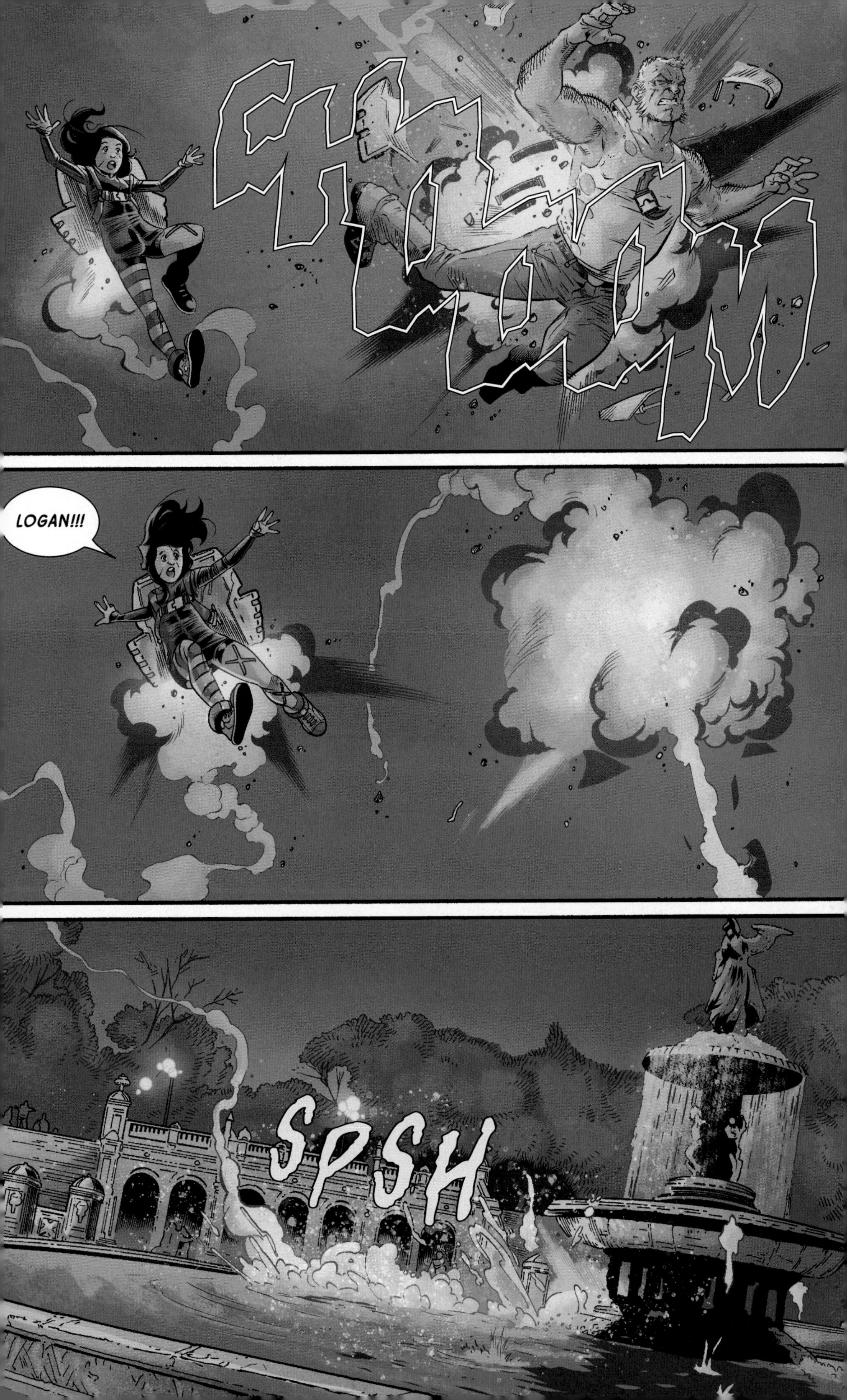
CHOOOM
LOGAN!!!
SPSH

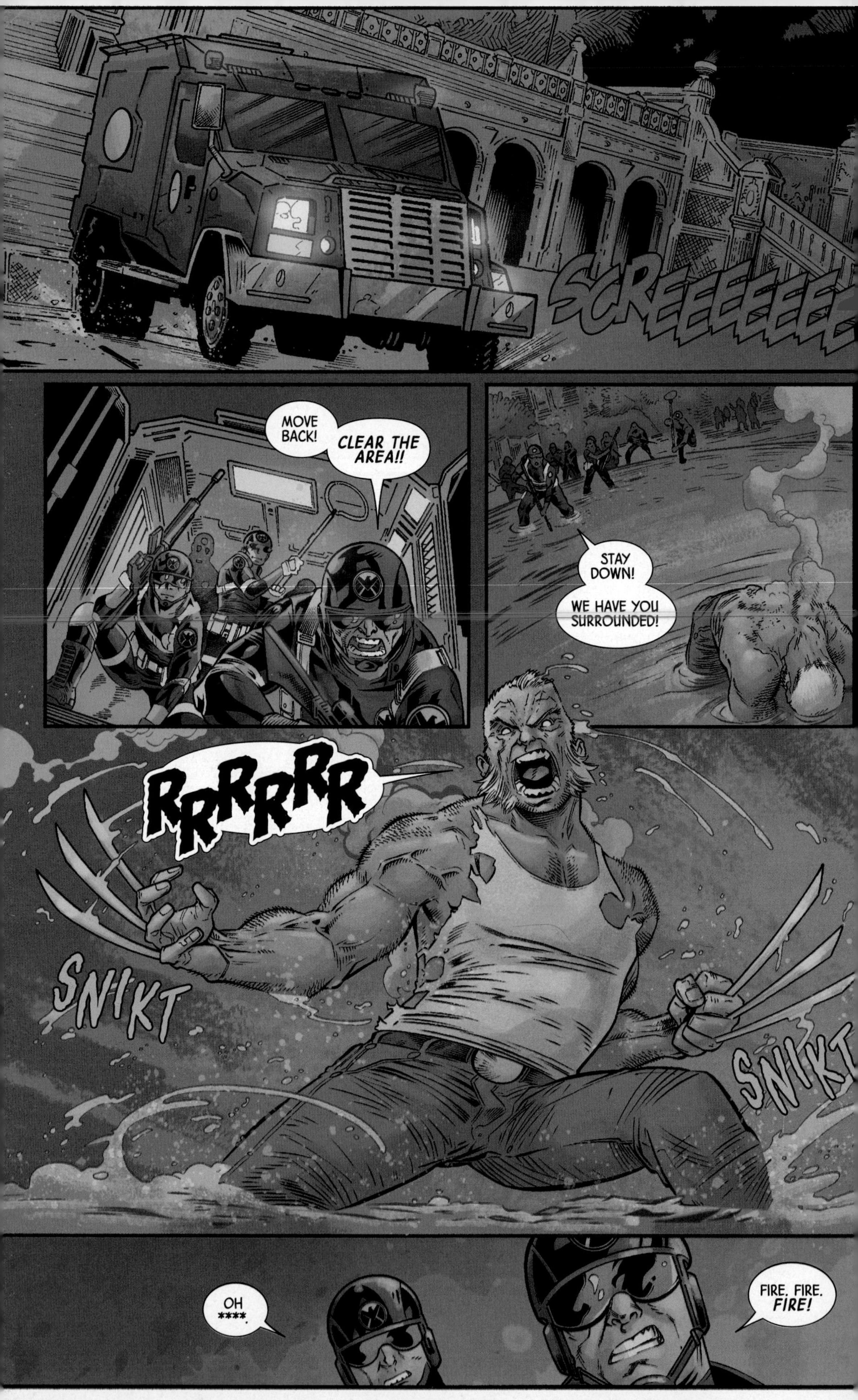
SCREEEEEEEE
MOVE BACK!
CLEAR THE AREA!!
STAY DOWN!
WE HAVE YOU SURROUNDED!
RRRRRR
SNIKT
SNIKT
OH ****.
FIRE. FIRE. FIRE!

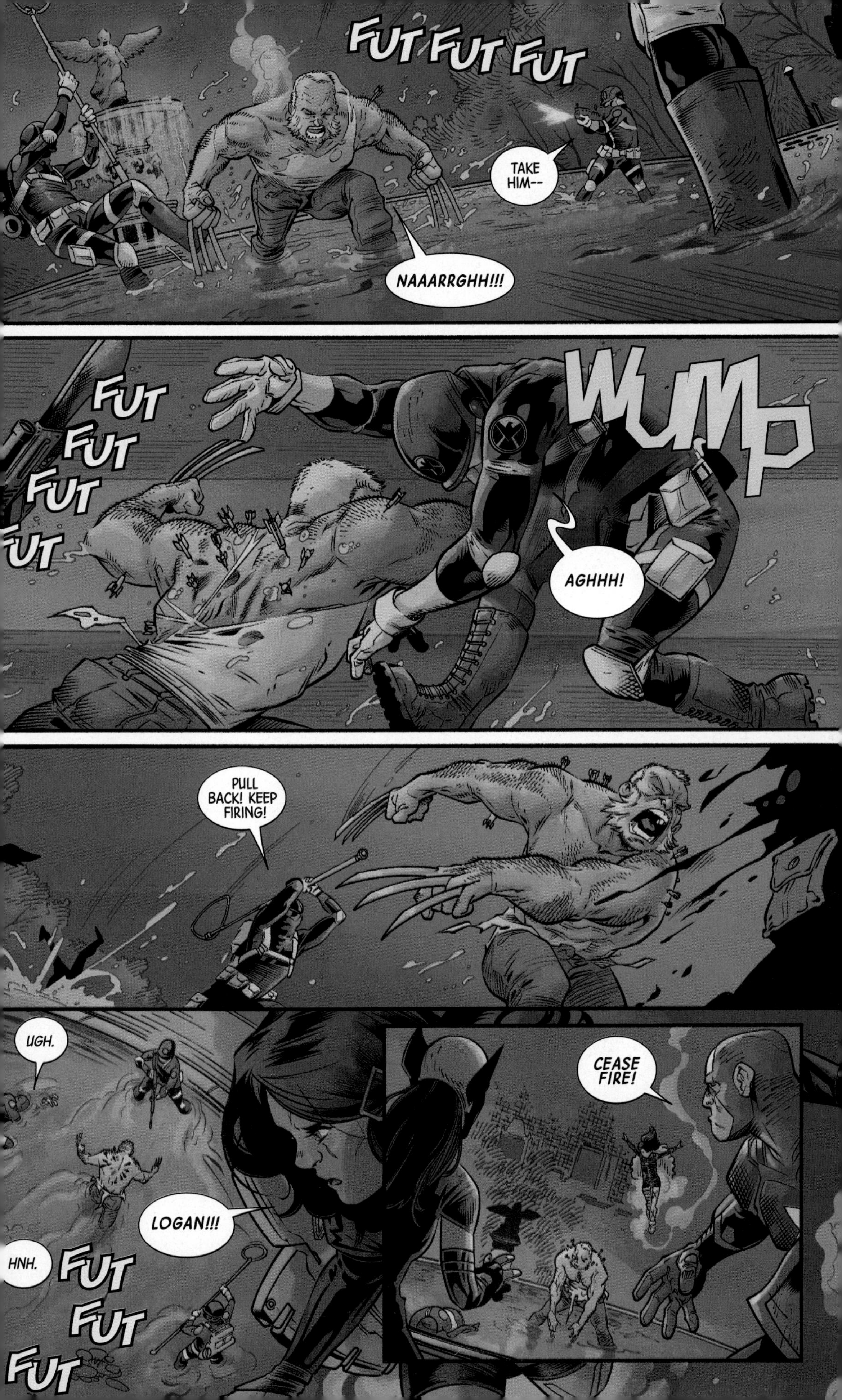
FUT FUT FUT
TAKE HIM--
NAAARRGHH!!!
FUT
FUT
FUT
FUT
WUMP
AGHHH!
PULL BACK! KEEP FIRING!
UGH.
LOGAN!!!
HNH.
FUT
FUT
FUT
CEASE FIRE!

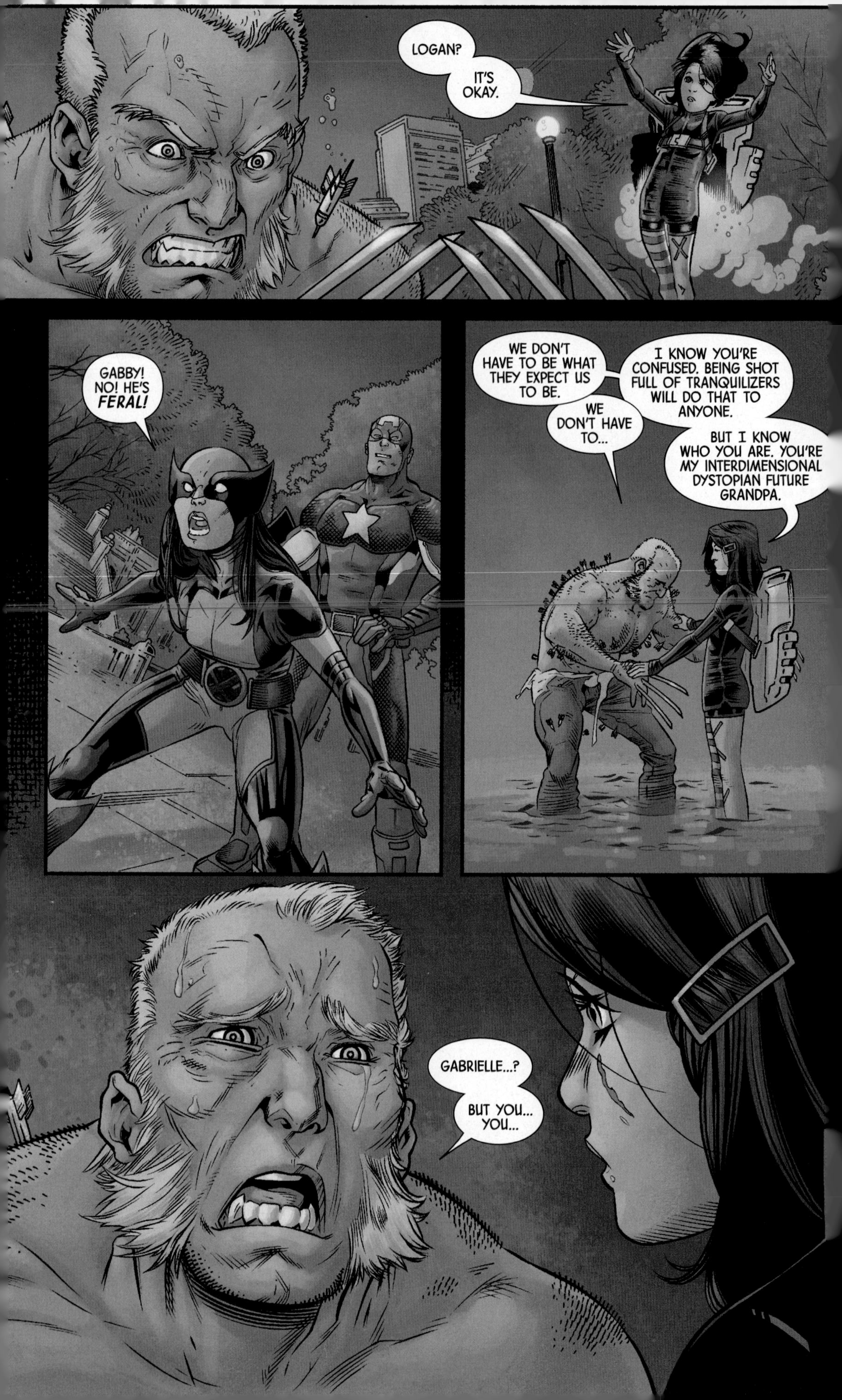
LOGAN?
IT'S OKAY.
GABBY! NO! HE'S *FERAL!*
WE DON'T HAVE TO BE WHAT THEY EXPECT US TO BE.
WE DON'T HAVE TO...
I KNOW YOU'RE CONFUSED. BEING SHOT FULL OF TRANQUILIZERS WILL DO THAT TO ANYONE.
BUT I KNOW WHO YOU ARE. YOU'RE MY INTERDIMENSIONAL DYSTOPIAN FUTURE GRANDPA.
GABRIELLE...?
BUT YOU... YOU...

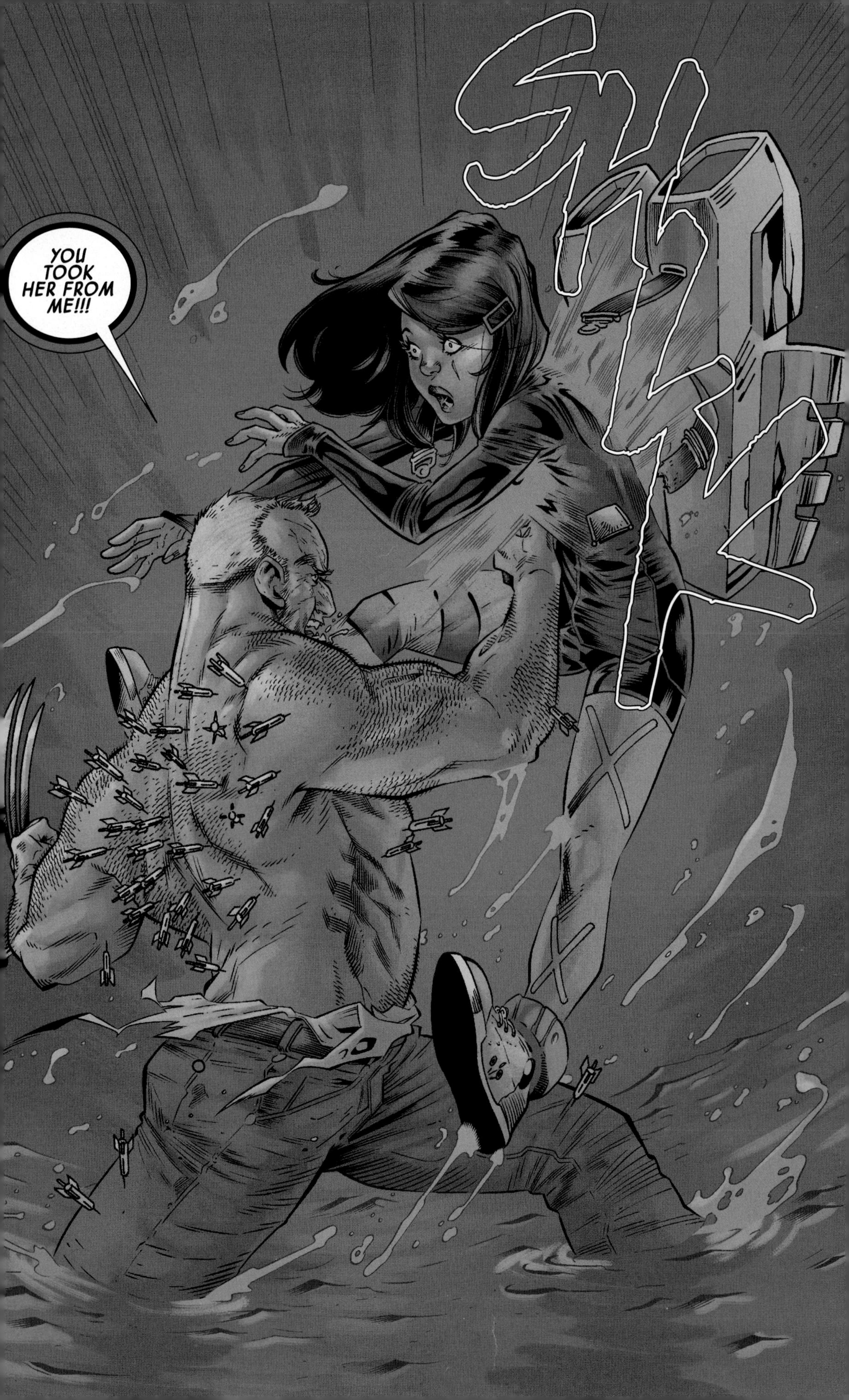
YOU TOOK HER FROM ME!!!

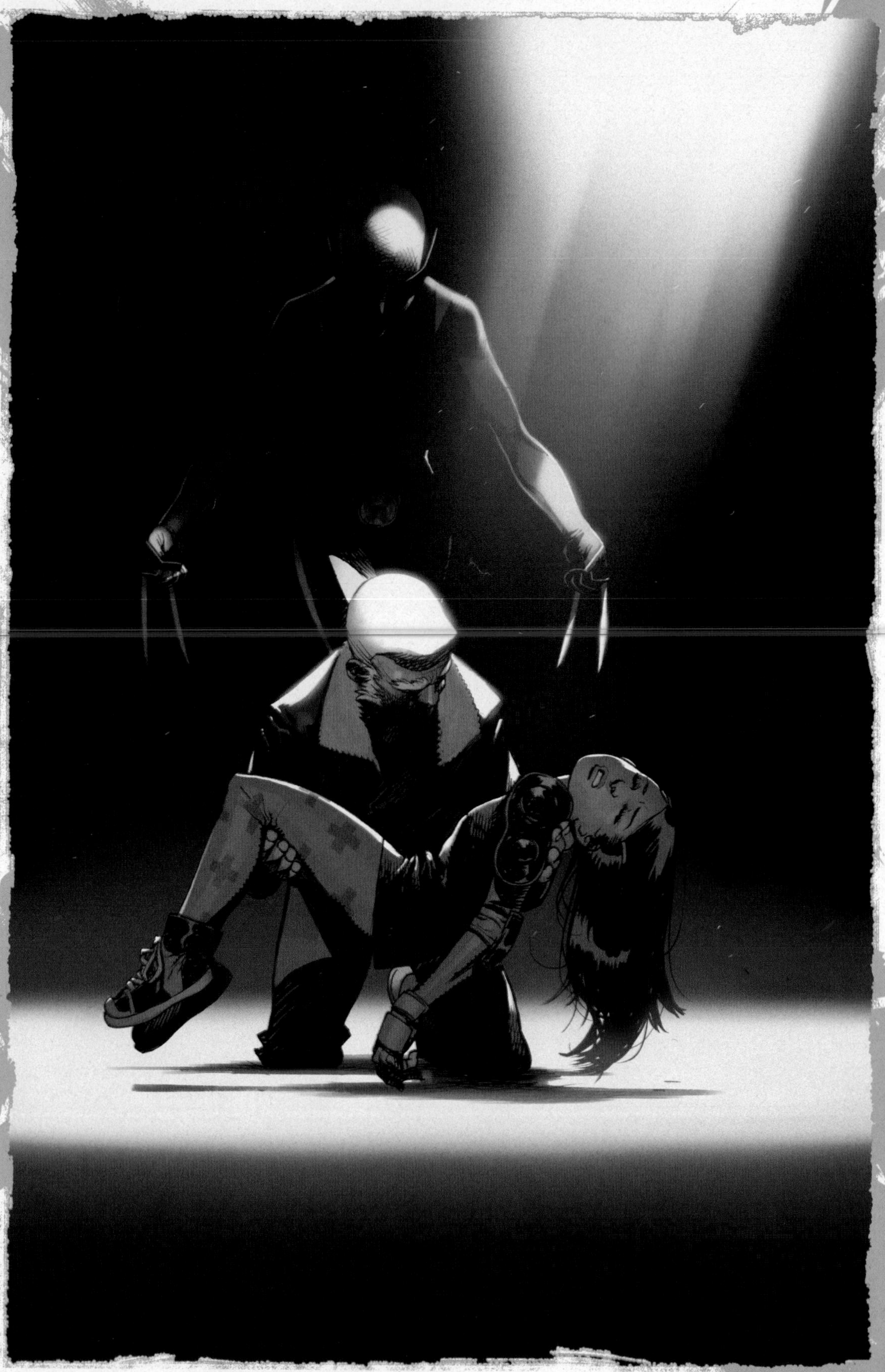

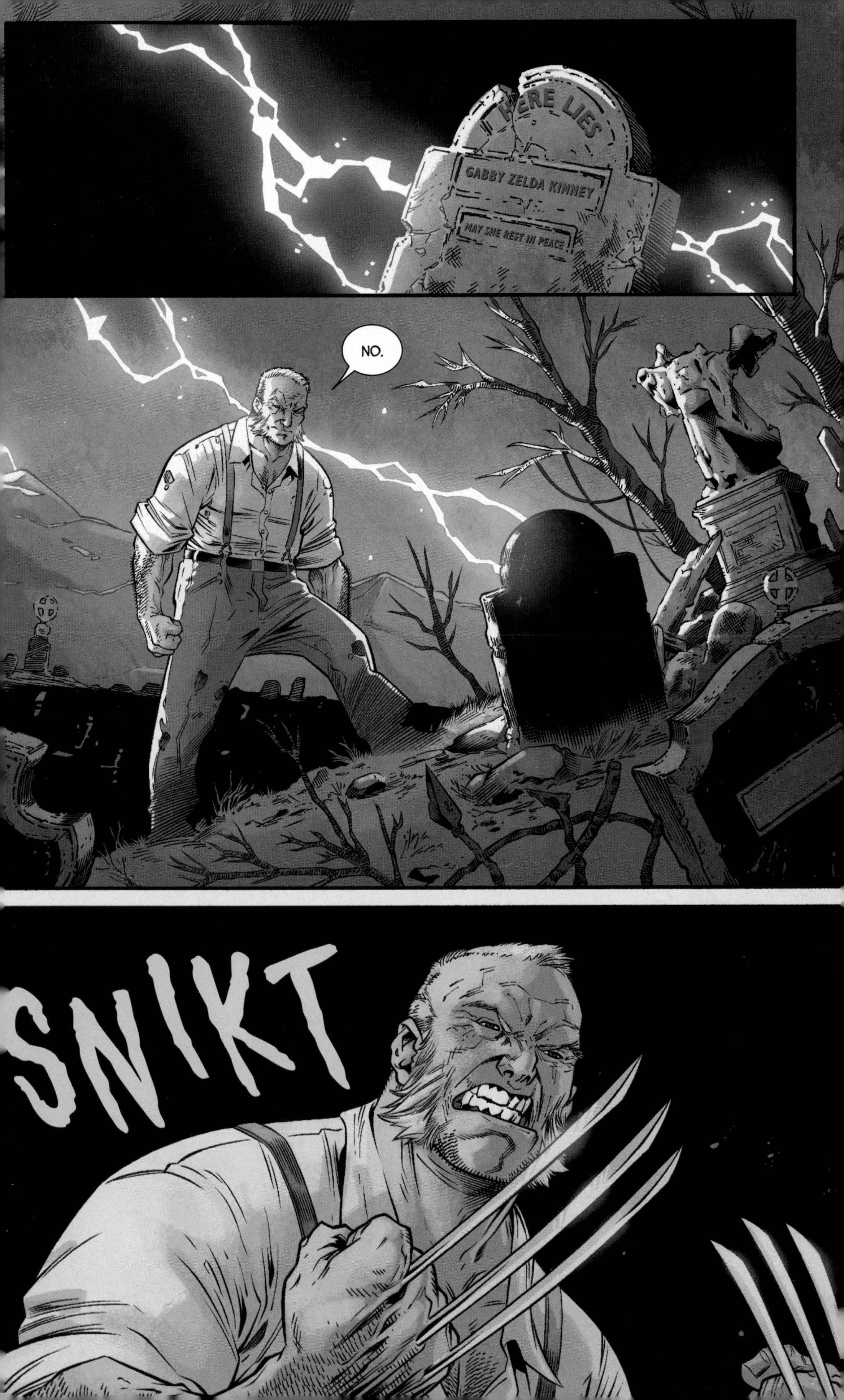
HERE LIES
GABBY ZELDA KINNEY
MAY SHE REST IN PEACE
NO.
SNIKT

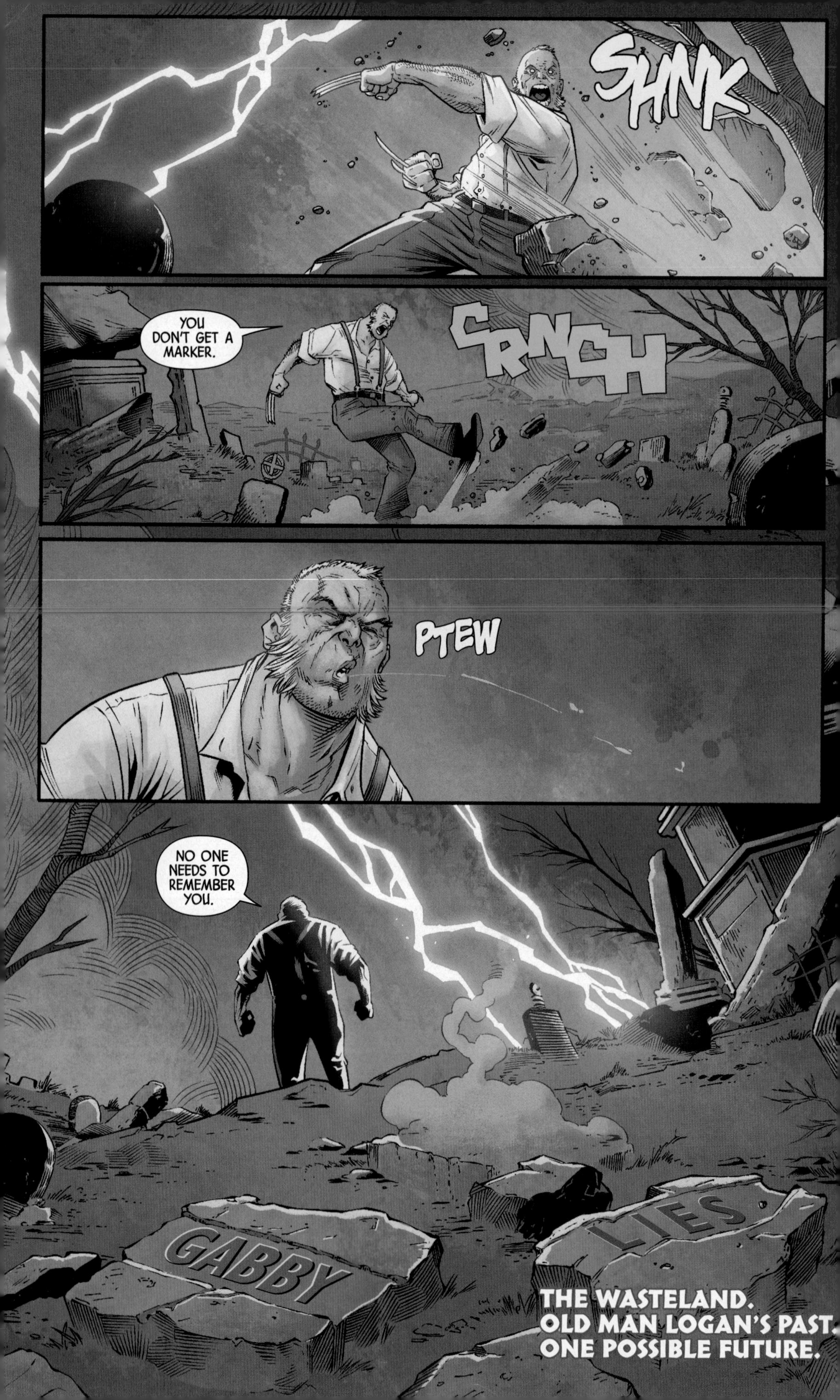
SHNK
YOU DON'T GET A MARKER.
CRNCH
PTEW
NO ONE NEEDS TO REMEMBER YOU.
GABBY
LIES
THE WASTELAND.
OLD MAN LOGAN'S PAST.
ONE POSSIBLE FUTURE.

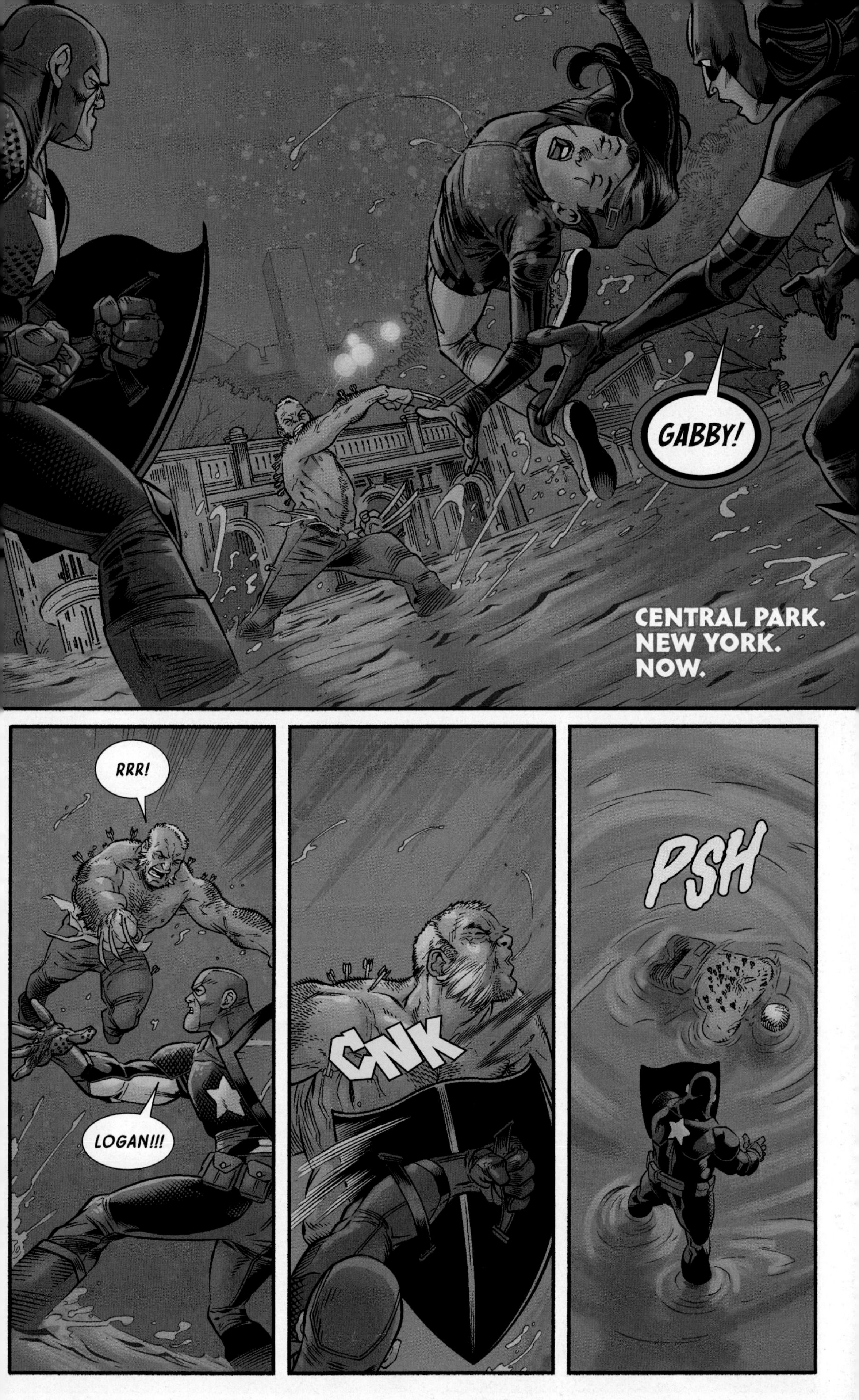
GABBY!
CENTRAL PARK.
NEW YORK.
NOW.
RRR!
LOGAN!!!
CNK
PSH

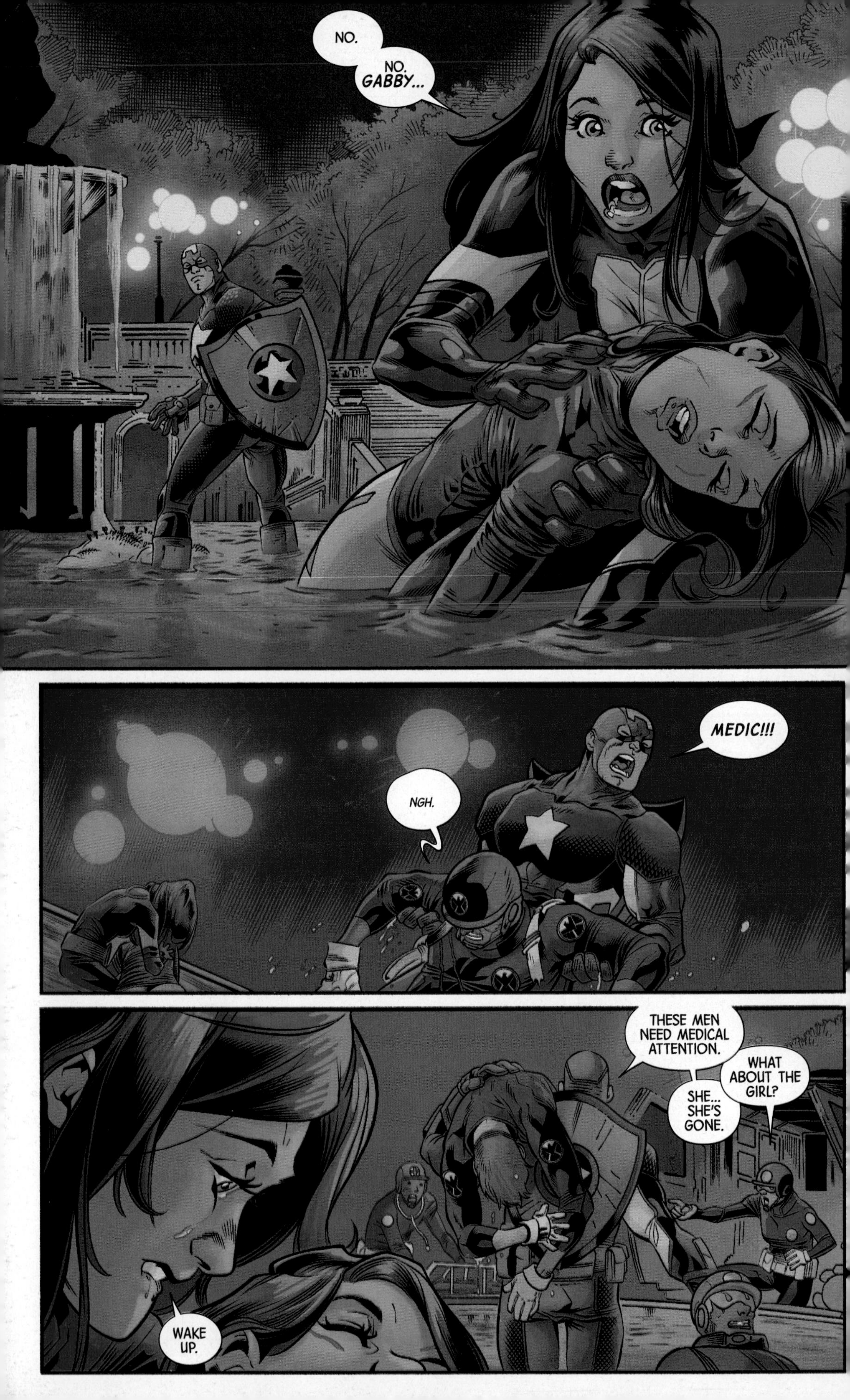
NO.
NO. GABBY...
NGH.
MEDIC!!!
THESE MEN NEED MEDICAL ATTENTION.
WHAT ABOUT THE GIRL?
SHE... SHE'S GONE.
WAKE UP.

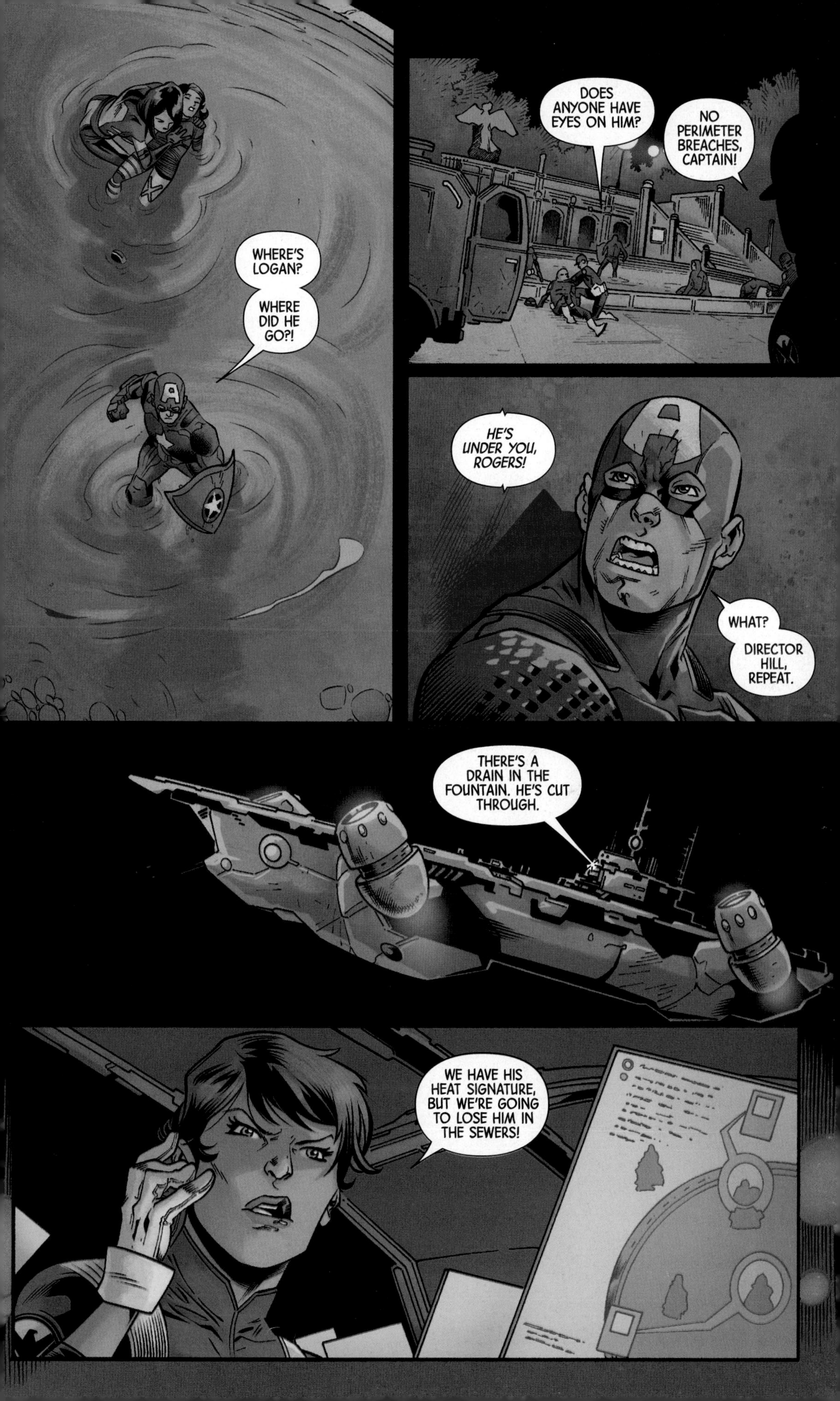
WHERE'S LOGAN?
WHERE DID HE GO?!
DOES ANYONE HAVE EYES ON HIM?
NO PERIMETER BREACHES, CAPTAIN!
HE'S UNDER YOU, ROGERS!
WHAT?
DIRECTOR HILL, REPEAT.
THERE'S A DRAIN IN THE FOUNTAIN. HE'S CUT THROUGH.
WE HAVE HIS HEAT SIGNATURE, BUT WE'RE GOING TO LOSE HIM IN THE SEWERS!

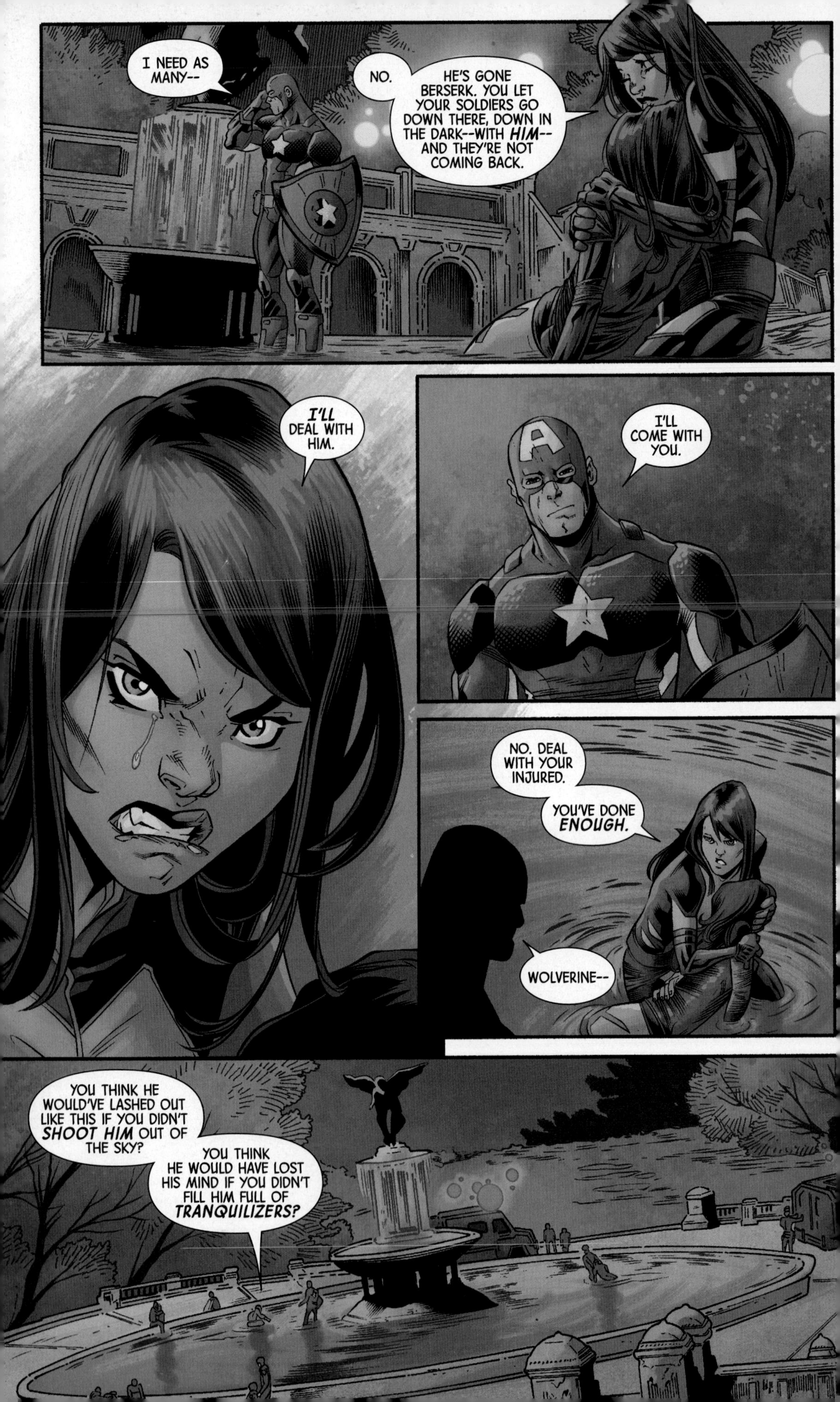
I NEED AS MANY--
NO.
HE'S GONE BERSERK. YOU LET YOUR SOLDIERS GO DOWN THERE, DOWN IN THE DARK--WITH *HIM*--AND THEY'RE NOT COMING BACK.
I'LL DEAL WITH HIM.
I'LL COME WITH YOU.
NO. DEAL WITH YOUR INJURED.
YOU'VE DONE *ENOUGH.*
WOLVERINE--
YOU THINK HE WOULD'VE LASHED OUT LIKE THIS IF YOU DIDN'T *SHOOT HIM* OUT OF THE SKY?
YOU THINK HE WOULD HAVE LOST HIS MIND IF YOU DIDN'T FILL HIM FULL OF *TRANQUILIZERS?*

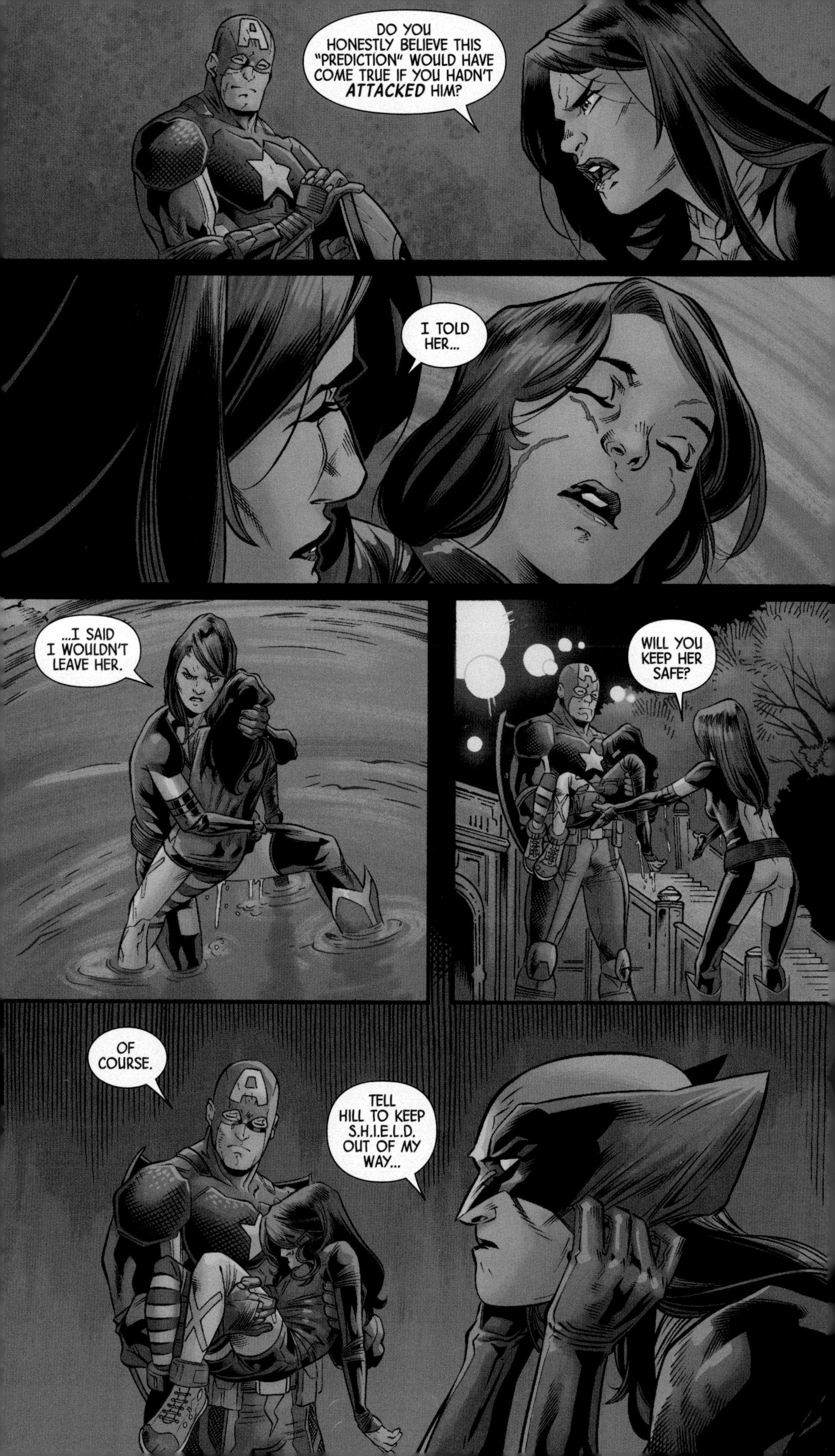
DO YOU HONESTLY BELIEVE THIS "PREDICTION" WOULD HAVE COME TRUE IF YOU HADN'T *ATTACKED* HIM?
I TOLD HER...
...I SAID I WOULDN'T LEAVE HER.
WILL YOU KEEP HER SAFE?
OF COURSE.
TELL HILL TO KEEP S.H.I.E.L.D. OUT OF MY WAY...

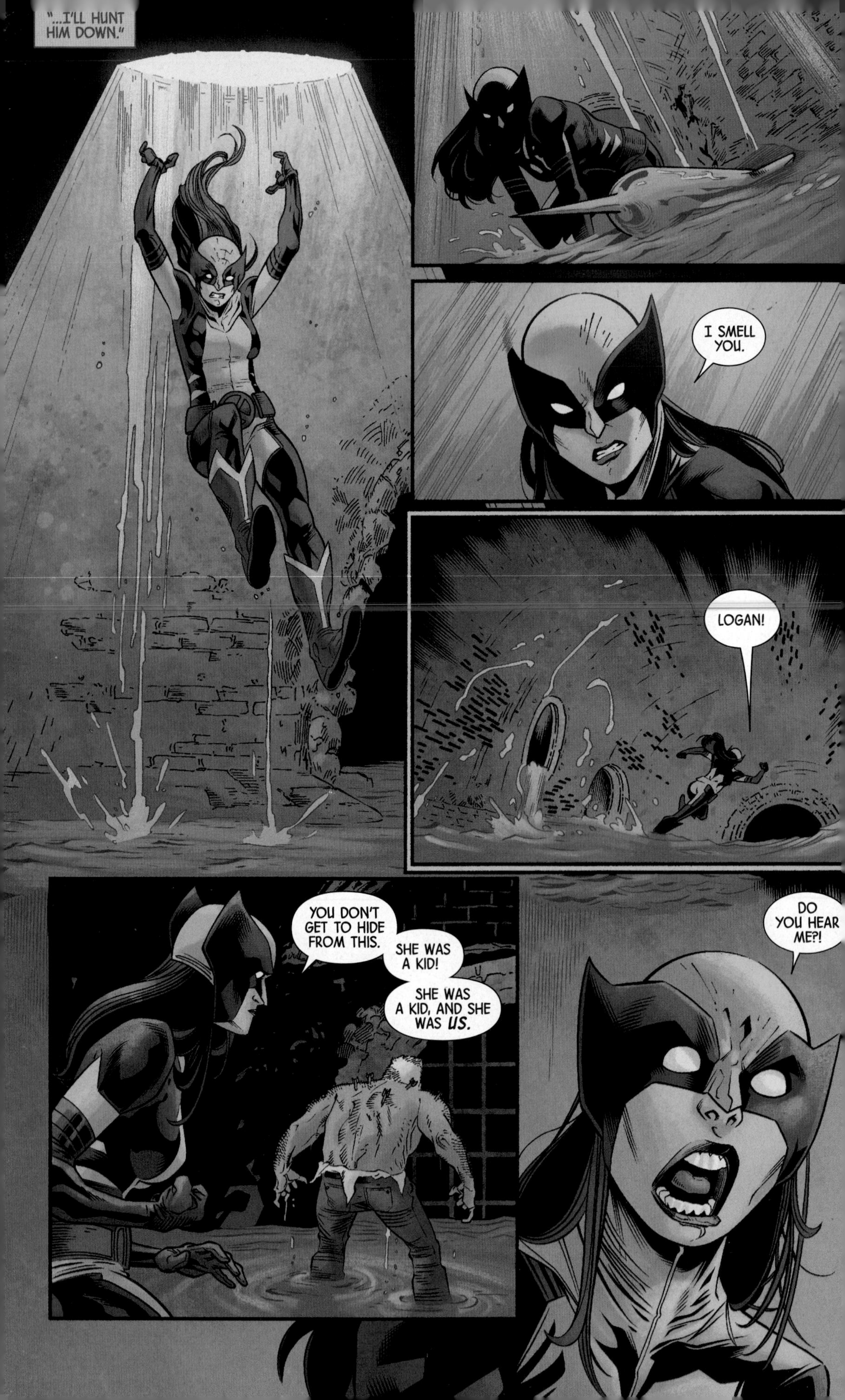
"...I'LL HUNT HIM DOWN."
I SMELL YOU.
LOGAN!
YOU DON'T GET TO HIDE FROM THIS.
SHE WAS A KID!
SHE WAS A KID, AND SHE WAS *US*.
DO YOU HEAR ME?!

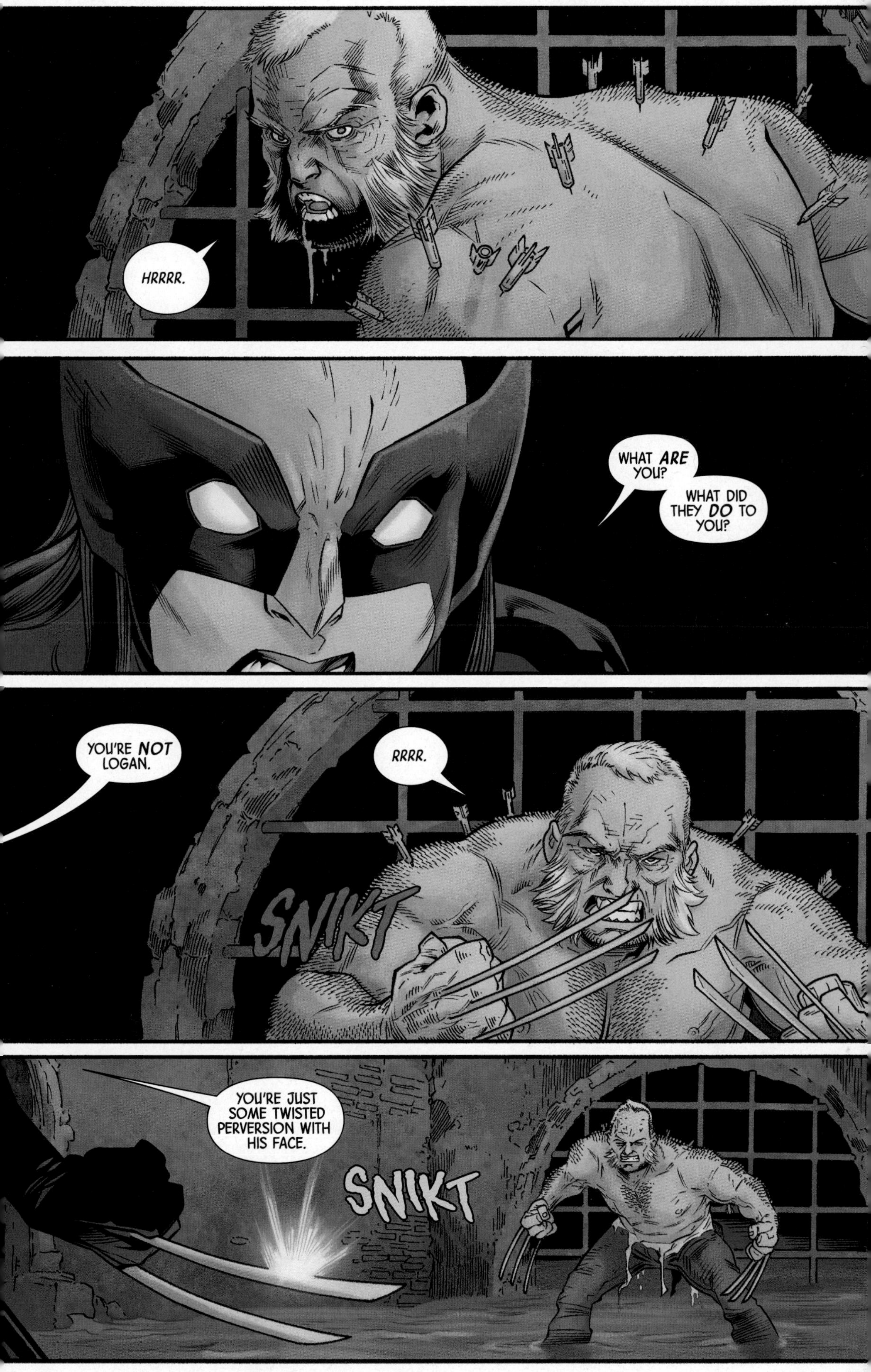
HRRRR.
WHAT ARE YOU?
WHAT DID THEY DO TO YOU?
YOU'RE NOT LOGAN.
RRRR.
SNIKT
YOU'RE JUST SOME TWISTED PERVERSION WITH HIS FACE.
SNIKT

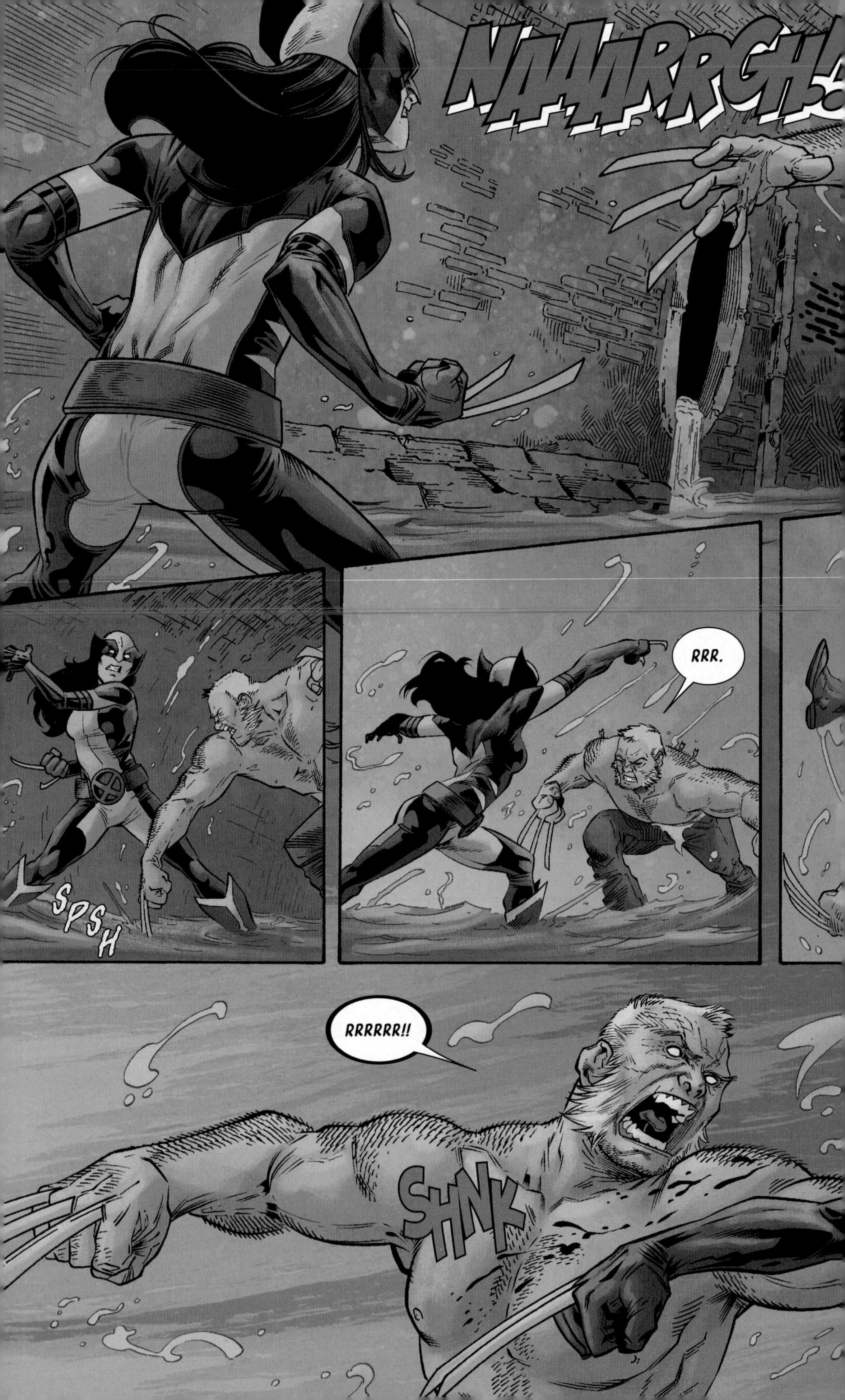
NAAARRGH!
SPSH
RRR.
RRRRRR!!
SHNK

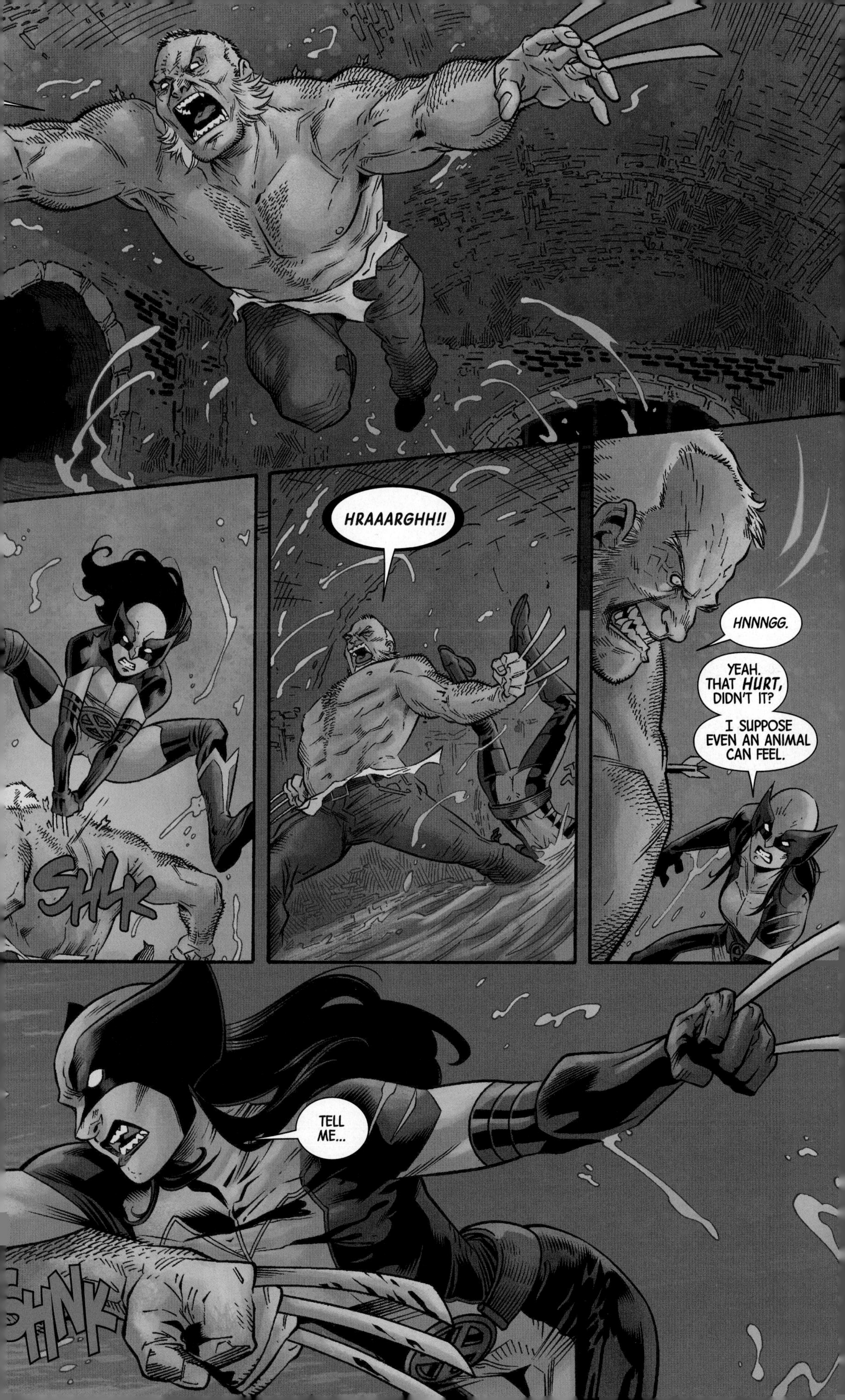
SHLK
HRAAARGHH!!
HNNNGG.
YEAH. THAT HURT, DIDN'T IT?
I SUPPOSE EVEN AN ANIMAL CAN FEEL.
TELL ME...
SHNK

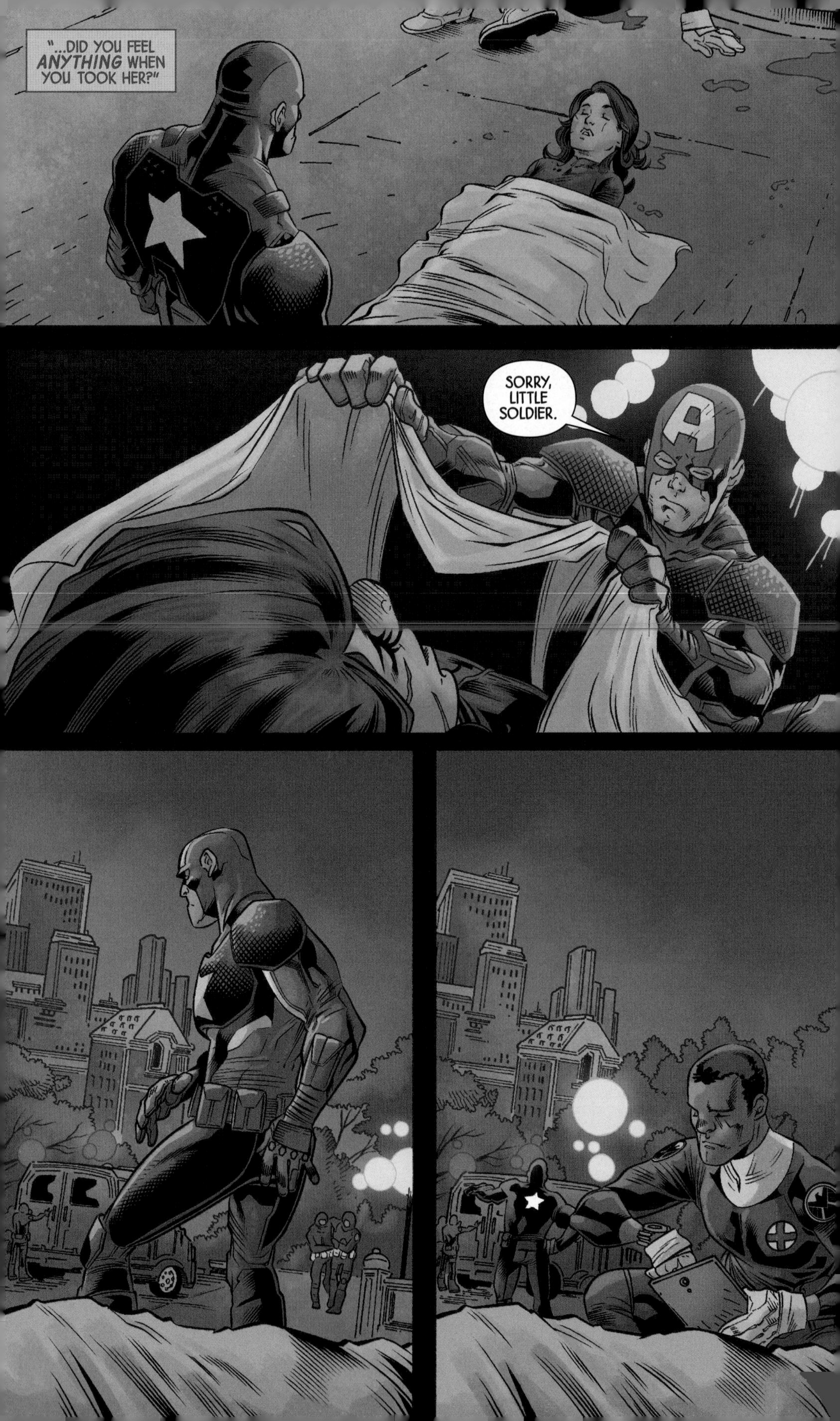
"...DID YOU FEEL ANYTHING WHEN YOU TOOK HER?"
SORRY, LITTLE SOLDIER.

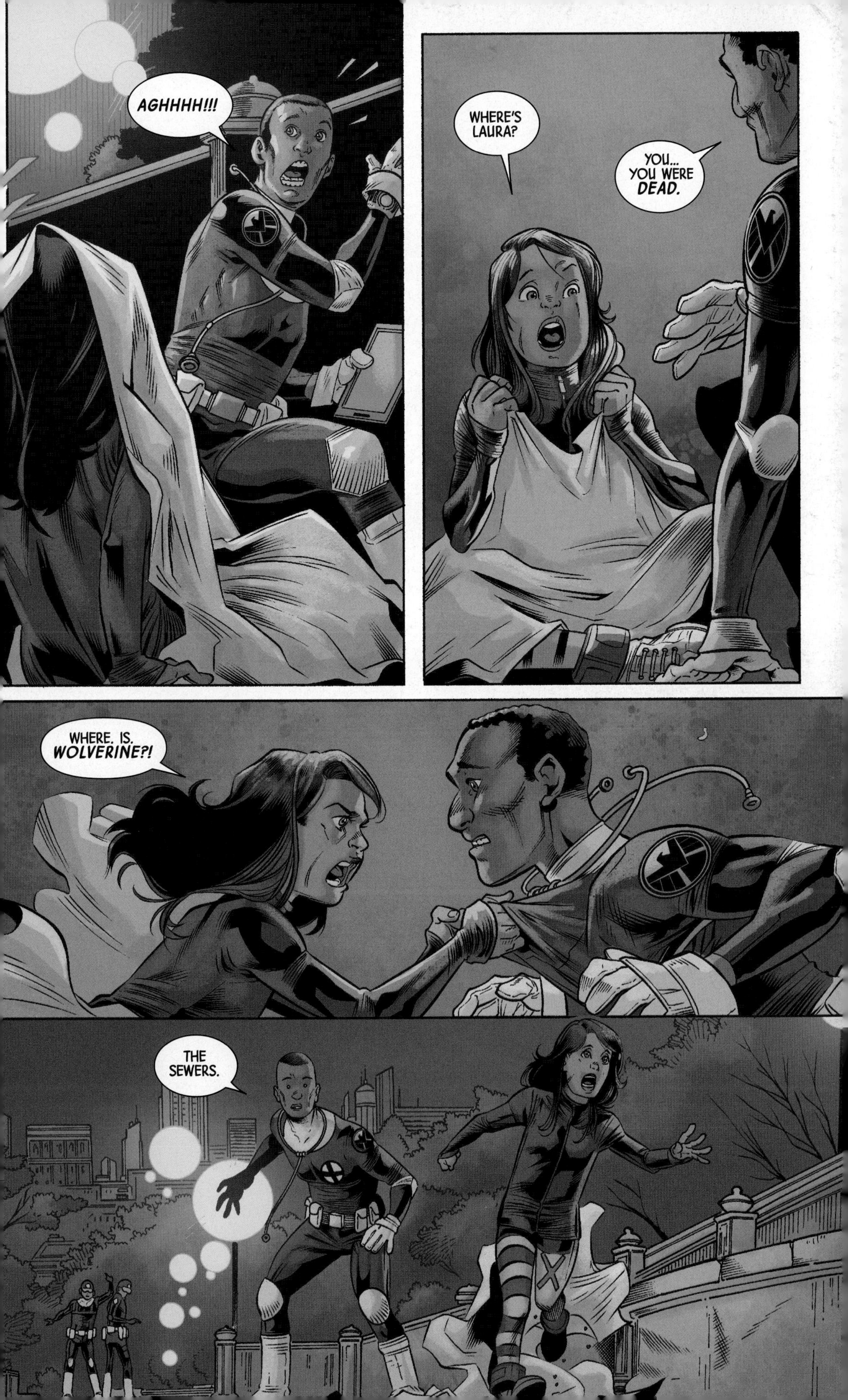
AGHHHH!!!
WHERE'S LAURA?
YOU... YOU WERE DEAD.
WHERE. IS. WOLVERINE?!
THE SEWERS.

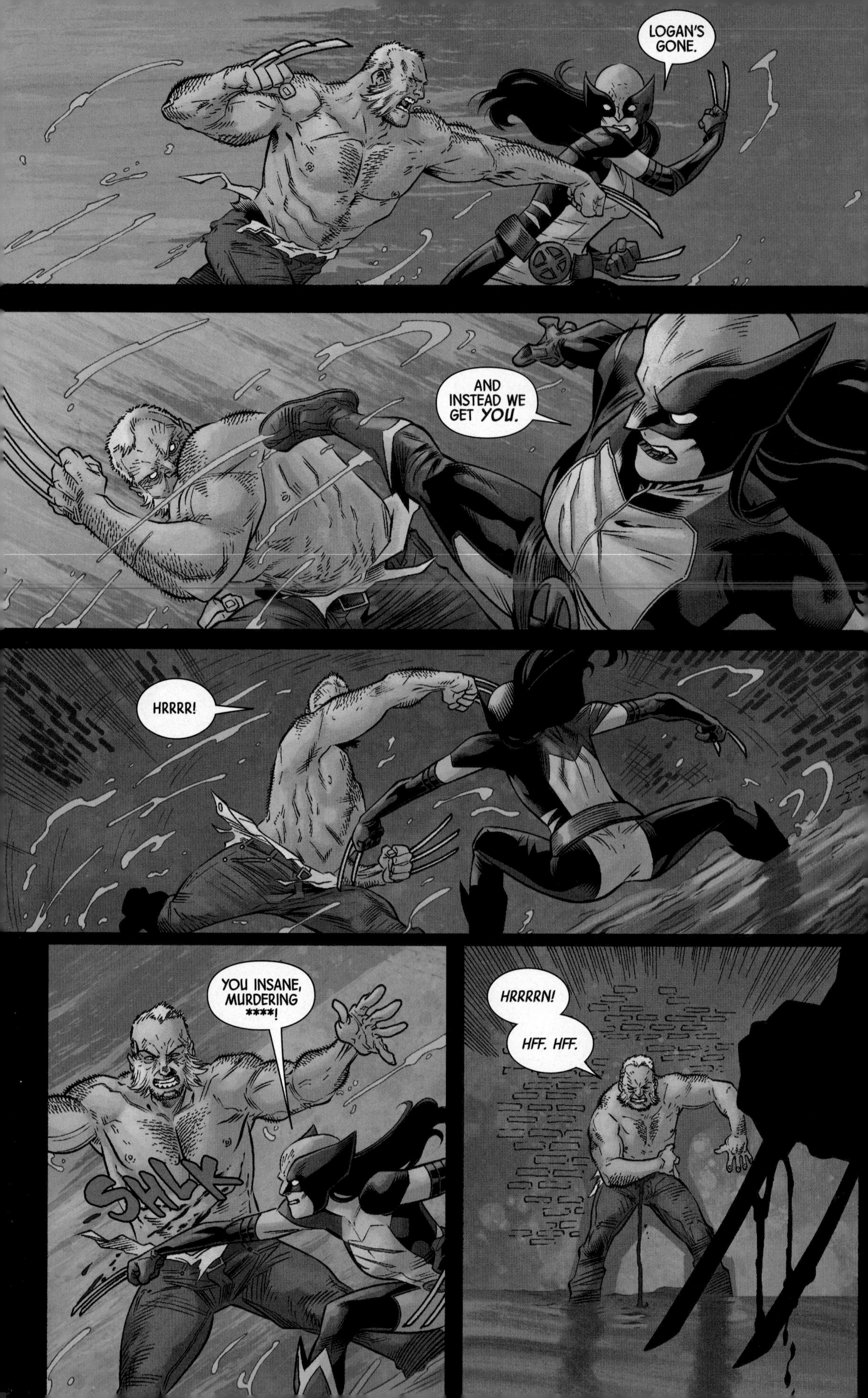
LOGAN'S GONE.
AND INSTEAD WE GET YOU.
HRRRR!
YOU INSANE, MURDERING ****!
SHLK
HRRRRN!
HFF. HFF.

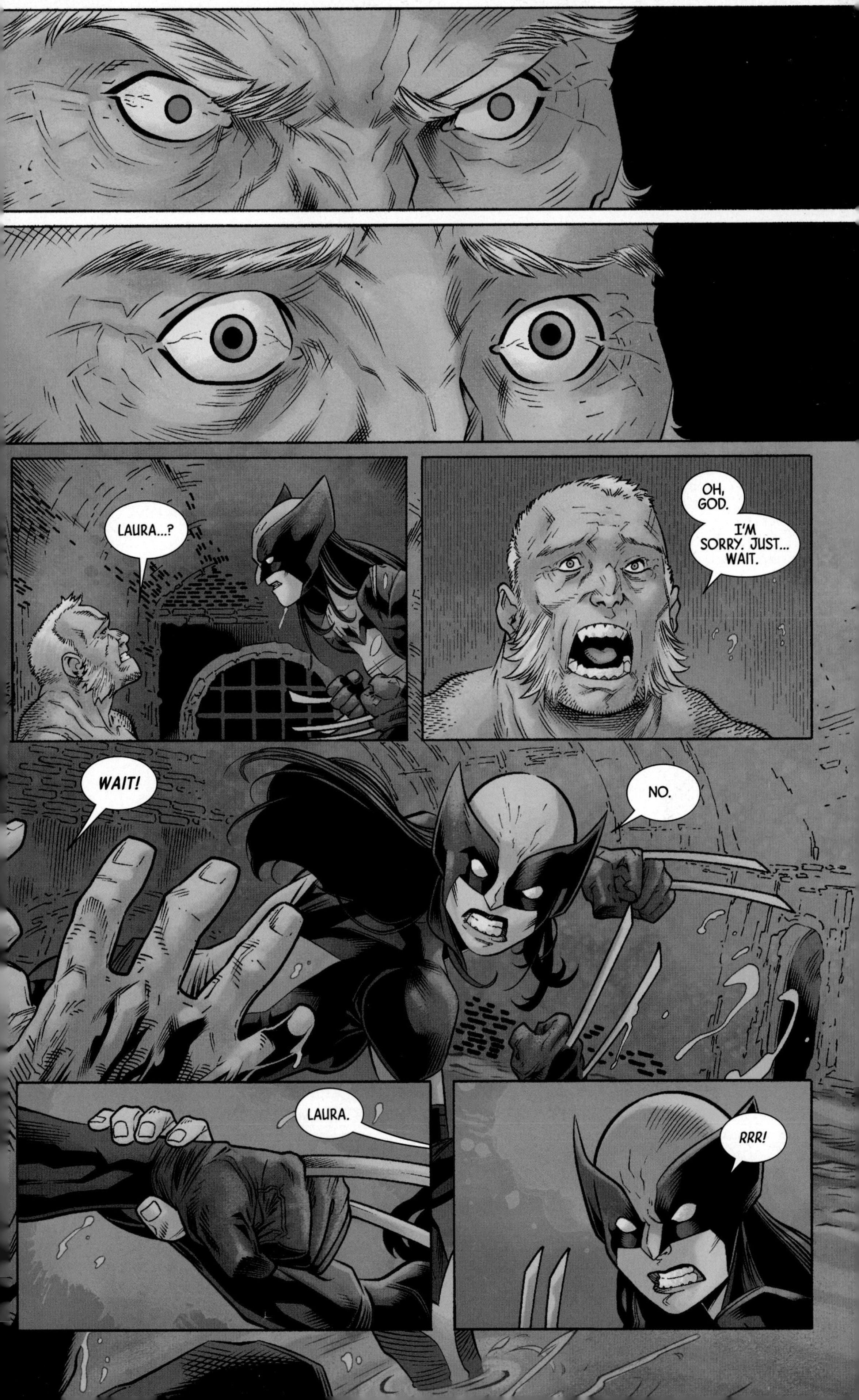
LAURA...?
OH, GOD.
I'M SORRY. JUST... WAIT.
WAIT!
NO.
LAURA.
RRR!

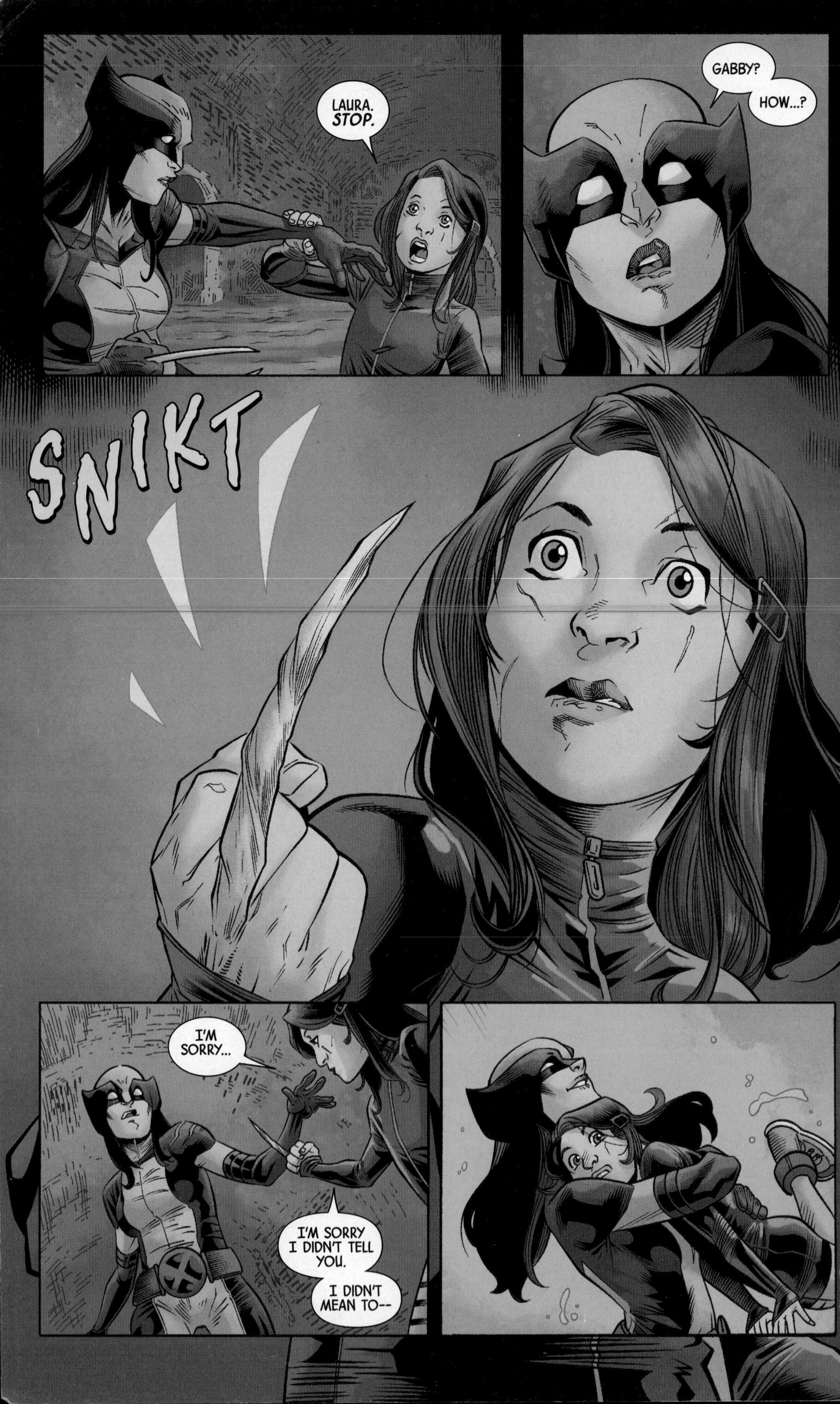
LAURA. STOP.
GABBY?
HOW...?
SNIKT
I'M SORRY...
I'M SORRY I DIDN'T TELL YOU.
I DIDN'T MEAN TO--

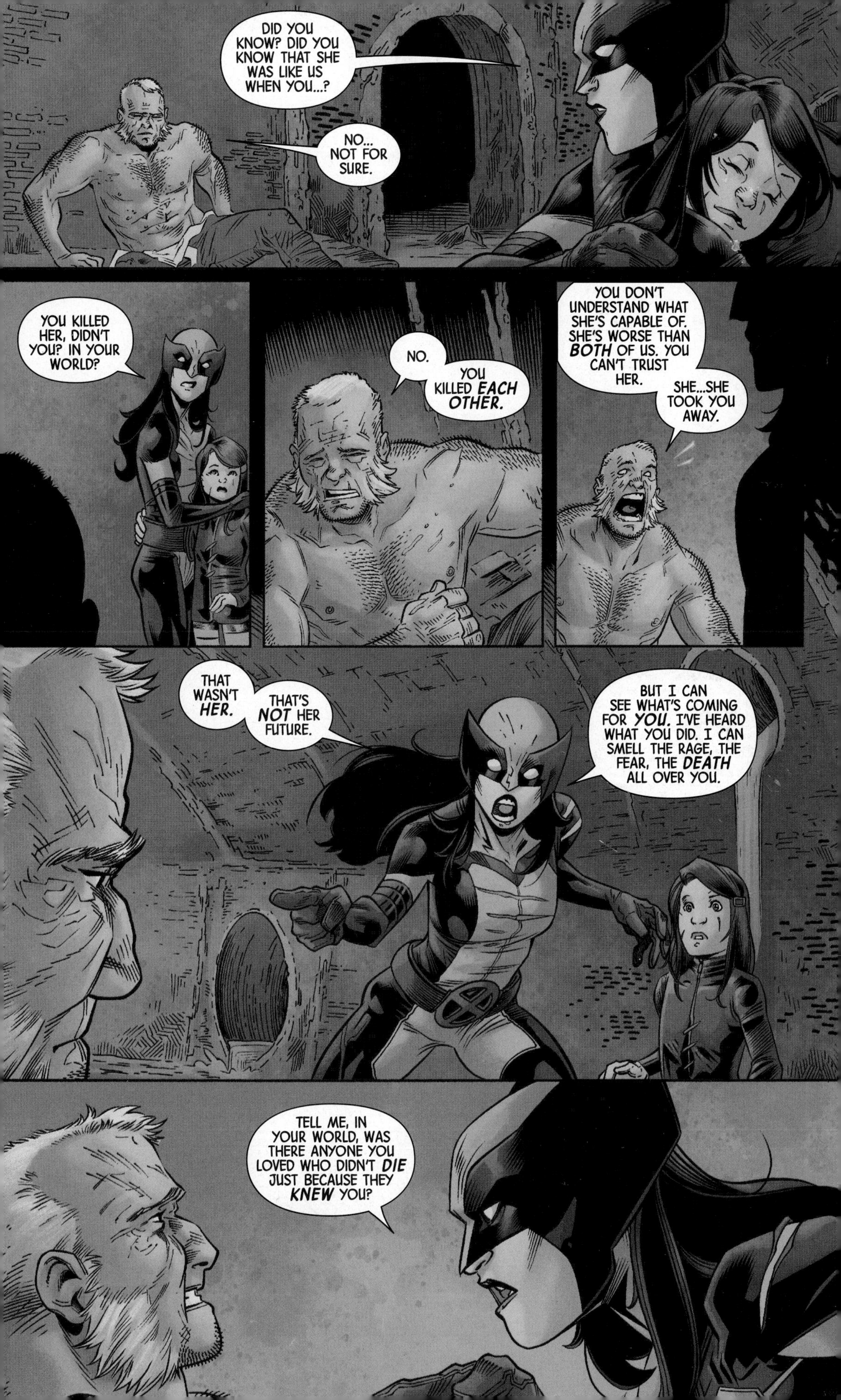
DID YOU KNOW? DID YOU KNOW THAT SHE WAS LIKE US WHEN YOU...?
NO... NOT FOR SURE.
YOU KILLED HER, DIDN'T YOU? IN YOUR WORLD?
NO.
YOU KILLED EACH OTHER.
YOU DON'T UNDERSTAND WHAT SHE'S CAPABLE OF. SHE'S WORSE THAN BOTH OF US. YOU CAN'T TRUST HER.
SHE...SHE TOOK YOU AWAY.
THAT WASN'T HER.
THAT'S NOT HER FUTURE.
BUT I CAN SEE WHAT'S COMING FOR YOU. I'VE HEARD WHAT YOU DID. I CAN SMELL THE RAGE, THE FEAR, THE DEATH ALL OVER YOU.
TELL ME, IN YOUR WORLD, WAS THERE ANYONE YOU LOVED WHO DIDN'T DIE JUST BECAUSE THEY KNEW YOU?

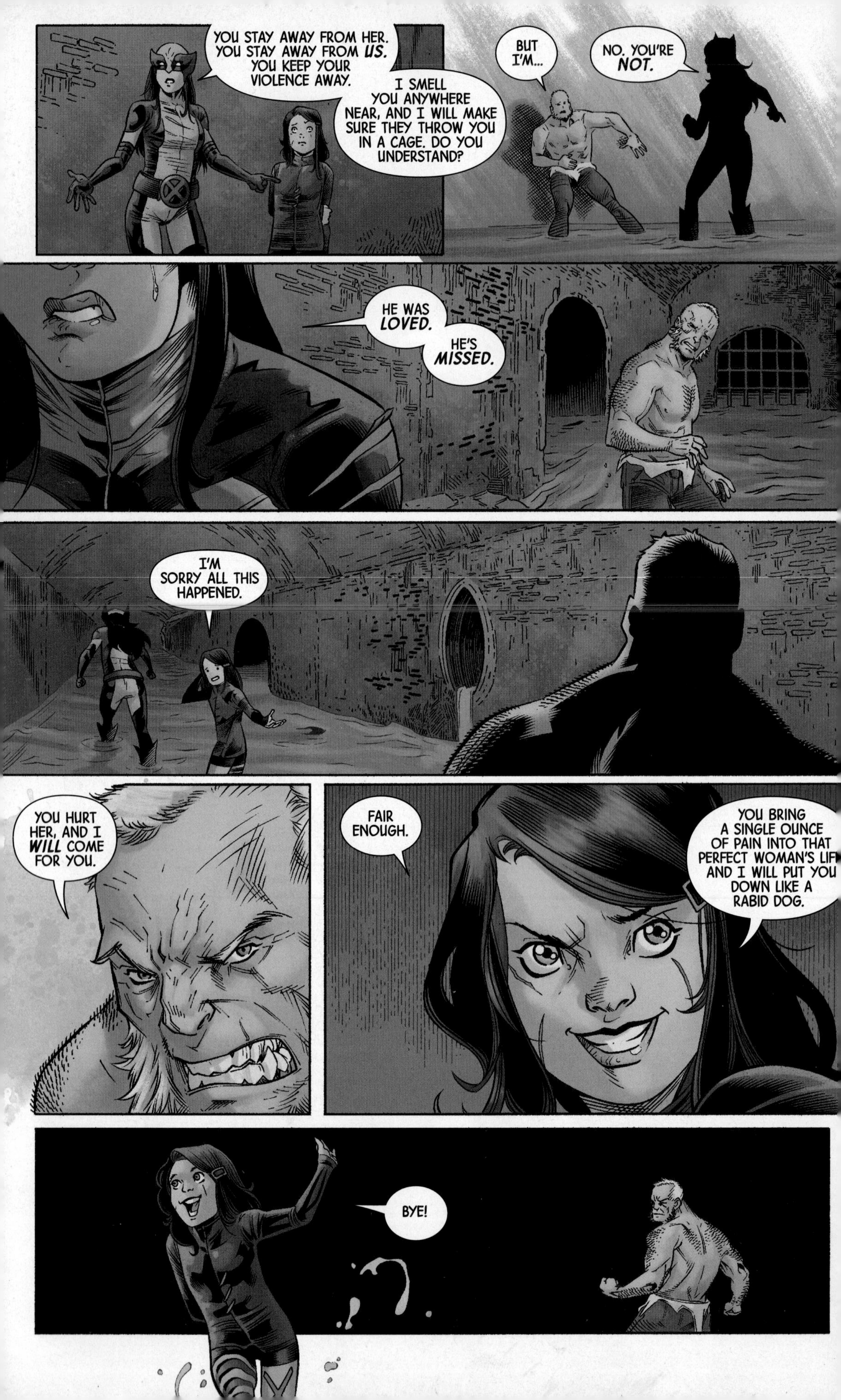
YOU STAY AWAY FROM HER. YOU STAY AWAY FROM US. YOU KEEP YOUR VIOLENCE AWAY.
I SMELL YOU ANYWHERE NEAR, AND I WILL MAKE SURE THEY THROW YOU IN A CAGE. DO YOU UNDERSTAND?
BUT I'M...
NO. YOU'RE NOT.
HE WAS LOVED.
HE'S MISSED.
I'M SORRY ALL THIS HAPPENED.
YOU HURT HER, AND I WILL COME FOR YOU.
FAIR ENOUGH.
YOU BRING A SINGLE OUNCE OF PAIN INTO THAT PERFECT WOMAN'S LIF
AND I WILL PUT YOU DOWN LIKE A RABID DOG.
BYE!

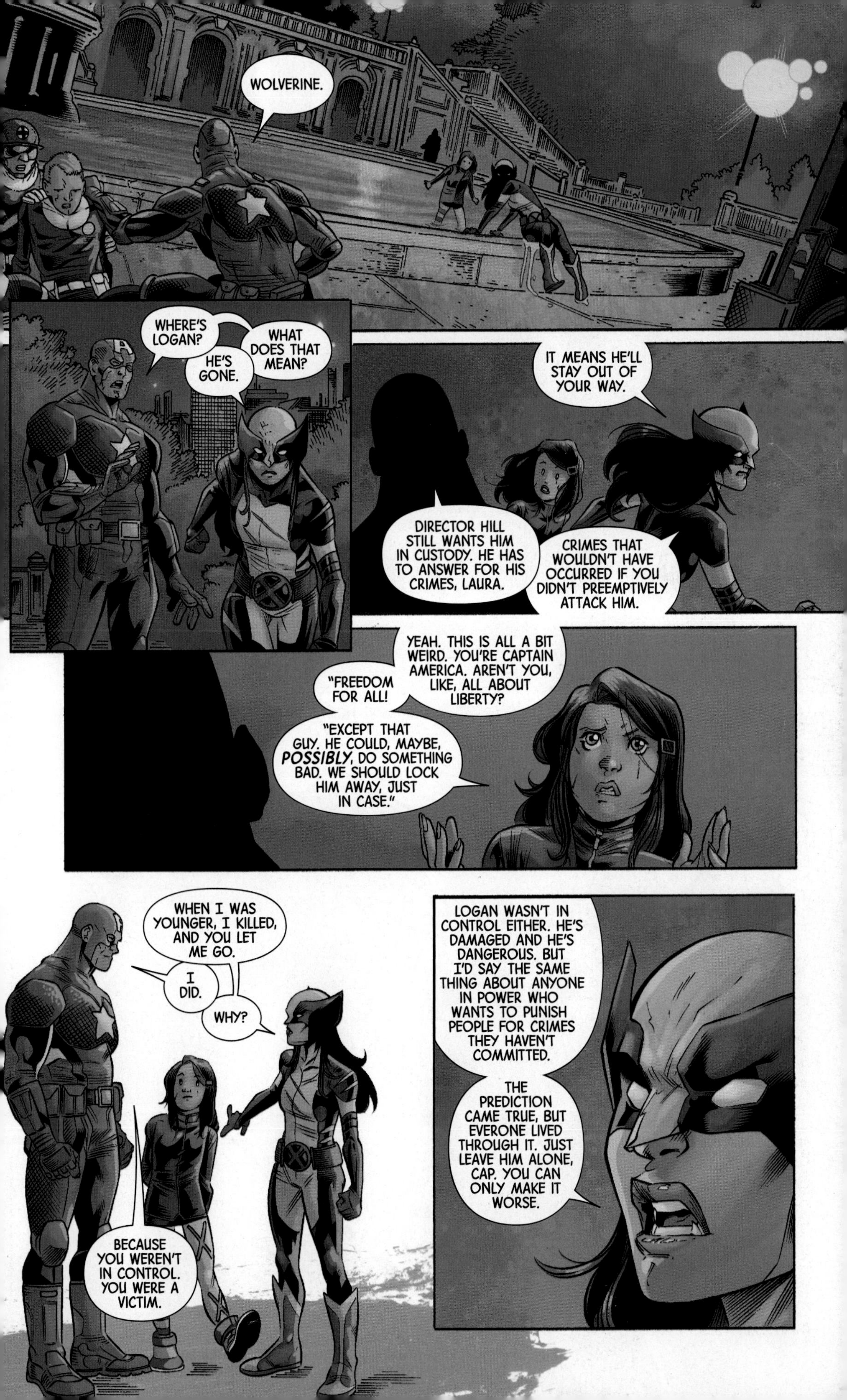
WOLVERINE.
WHERE'S LOGAN?
HE'S GONE.
WHAT DOES THAT MEAN?
IT MEANS HE'LL STAY OUT OF YOUR WAY.
DIRECTOR HILL STILL WANTS HIM IN CUSTODY. HE HAS TO ANSWER FOR HIS CRIMES, LAURA.
CRIMES THAT WOULDN'T HAVE OCCURRED IF YOU DIDN'T PREEMPTIVELY ATTACK HIM.
YEAH. THIS IS ALL A BIT WEIRD. YOU'RE CAPTAIN AMERICA. AREN'T YOU, LIKE, ALL ABOUT LIBERTY?
"FREEDOM FOR ALL!
"EXCEPT THAT GUY. HE COULD, MAYBE, POSSIBLY, DO SOMETHING BAD. WE SHOULD LOCK HIM AWAY, JUST IN CASE."
WHEN I WAS YOUNGER, I KILLED, AND YOU LET ME GO.
I DID.
WHY?
BECAUSE YOU WEREN'T IN CONTROL. YOU WERE A VICTIM.
LOGAN WASN'T IN CONTROL EITHER. HE'S DAMAGED AND HE'S DANGEROUS. BUT I'D SAY THE SAME THING ABOUT ANYONE IN POWER WHO WANTS TO PUNISH PEOPLE FOR CRIMES THEY HAVEN'T COMMITTED.
THE PREDICTION CAME TRUE, BUT EVERONE LIVED THROUGH IT. JUST LEAVE HIM ALONE, CAP. YOU CAN ONLY MAKE IT WORSE.

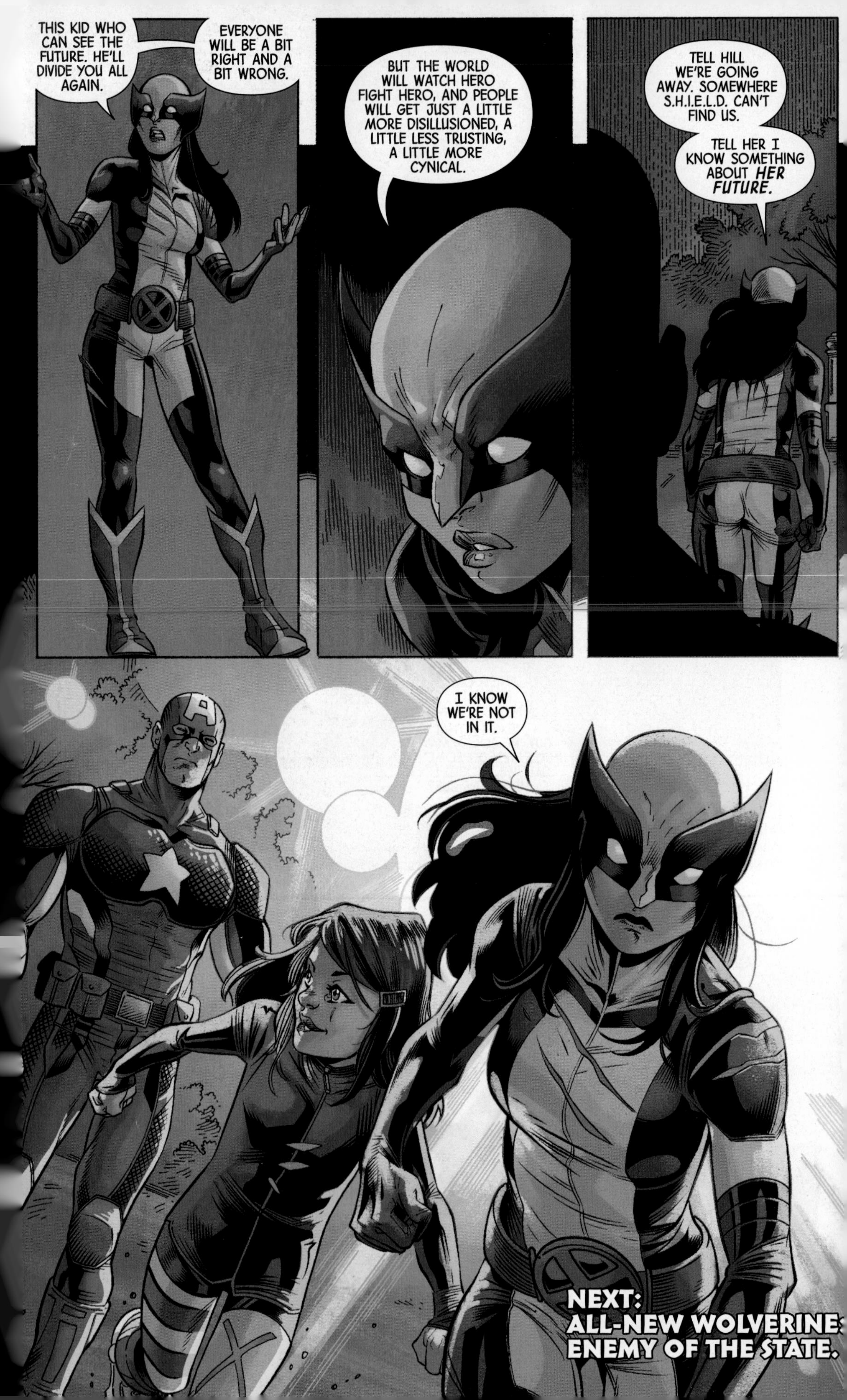
THIS KID WHO CAN SEE THE FUTURE. HE'LL DIVIDE YOU ALL AGAIN.
EVERYONE WILL BE A BIT RIGHT AND A BIT WRONG.
BUT THE WORLD WILL WATCH HERO FIGHT HERO, AND PEOPLE WILL GET JUST A LITTLE MORE DISILLUSIONED, A LITTLE LESS TRUSTING, A LITTLE MORE CYNICAL.
TELL HILL WE'RE GOING AWAY. SOMEWHERE S.H.I.E.L.D. CAN'T FIND US.
TELL HER I KNOW SOMETHING ABOUT *HER FUTURE.*
I KNOW WE'RE NOT IN IT.
NEXT:
ALL-NEW WOLVERINE: ENEMY OF THE STATE.

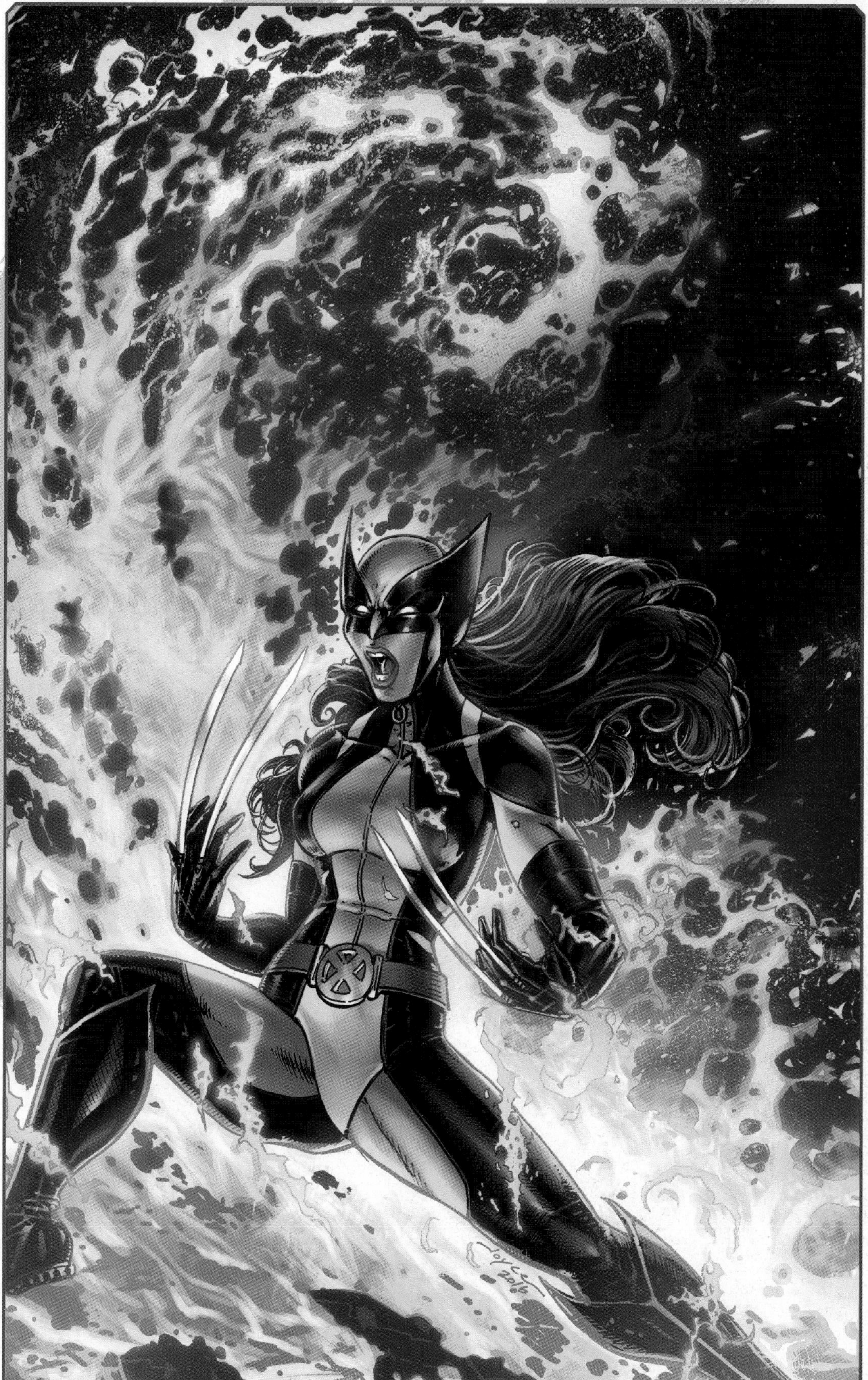

#9 Civil War Reenactment variant by
JOYCE CHIN & **NEI RUFFINO**

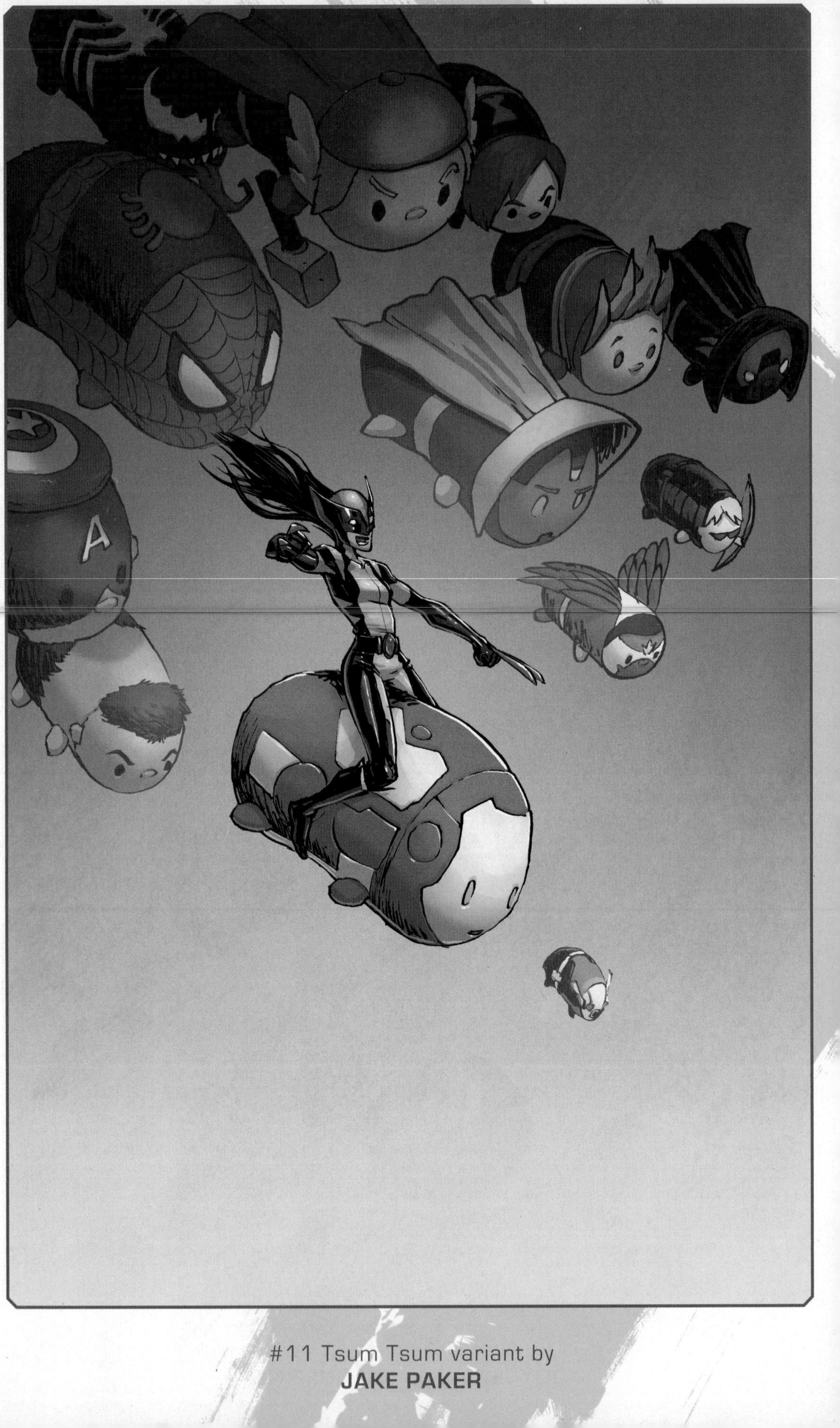

#11 Tsum Tsum variant by
JAKE PAKER

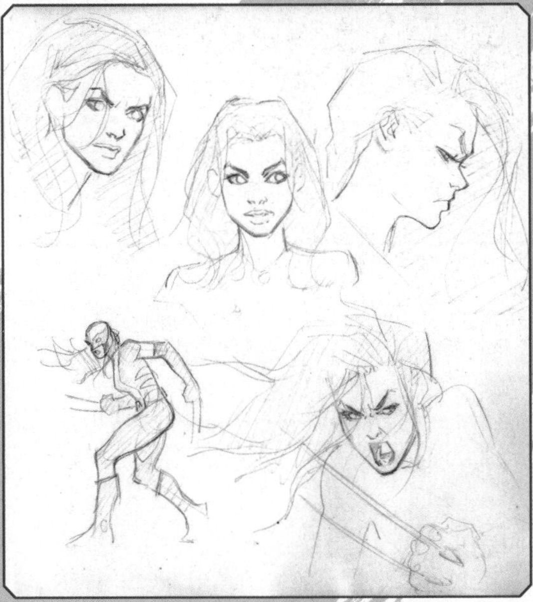

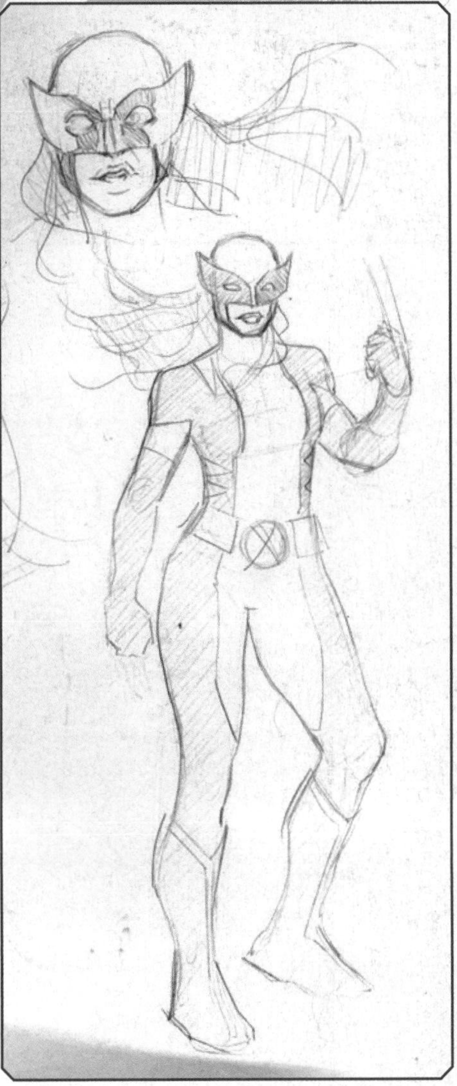

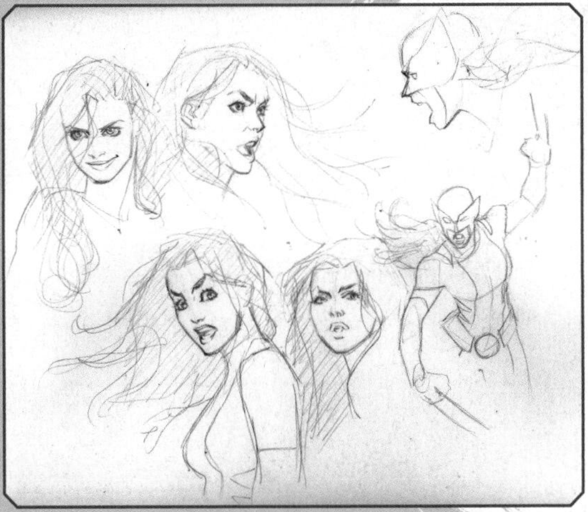

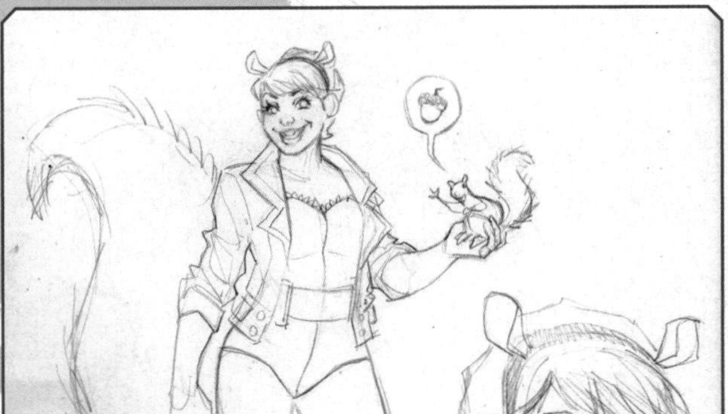

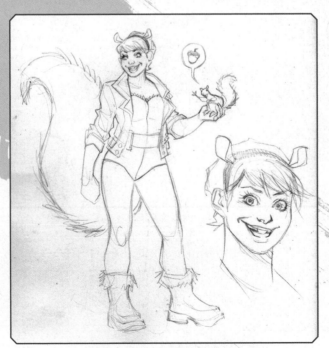

character sketches by
MARCO TAKARA

character sketches by
IG GUARA